STAGING A
revolution:

STAGING A

revolution:

THE ART OF PERSUASION IN THE
islamic republic of iran

peter chelkowski | hamid dabashi

First published in the U.S.A. in 1999 by
NEW YORK UNIVERSITY PRESS
Washington Square
New York, NY 10003

First published in the UK by Booth-Clibborn Editions

Design: Jason Beard and Jonathan Barnbrook

Library of Congress Cataloging-in-Publication Data
Chelkowski, Peter J.
Staging a revolution: the art of persuasion in the Islamic
Republic of Iran / Peter Chelkowski and Hamid Dabashi
p.   cm.
Includes bibliographical references (p.   ) and index.
ISBN 0-8147-1597-4 (cloth)
1.   Iran–History–Revolution, 1979–Propaganda. 2. Iran-Iraq War, 1980-
1988–Propaganda. 3. Propaganda, Iranian. I. Dabashi, Hamid, 1951- .
II. Title.
DS318.825.C44   1999
320'. 01' 4095509047–DC21   99-20633
                                              CIP

The illustrative material in this book comes primarily from the
Archives of the Hoover Institution on War, Revolution and Peace,
Stanford, CA, and the University of Chicago library, as well as from
private archives in the United States and Europe. Several of the
photographs included herein are the works of internationally
known photographers who were witnesses to the events in
Revolutionary Iran.

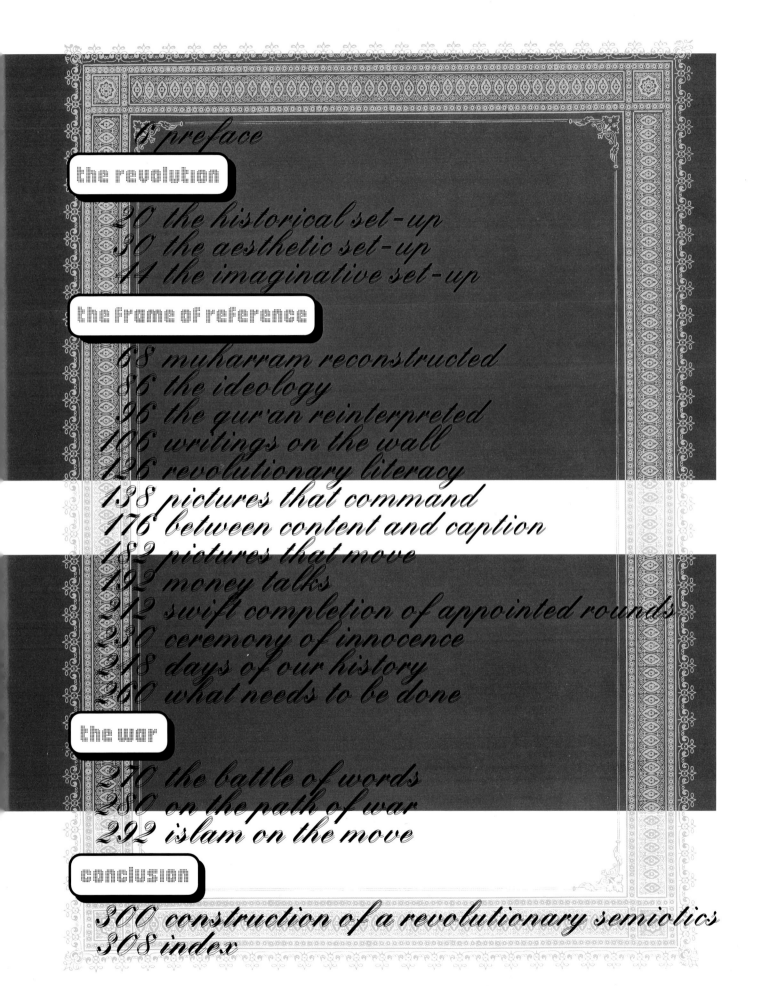

THE PURPOSE OF THIS BOOK IS TO EXAMINE THE MASSIVE ORCHESTRATION OF PUBLIC MYTHS AND COLLECTIVE SYMBOLS IN THE MAKING OF THE ISLAMIC REVOLUTION OF 1978-9 IN IRAN AND THE WAR WITH IRAQ THAT FOLLOWED IT BETWEEN 1980 AND 1988.

The Islamic Revolution in Iran has been one of those remarkable occasions in history when the power of words and images has successfully challenged the military might of an established state. How exactly the plethora of collectively constructed myths and symbols has been mobilized to stir a nation into revolutionary trance is at the root of our understanding of the whole revolutionary movement that occasioned it. The mechanism of revolutionary build-up during the eight-year-long bloody war with Iraq, too, needs to be studied in terms of the crescendo of common memories and shared sentiments conducive to sacrificial and martyrological dispositions. From the fiery words of Ayatollah Khomeini, the charismatic leader of the Revolution, transmitted to Iran through cassette tapes, to graffiti, slogans, and murals on walls and bridge columns, to revolutionary posters and banners, to songs, poems, declamations, and oratorical devices, to the creation of vivid and compelling mental images from the shared sacred history, an avalanche of public sentiments were mobilized by the leading figures of the revolutionary movement. Popular belief and rituals were converted into stamps, banknotes, and chewing-gum wrappers, and directed towards mass mobilization for revolution and war. To oppose the established authority of the state, this relentless resuscitation of the shared sacred history was directed to delegitimate the status quo. Every genre of these mobilizing mechanisms, every mood of these systematic orchestrations of public sentiments, ought to be understood carefully, and documented appropriately, before we can begin to comprehend both the semiological and the dramaturgical dimensions of this Revolution. The drama of the Islamic Revolution, this massive staging of the most sacred symbolics of an ancient culture, is inseparable from, indeed indispensable to, the quintessential nature of its causes and consequences. Approaching an understanding of the Islamic Revolution from an angle of vision sharpened by the vivid images of a resurrected nation is a crucial step towards a more

سپاه ما مخصوص به برادران ارتشی
ما نیست ، زن و مرد ما کوچک وبزرگ
ما سپاه اسلامیند و پاسدار
اسلام .

آیت الله طالقانی

Our army does not belong
only to our brothers in the
armed forces. Men and women,
young and old in our country
are the members of Islamic
Army, and are guardians of
Islam.

"Ayatollah Taleqani"

(left) The revolution was launched against both internal reactionary forces and Imperialism.

(bottom) Here an early Mojahedin-e Khalq Organisation poster, celebrates Shari⁣ati and Khomeini, and "the march towards the Unitary, classless society."

The 28th of Mordad was a national holiday declared upon the Shah's triumphant return to Iran (August 22, 1953) after five days of "enforced exile". This poster (opposite) proclaims that day "National Resurrection Day" and links it with another milestone in the Shah's vision of Iran: the "White Revolution" which was approved in a "national referendum" on the 6th of Bahman (January 26, 1963). Here the artist unrolls a panorama of the "Great Civilisation."

accurate grasp of the event itself. But, perhaps even more important, a reading of the constellation of revolutionary images is indispensable in comprehending the more compelling question of how public sentiments and collectively held symbolics are used to mobilize a people for radical and revolutionary purposes.

Addressing these issues with semiotic sensitivity, and with detailed attention to Iranian history and the Shi⁣i religion, is one thing; accumulating, typifying, and accurately reading the range of mental and pictorial images produced in the course of the revolutionary movement, is another. During the last decade and a half, a wealth of primary sources—posters, cassette tapes, pictures, graffiti, stamps, banknotes, etc.—have been produced by the various active organs of the Islamic Revolution. We now

have at our disposal the widest possible sample of these revolutionary images. Our study of the varieties of ways in which the Islamic Revolution has been propagated will rest on these detailed materials documenting the Iranian and Shi⁣i art of persuasion. Without such detailed attention to the primary sources, and without balanced attention to Iranian history and the Shi⁣i faith, no study of this colossal political event can claim to have taught us something about the nature and organization of revolutionary mobilization.

Located in the context of the Shi⁣i political culture, however, this was primarily a pictorial revolution, a revolution in full semiotic control of the representation of itself. In this revolutionary representation, pictures "talk." The "talking" that these pictures do is not audible but visible. Imagine a people who hear with their eyes! Almost all pictures talk. But we are going to

Early in the year 1971, when preparations for the commemoration of the 2500 years of the Persian Empire were in full swing, thirteen heavily-armed young men with leftist leanings attacked a gendarmerie post in the village of Siahkal on the shores of the Caspian. This poster proclaims "We shall make Iran Siahkal from end to end." In the years between the Siahkal incident and the beginning of the Islamic Revolution, urban guerrillas launched many attacks against the Shah's regime.

tell the story of an archive of pictures that was produced during the revolutionary period of the late 1970s and then all through the 1980s in revolutionary Iran. These pictures were produced by a nation mobilized to its highest sacred sensibilities, set on a course of self-revelation, exposing itself to the world, for the whole world to see. Imagine a nation that goes public, becomes transparent, reveals, discovers, unveils itself, puts itself on exhibition—a whole national psyche that turns itself into a museum of—if not so "fine" then at least—furious art. "The Museum of Furious Art"— that is the Iran of the 1980s, a nation engaged in a revolution and a war, relentlessly remaking itself in images and forms, shapes and colors, frames of angers and anxieties.

"Independence, Freedom, the Islamic Republic": the defining moment of the Revolution as "Islamic".

We are going to tell the stories of these pictures as they narrate themselves on posters and walls, stamps and textbooks, banknotes and coins. But we are also going to trace them to the inner corners of the mind—of those who produced them, of those who saw and read them, interpreted and acted upon them. This is thus the story of the Iranian Revolution in pictures—with some necessary words.

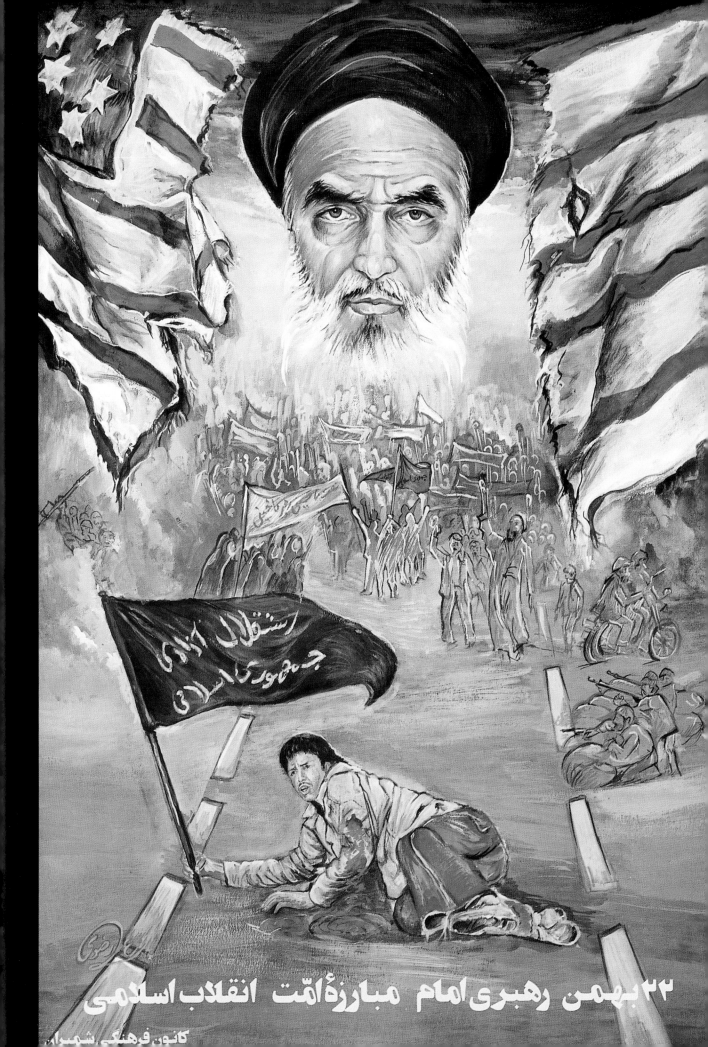

۲۲ بهمن رهبری امام مبارزهٔ اُمّت انقلاب اسلامی

کانون فرهنگی شهید...

Ayatollah Khomeini's funeral, see page 224 of chapter 13.

The seventh day mourning at the temporary tomb of Ayatollah Khomeini.

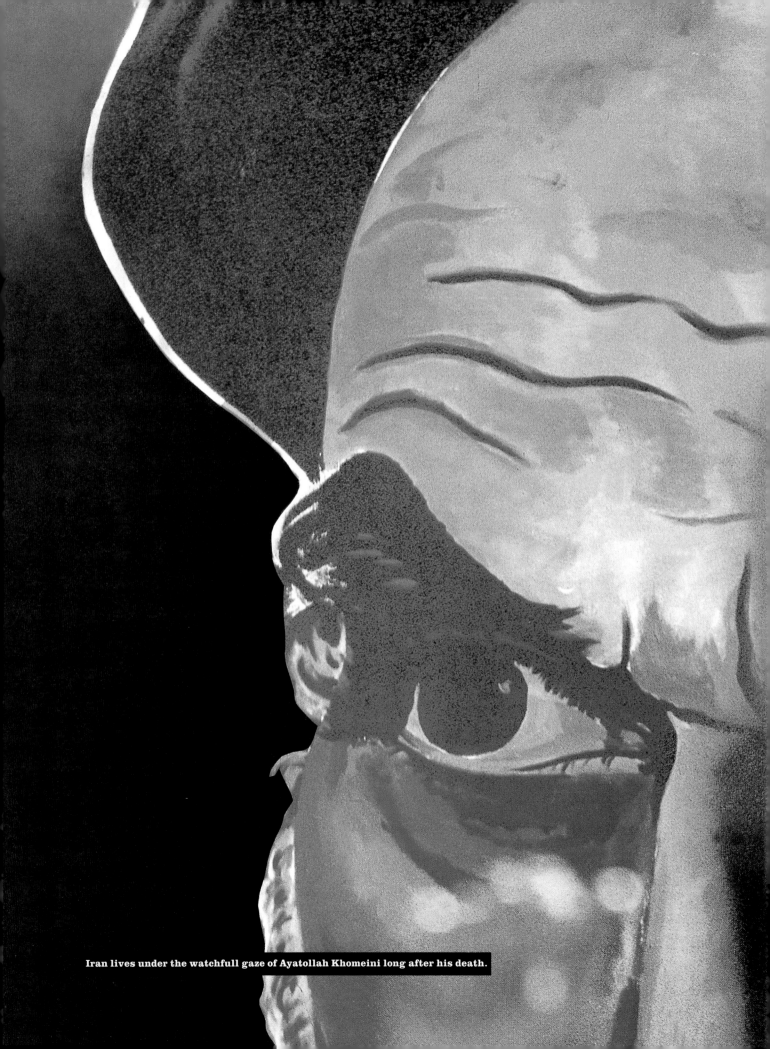

Iran lives under the watchfull gaze of Ayatollah Khomeini long after his death.

آمریکایی پس غلطی نمی تونید بکنید

U.S. CAN NOT DO ANYTHING

Part One:

THEIR *PURPOSE*

and their objective is not to conquer lands. Those who talk about the [early] Islamic expansionism, they have absolutely no idea what Islam is. They think, Islam is like the United States, the larger the size of its domain the better. The expansionism of the prophets is different from the expansionism of rulers. [The rulers] struggle for this world, conquer for this world, for their own diabolical power, The prophets [or the contrary,] intend to humanize a multitude, They whip them to become humans. Their expansionism is to make humans. – AYATOLLAH KHOMEINI

It is a very bad temptation for the faithful, when things in the world are confused and it seems that God no longer engages with them but that fortune governs and rules. This has been the cause of these diabolical proverbs that everything is ruled by chance, that things happen blindly, and that God plays with men like tennis balls, that there is no reason or measure, or indeed that everything is governed by some secret necessity and that God does not bother to think of us. These are blasphemies that have always ruled. And why? Because the human mind is bewildered when we try to grasp confused things that surpass our judgment and reason.
John Calvin

the frame of reference

the historical setup:
causesandconditions

of the iniran

islamic revolution

One

LET US PUT THE UNFOLDING OF THIS UNFORGETTABLE DRAMA IN ITS IMMEDIATE HISTORICAL SET-UP. IT WOULD NOT BE AN EXAGGERATION TO SUGGEST THAT THE REVOLUTIONARY ART THAT IMMEDIATELY PRECEDED AND THAT CONTINUED AFTER THE SUCCESS OF THE IRANIAN REVOLUTION OF 1978-9, MORE THAN ANY OTHER PROPAGANDA MACHINERY, SERVED TO MARK AND REPRESENT THE CATACLYSMIC EVENT AS AN "ISLAMIC REVOLUTION." THE REVOLUTION IN IRAN WAS AN EVENT OF UNIVERSAL SIGNIFICANCE IN THE MODERN HISTORY OF THE MIDDLE EAST. IT RESULTED FROM THE COMBINED CIRCUMSTANCES AND CONDITIONS CREATED BY A MULTIPLE SET OF MATERIAL AND IDEOLOGICAL FORCES.[1] SOME SEVEN DECADES AFTER THE CONSTITUTIONAL REVOLUTION OF 1906-11,[2] THE ISLAMIC REVOLUTION OF

1978-9 PICKED UP SOME OF THE MAINLY UN-RESOLVED THEMES OF THAT MOMENTOUS EVENT AND CARRIED THEM TO SOME OF THE POTENTIAL CONCLUSIONS.[3] DEEPLY ROOTED IN CERTAIN ENDURING FEATURES OF THE SHI[C]I FAITH,[4] THE REVOLUTION OF 1978-9 RESUSCITATED THE MOST RADICAL AND SUBVERSIVE FEATURES OF THAT FAITH AND PUT THEM TO IMMEDIATE POLITICAL USE.[5] AFTER MORE THAN 500 YEARS OF PERVASIVE INSTITUTIONALIZATION, SHI[C]ISM WAS THE MOST COMMON DENOMINATOR OF POLITICAL CULTURE IN IRAN.[6] ALL THROUGH THE NINETEENTH CEN-TURY, SHI[C]ISM WAS THE MOST POWERFUL SOURCE OF REVOLUTIONARY MOVEMENTS IN IRAN.[7] IN ITS RHETORICS AND SENTIMENTS, IDEOLOGY AND HISTORICAL MEMORY, THE ISLAMIC REVOLUTION OF 1978-9 TOOK FULL ADVANTAGE OF ITS RECONSTRUCTED HISTORICAL ANTECEDENTS.[8]

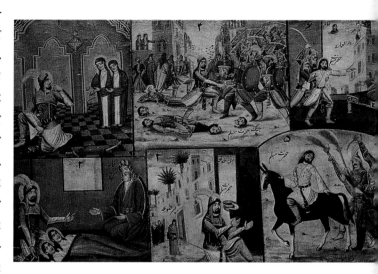

The modern manifestations of Shi[c]ism were of course not limited to Iran. In Iraq and Lebanon in particular, and the rest of the Muslim world in general, Shi[c]ism had played a significant role in active and radical political awareness.[9] But as the political and cultural arena of Shi[c]ism for more than 500 consecutive years, Iran has been the birthplace of the most salient features of this branch of Islam.[10] Although deeply rooted in material and ideological conditions of diverse nature and origin, the Islamic Revolution of Iran increasingly assumed the most radical rhetorics of Shi[c]ism as its defining character.[11] Playing on both the doctrinal and the popular dimensions of Shi[c]ism,[12] the Islamic Revolution extended the full metaphysical possibilities of the ancestral faith to the furthest corners of radical political life. The active institutionalization of Shi[c]ism in specific political organizations such as the Freedom Movement of Iran[13] was but a specific case of a much wider presence of the faith in the fullest unfoldings of routine, daily life. From the most material economic conditions,[14] to the literary and dramatic arts,[15] Shi[c]ism was critically and consciously present in Iranian life. More than 200 years of exposure to secular (radical and liberal) ideas[16] came to no effective result in the wake of the Iranian Revolution of 1978-9 which successfully identified and institutionalized itself as "Islamic."

1.1 and 1.2 Themes and motifs from Shi[c]i iconography played a significant role in the making of the revolutionary ideology.

Samuel R. Peterson

القدس ملك للمسلمين و يجب أن تعود اليهم

الإمام الخميني

**QODS BELONGS TO MUSLIMS
AND SHOULD BE RETURNED TO THEM**

IMAM KHOMEINI

جمهورية ايران الاسلامية
وزارة الارشاد الاسلامي
ISLAMIC REPUBLIC OF IRAN
MINISTRY OF ISLAMIC GUIDANCE

1.3 While nationalist icons like Muhammad Mosaddeq were incorporated into the revolutionary slogans, it was patently Islamic symbols that defined the movement.

1.4 Competing ideologies vied for power in the course of the revolutionary movement. But Shi͑i martyrology emerged as the supreme symbolic significance of the event.

How did that comprehensive "Islamic" identification occur? Upon the initial success of the revolutionary movement of 1978-9, the idealizing forces mobilizing the event were effectively renarrated and reinstitutionalized into a number of competing ideologies struggling for political power. Very broadly, three major ideological claims were laid on the Revolution of 1979: nationalist, Marxist, and Islamic. The nationalist ideology, institutionalized in and represented by the enduring memory of Muhammad Mosaddeq,[17] was the least successful of noticeable measures to claim and control the Revolution. The Marxist (or socialist) ideology, permeated in and represented by both the Tudeh Party and the Guerilla Organization of People's Fada'ian, was much more successful than the nationalist elements in mobilizing a considerable portion of the population and claiming a sizeable measure of revolutionary rhetorics. But by far the most successful ideological appropriation of the revolutionary movement was by the Islamic forces, institutionalized in the People's Mujahedin and the wide spectrum of groups and classes rallying behind Ayatollah Khomeini. The People's Mujahedin, a syncretic movement that successfully wed certain socialist ideas with the most radical aspects of Shiʿism, initially joined forces with the supporters and followers of Ayatollah Khomeini. Very soon, however, it recognized that Khomeini's immediate lieutenants were not ready to share power with it, and thus it seceded and engaged in a protracted period of active opposition to the nascent Islamic Republic, which continues to the present day. Patently victorious from this multifaceted struggle for ideological and political supremacy in Iran were the immediate followers of Ayatollah Khomeini, for whom the aged revolutionary sage became the most persuasive spokesman.

While the nationalists and the Marxists (socialists) tried in vain to give their respective colorations to the unfolding revolutionary event, the Islamic ideologues won the day in defining and characterizing the cataclysmic event as nothing but an "Islamic Revolution." This was the most pervasive and systematic aspect of the revolutionary movement. While engaged in a relentless and systematic outmaneuvering of their ideological and political rivals, the Islamic ideologues launched a massive propaganda program to claim the Revolution exclusively for themselves. As militant supporters of Ayatollah Khomeini appropriated and took control of the organs of the state apparatus, a massive propaganda machinery was gradually set in motion to color the event "Islamic." While the ideological and political rivals and opponents of this deliberate Islamicization of the social revolution were being either eliminated or effectively neutralized, a colossal revolutionary narrative was

1.5 Targetting a foreign audience was one way of Islamicizing the revolution.

unleashed into the mass media—the radio, television, newspapers, public sermons, etc.—and began to claim the entirety of the Revolution for itself. But given the semi-illiterate character of the society, where a considerable population with immediate political significance could not read and write, the ideologues very soon realized the power and potency of the spoken word and the drawn picture—and dramatically delivered them with razor-sharp effectiveness.

This book is devoted to a study of those dramatically spoken words and those drawn pictures, which were massively mobilized and orchestrated in order to define the cataclysmic events of the Iranian Revolution of 1978-9 and the brutal Iraq-Iran war of 1980-8, as having an innately "Islamic" origin, nature, purpose, and destination. The belated advent of modernity—the ideological institutionalization of the epistemic suppositions of reason, progress, and nationhood—ushered in a rapid period of acculturation in Iran. A new bourgeois class, ideologically and institutionally connected to the European commercial and cultural imaginations, came to dominate the social organization of political and economic life. Through the bourgeois revolution of 1906-11, the traditional contentions between the religious and political authorities came once again into sharper focus. A historical coalition between the traditional merchant class, represented and supported by the clergy, and the rising modern bourgeoisie resulted in the Constitutional Revolution and a radical curtailment of the absolutist monarchy. Following the Constitutional Revolution, the monarchy was forced to submit to certain democratic measures, and a parliament was established to give institutional voice to the class interests of the traditional merchant class, represented by the clergy, and of the emerging modern bourgeoisie, represented by the bourgeois liberals in the newly established core of European-educated technocrats. Between the late 1900s and the mid-1920s, Iranian revolutionary politics witnessed a serious contention between the traditional merchant class and clergy on one side and the emerging modern bourgeoisie and their liberal or radical representatives on the other. The *coup d'état* of Reza Shah in 1926 aborted this crucial tension in favor of a military dictatorship. After the military coup of 1926 and the establishment of the Pahlavi dynasty, the ideological and institutional development of liberal, radical (both secular), and religious forces entered a period of radical retardation. It was not until much later in Reza Shah's reign that these forces took advantage of the Allied occupation of Iran, released themselves from under the yoke of a military dictatorship, and began to reinvigorate their ideological and institutional bases.

Reza Shah was forced by the Allied forces to abdicate in 1941 in favor of his son, Muhammad Reza Shah. Between 1941 and 1953, the radical, liberal, and religious forces again took advantage of a weak monarchy and gathered considerable political momentum. The Tudeh Party was established almost immediately after the abdication of Reza Shah to give full-fledged institutional expression to earlier forces and sentiments of Iranian communism. Later into the weak monarchy of Muhammad Reza Shah, Muhammad Mosaddeq became the charismatic champion of the National Front, the institutional foundation of Iranian parliamentary liberalism. In the mean time, organizations such as Fada'ian-e Islam and Jebheh-ye Azadi, and religious figures such as Kashani, gave radical or liberal (but both religious) expression to Islamic sentiments.

The CIA-sponsored *coup* of 1953 introduced yet another subversive moment in these crucial developments in Iranian national politics. After the *coup*, the Tudeh Party was first forced to go underground and then totally banned, Mosaddeq's democratically elected government was deposed, and both liberal and radical religious organizations were forced to submit to the increasingly belligerent rule of Muhammad Reza Shah. All possibilities of secular—liberal or radical—institutions of political activity were suppressed, and when moderate religious resistance was offered to Muhammad Reza Shah's power, he effectively put an end to it. From the June 1963 uprising in Qom and other Iranian cities Ayatollah Khomeini emerged as the most effective and popular representative of religious resistance in his reign.

While Khomeini initially represented the more "liberal" (merchant class) branch of religious resistance to the Pahlavi dictatorship, from the 1960s an increasingly "radical" religious resistance emerged around the Mujahedin-e Khalq Organizations, with Ali Shari'ati and Ayatollah Taleqani as their chief ideologues. In the mean time, on the secular front the banned and discredited Tudeh Party, its leaders having fled the country, gradually gave way to a much more robust and active radical organization, the Fada'ian-e Khalq Guerilla Organization. Through daring and subversive acts of urban and rural terrorism, the organization seriously challenged the *status quo* and publicly exposed the Shah's self-delusions. Under these circumstances, when the urban and rural guerrillas of both Mujahedin-e Khalq and Fada'ian-e Khalq battled the Shah's security forces, liberal ideology had no opportunity or institutional basis to sustain and accredit itself. Weak and jaundiced leadership, and malnourished and outdated ideological debates became the hallmark of Iranian liberalism in the 1960s and 1970s. It lacked the innovative ideological radicalism and the daring political initiatives of both the Mujahedin and the Fada'ian, and thus the cause of Iranian secular liberalism remained singularly unattended.

As the Mujahedin and the Fada'ian fought fiercely against the Shah's regime, Khomeini, now exiled to Najaf in Iraq, began to gather his forces both within and outside Iran from among the traditional merchant class, the clerical establishment, as well as the Muslim student associations. In the mean time, the Shah was forced in 1977 to initiate a rapid process of "liberalization" encouraged by President Carter's "human rights" promises in his presidential election campaign. Taking advantage of this short period of liberalization, political organizations began to make their presence

1.6 Ayatollah Khomeini's principal achievement was to speak in
a language that unified an entire spectrum of Iranian population.

felt. Khomeini intensified his war of words from Iraq, the Muja-hedin and the Fada'ian actively resisted the monarchy, and the National Front emerged from virtual oblivion and sent an "open letter" to the king reminding him of his abuses of power and the institutional lack of democracy. President Carter responded to the emerging crisis in Iran by cancelling the Shah's order for AWACS. In order to alleviate the situation, the Shah dismissed Amir ʿAbbas Hoveyda, his prime minister for over a decade, and put Jamshid Amuzegar in his seat. Under the newly created liberal conditions, the Iranian intellectuals and literati began to be more active on the political scene, and arranged for regular sessions of political poetry readings. They gave a distinctly secular voice to the emerging revolutionary momentum, but there was no institutional beneficiary of their sentiments and force.

On 31 December 1977, President Carter paid a visit to Iran in order to demonstrate his support for the troubled monarch. In the mean time, the publication of a derogatory newspaper article in Tehran against Ayatollah Khomeini, who had now increased his anti-Shah activities, caused a massive demonstration in Qom. The security forces fired into the crowd and casualties were reported. By late February 1978, a chain of forty-day mournings-cum-demonstrations had extended the riot from Qom to Tabriz and other major cities. As a sign of anti-government protest, a number of banks and movie-houses were set on fire. By April, Tehran University had joined the open rebellion. In May, as Tehran, Shiraz, Isfahan, and other major urban centers witnessed massive anti-Shah demonstrations, two seminary students were reported killed

in Qom. The Shah left Iran for a short visit to Eastern Europe. In a major act of appropriation, Khomeini called for a massive anniversary demonstration in June. By July, the religious establish-ment felt confident enough for Ayatollah Shariʿatmadari, then a major ally of the exiled Khomeini, to call for parliamentary elections. But by August the brutal burning of hundreds of Iranians in a movie-theater which had been intentionally set on fire pushed the revolutionary movement into a new, even more serious, phase. The Shah dismissed Amuzegar, appointed Sharif-Imami as his prime minister, promised elections and further liberal-ization, but all this seemed futile as the outside world watched on television the burning of His Majesty's picture in downtown Tehran.

By September, the Shah was forced to put Tehran and many other cities under martial law. Martial law was defied and a major massacre occurred in Zhaleh Square in Tehran, an event which was to be remembered as "Black Friday." Very soon major industries, such as telecommunications and the oil industry, actively joined the Revolution, while the demonstrations in Tehran and other cities demanded Ayatollah Khomeini's return from exile. The call for an "Islamic Republic" came loud and clear from the crowds and their organizers. In October, Khomeini was forced to leave Iraq. His forced landing in a small suburb of Paris put the old revolutionary sage at the center of world media attention. In November, the Shah changed his prime minister yet again, replacing Sharif-Imami with a military man, General Azhari. The move was futile. Demonstrations continued. The workers of the Iranian National Oil Company, the employees of the National Television, as well as those of the Central Bank, joined the revolutionary ranks. By December (Muharram) of this fateful year of 1978, the Shah was forced to dismiss Azhari and appoint Shahpour Bakhtiar, an old National Front figure, as his last prime minister.

In January 1979, the Shah recognized that he must follow Khomeini's emphatic demand that he leave the country. He left, and Khomeini returned to a historic welcome by his devoted supporters and admirers. In less than a month, the government of Bakhtiar collapsed and Khomeini triumphantly appointed Mahdi Bazargan, an old ally, as the prime minister in charge of the transitional government. By December, Khomeini and his supporters managed to outmaneuver the other religious and secular forces that had participated in the Revolution and take full control of all the institutions and organs of the newly established "Islamic Republic of Iran," with a constitution of its own. But the phenomenal project of appropriating the monumental Revolution as an "Islamic" event had just started.

1 For a comprehensive study of the ideological foundations of the Islamic Revolution in Iran, see Hamid Dabashi, Theology of Discontent: The Ideological Foundations of the Islamic Revolution in Iran (New York, 1993). **2** For the most recent study of the Constitutional Revolution, see Mangol Bayat, Iran's First Revolution: Shiʿism and the Constitutional Revolution of 1905-1906 (Oxford, 1991). **3** See Ervand Abrahamian's Iran between Two Revolutions (Princeton, 1988) for a political history of Iran between the 1900s and the 1970s. **4** For a concise account of Shiʿism, see Moojan Momen, An Introduction to Shiʿism (New Haven, 1985). For an anthology of primary sources on Shiʿism, see S. H. Nasr et al. (eds.), Shiʿism: Doctrines, Thought, and Spirituality (Albany, NY, 1988), and S. H. Nasr et al. (eds.), Expectation of Millennium: Shiʿism in History (Albany, NY, 1989). **5** For a collection of Khomeini's writings best representing this resuscitation of Shiʿi doctrines and sentiments, see Khomeini, Islam and Revolution: Writings and Declarations, trans. and annotated by Hamid Algar (London, 1985). **6** For the most authoritative sociological study of Shiʿism and its political institutionalizations in Iran, see Amir Arjomand, The Shadow of God and the Hidden Imam: Religion, Political Order, and Societal Changes in Shiʿite Iran from the Beginning to 1890 (Chicago, 1988). **7** See Abbas Amanat's Resurrection and Renewal: The Making of the Babi Movement in Iran, 1844-1850 (Ithaca, NY, 1989) for a thorough examination of the Babi movement, the most radical expression of Shiʿi potential for revolutionary outbursts in nineteenth-century Iran. **8** For a brilliant historical narrative of the cultural foundation of the Islamic Revolution in Iran, see Roy Mottahedeh, The Mantle of the Prophet: Religion and Politics in Iran (New York, 1985). **9** For an exposure to non-Iranian manifestations of political Shiʿism in modern times, see Karl-Heinrich Göbel, Moderne Schiitische Politik und Staatsidee˘ (Opladen, Germany, 1984), and Fouad Ajami, The Vanished Imam: Musa al-Sadr and the Shiʿa of Lebanon˘ (Ithaca, NY, 1986). **10** For various studies exploring Shiʿism as a political culture, see Said Amir Arjomand (ed.), Authority and Political Culture in Shiʿism (Albany, NY, 1988). **11** See Said Amir Arjomand's The Turban for the Crown: The Islamic Revolution in Iran (New York, 1988) for a critical assessment of how this gradual adoption occurred. See also Nikki Keddie's Roots of the Revolution: An Interpretative History of Modern Iran (New Haven, 1981) for further historical background. **12** For two brilliant assessments of these complementary aspects, see Michael Fischer and Mehdi Abedi, Debating Muslims: Cultural Dialogues in Postmodernity and Tradition (Madison, 1990). **13** For a comprehensive study of this political organization, see Houchang E. Chehabi, Iranian Politics and Religious Modernism: The Liberation Movement of Iran under the Shah and Khomeini (Ithaca, NY, 1990). **14** See Homa Katouzian's The Political Economy of Iran: Despotism and Pseudo-Modernism (New York, 1981) for an account of this aspect. **15** For this aspect of Shiʿism, see Peter J. Chelkowski (ed.), Taʿziyeh: Ritual and Drama in Iran (New York, 1979). **16** For some salient observations on the fate of secular ideas in Iran, see Homa Katouzian, Musaddiq and the Struggle for Power in Iran (London, 1990). **17** For a good introduction to Mosaddeq's political life and ideas, see ibid.

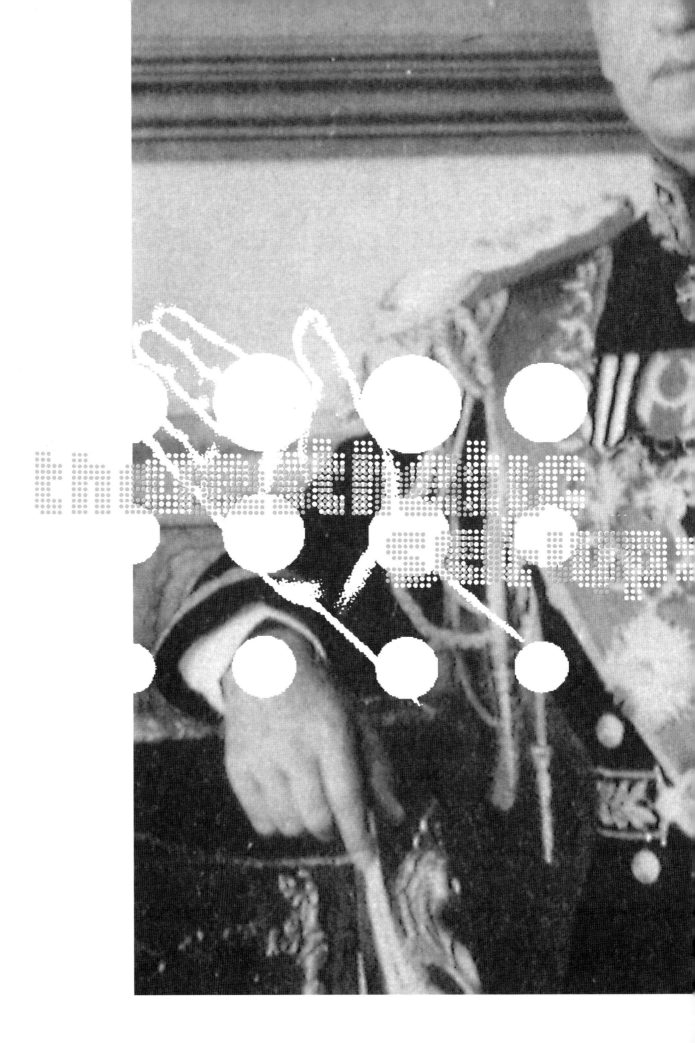

from the myth of

to the art of

Two

How exactly is a revolution appropriated? How was an event so deeply rooted in diverse—religious and secular—social and ideological forces so thoroughly and successfully brought into the wide and all-inclusive bosom of "the Islamic Ideology"? We must begin from the very heart and center of the Revolution itself. The following statement, by a young revolutionary, should take us right into the midst of the revolutionary sentiment:

I was born into a poor family, to a father whose loving care I did not have for more than nine years. Then I spent my childhood reminiscing about the stories which were told about him. These were stories of his facing up to injustice and tyranny, of his standing up against dictatorship and repression. Visible in his old and broken face were years of pain and suffering, of fighting against those who tyrannized him relentlessly. In our home, there was always a scarcity of bread, and the most beautiful music we ever heard was the sound of my father's prayers. So long as he was alive, injustice did not dare to intrude through the small window of our humid room. When the music of his prayers stopped, I remained with my mother, four brothers, and twenty-five years of suffering under tyranny, sorrow, and anxiety. Throughout the reign of Muhammad Reza Shah the tyrant, which occupied all my life, I always searched for someone who, like my father, would stand up to tyranny and without fear fight with the landlord, slap the chief of the police in the face, go to jail for having defended an old woman, and recite his prayers in a loud music. Suddenly, in the wake of the Revolution, I heard the voice of a man from the most noble city of Najaf. The voice was one thousand times louder than my father's. A man whose cry penetrated deep into the very existence of the deprived people. His words were each like a sacred sword coming down on the fake regime of the Shah. I realized that this is my expected savior who is coming from Najaf. He has arisen from the site of Ali's grave, peace be upon him.[1]

This is the voice of a revolution in the making, the self-revealing confessions of a young man about to tell his revolutionary tale, and thus to help appoint and appropriate it as "Islamic." How does this tale compose itself? There is a point where scattered sentiments of an injured self, personal and collective, meet the particulars of an expectation of massive revolt. That revolt invests in the validity of those sentiments and reaches out for the effective mobilization of symbolics sacred to that collectivity, to every individual of that society. A particular delivery of the rhetorical images of convictions—the art of persuasion, the ability to move the individuals in a mass—is designed to make legitimate claims on political obedience, on measures of mass mobilization. To the degree that such rhetoricals of images are rooted in deep and surviving cultural paradigms, they expose a wide angle of vision on the dominant moral matters of a political culture. The purpose, whether or not self-conscious, of aesthetics in any art of persuasion is to transform the experience of rhyme and reason, shape and beauty, into elements of mobilizing conviction. Even more fundamental to the art of persuasion is the built-in mechanism of moralizing enterprise—it moves as it pleases, it convinces as it offers its colorful interpretation of the world. From convictions and moralities, ethics of ultimate ends are made, and the radical aesthetic gives birth to a new revolutionary (wo)man whose past, present, and future are mere extensions of a presumed sense of present ideological identity.

The fountain-head of aesthetic imagination that lends itself to revolutionary mobilization ultimately derives its energy from an enduring and/or renovated enchantment with the world. With a relentless tenacity, the picture of a perfect world, released from all tension and hostility, captivates a revolutionary generation and redefines, and thus re-creates, its radical agenda. Any theoretical, or even analytical, attendance upon the aesthetics of this tenacity, and of this revolutionary use of art, is bound to demythologize the process of creative imagination. "With the birth of aesthetic," we may extend Terry Eagleton's distinction between the theory and the practice of art, "the sphere of art itself begins to suffer something of the abstraction and formalization characteristic of modern theory in general."[2] The necessity of abstraction and formalization for any theoretical or analytical grasp of an act of persuasion is, at the same time conducive to, even concurrent with, a simultaneous deconstruction of the revolutionary mythology. How—and through the revolutionary activation of what particular mechanisms—is this myth mobilized? There is a point at which revolutionary ideologues part company with their detached theorists.

The Parsonian assumption that, in contrast to "propaganda," there is a genuine act of "rational enlightenment"[3] is simply too naive to be taken seriously. There is no discounting the rhetoric of conviction equally operative in both the acts of "enlightenment" and of "persuasion." Any act of propaganda is by definition a collective enterprise in making realities speak an interpretative language. As Parsons himself attested, "most propaganda is oriented

2.1 Resistance to victory.

to the influencing not of single persons, but of large numbers in such a way that its effectiveness will lead to an appreciable alteration of the 'state of the social system' of which they are a part."[4] As a collective enterprise, any act of persuasion is directed not at the analytical but at the symbolic faculties of the collective consciousness. In a very significant way, the rhetoric of the revolutionary pictures which we observe in this book is to persuade, not to argue. At the collective symbolic level, there is no separating the rational and the non-rational, enlightenment and propaganda. The art of persuasion, successfully executed, is an invitation to a symbolic realm of operation in which identities are defined, destinies articulated, the sense of purpose in life and of meaning in the world suggested and legitimated. This is the most salient aspect of revolutionary posters, for example. Once part and parcel of this symbolic realm of conviction, individuals are not merely

persuaded—they are changed for good. The transmutative power of propaganda derives its energy from the permanent need of man to be perpetually enchanted with the world. "The Islamic Revolution" of Iran, with all its orchestrated acts of pictorial persuasion, was a grand occasion of enchantment. Revolutionary rhetorics, both verbal and visual, are heightened moments of re-enchantment through the explosion of a charismatic moment in an otherwise routine history.

The charismatic moment derives its historical energy from an innate force in human collectivity that Ernst Cassirer identified as *animal symbolicum* (the symbolic animal). This quintessential constitution in man Cassirer preferred over and above the illusion of *animal rationale* (the rational animal). "Human rationality" itself was perhaps one of the most successful productions of man's symbolic repertoire. The production was so successful that for a time it was taken for the real thing. Symbolically predisposed, man is more responsive to the visual than to the verbal. Even verbal stimuli must become visual interpretants before they can reach their vast public constituency. Nowhere is this pictoral aspect of the written word more evident than in Islamic calligraphy, which had a profound influence on the revolutionary art of the late 1970s. Collective mobilization for revolutionary purposes can measure the degree of its success only to the extent that it can respond to the innate expectation of the *animal symbolicum*.

In every act of persuasion, mobilizing all forces of symbolic participation in communal identity, there is an active representation of Truth, thus bluntly put outside any modifying or compromising quotation marks. There is no compromising this Truth in any particular ontology or theology. Khomeini, like many other Muslim ideologues, spoke with absolute certainty. The ideological conviction surpasses all the troubles of minor uncertainties. Representation of Truth in every act of persuasion *is* the Truth. Under such revolutionary circumstances, individuals are made to live out the compelling aesthetics of their collective imagination. Living that imagination becomes the functional equivalent of life itself. As social artifacts, the particulars of this collective imagination reveal the most pressing problems of a community—real or relative. A collective imagination reveals its fears and fantasies in its revolutionary art, and then in turn lets the work of art thus produced recreate its place in world history. The revolutionary art of persuasion produced in Iran in the 1980s is thus the most compelling act of self-representation with which Iranians themselves decided to attend their history.

2.2 Symbolizing and destroying the enemies.

Any art of persuasion is the collective construction of a handful of manipulative practitioners of what is quintessential to a culture. They are, whether consciously or otherwise, in direct communication with the most sacred symbolics that at once make and break a communal identity, the particulars of a representation of Truth. Practitioners of the communal culture, these artists/ideologues formulate their immediate political aims, as well as their distant ideological objectives, in terms of mental pictures that immediately register an instant cause of commitment and action. The pictures we observe in this book were not meant to entertain, they were meant to move, mobilize, commit to action.

A commitment to action rests on the active construction of myth. Ernst Cassirer ought to be credited with the monumental achievement of having rescued the central significance of myth, its representing mechanism, in collective human behavior from its hasty dismissal by the Enlightenment as the mere figment of imagination. Figment of imagination indeed the mythical views of the world it might be, but it is precisely in terms of such imaginings

that reality is not only perceived but, more important, constructed. Cassirer's theoretical observations on the nature and function of myth were particularly enriched by the empirical data afforded him during Nazi Germany. Notions of a "master race" and a "superior man" gave the German theorist ample opportunity to see the specifics of a mythical construction of reality and identity. Such mythical constructions are not limited to any particular society or culture. They are constitutional to any human collectivity.[5] Revolutionary Iran of the 1970s and 1980s produced a monumental body of mythological artifacts, literal and pictoral tropes from which the historical reality of something called "the Islamic Revolution" was made. Every constellation of images and words— every revolutionary poster or banknote or postage stamp, for example— contained the constitutional forces of a myth in the making.

A mythical view of reality assumes a reality *sui generis*. It may borrow the specific materials of its construction from the communal culture, from the shared memory of a near or distant history, from the semiotic bonds of a common language, or even from the collective sentiments of a religion. Yet its construction—and continuity—sustains a legitimate reality all unto itself. One is either in or out of this constructed reality. There is no denying it legitimacy on cultural, historical, logical, linguistic, or religious grounds. A mythical view of reality is a self-fulfilling prophecy. It proves itself. Upon the initial political success of the Iranian Revolution of 1978-9, an army of graphic artists was mobilized to name and appropriate it as "Islamic." The self-generating myth of "the Islamic Revolution" never had a more powerful mechanism of persuasion than the art it engendered and sustained.

Hans Blumenberg's brilliant achievement in pointing even beyond Cassirer's insight has permanently secured the central significance of myth in making sense and legitimacy in human existence possible. He has convincingly argued for the coeternality of both mythos and logos in rendering the totality of life in its stable or turbulent phases intelligible and trustworthy. As he successfully demonstrated, myth is not a "primitive" stage in the historical formation of human faculties. While for Cassirer the emergence of Nazi Germany may have appeared as a particular reversion in the unilateral line of progress from logos to mythos, for Blumenberg it is a mere realization of something fundamental to human existence.[6] The reconstruction of the Shiʿi mythos for the specific revolutionary purposes of the late 1970s should not be understood in terms of a successful alternative to its failed secular counterparts. That, more than anything else, is anachronistic. The Shiʿi, as any other, mythos is coaccidental with the believer's insatiable need to ask for an explanation, to demand an answer. Shiʿism, particularly when redefined by contemporary Shiʿi ideologues, explains the world. Any mythological construction of reality has a built-in narrative of interpretation which explains not only itself but also the rest of the world, no matter how tumultuous, with it. Alternative (secular) ideologies may claim a closer affinity with their logos than with their mythos, yet "the Islamic Ideology" always begins with a point of origin that predates its own particular historicity. Understanding its own historicity in terms of an atemporal claim on the believer's credulity, "the Islamic Ideology" explains the rest of the universe to the fullest satisfaction of that believer. When entering its momentous phases of revolutionary attestations, this ideology unleashes every ounce of energy at its disposal to re-create the world in its own image, in the particulars of its mythical reality.

Myth, particularly in acute moments of revolutionary self-redefinitions, rationalizes the world. It brings life under control. Under transitional and tumultuous circumstances, when the historical person in both private and communal realizations of an identity ceases to trust the existing environment, new and powerful myths are created. Beyond securing and signifying the world through their rationalized interpretation of this and any other world, myths promise every measure of eternal safety and salvation. But explaining this world would always have primacy over and above securing salvation in the one to come. The two are related. When, on their way to the battle-lines of the Iraq–Iran war, the Iranian youths were inculcated with the Shiʿi martyrology, the significance of the resuscitated myth is in its explaining the brutality of this world, not least the unfathomable brutality of sending a child to his "voluntary" death. That it also promises eternal bliss in the world to come has less tangible truth and reality than that the orchestrated myth makes this world meaningful and trustworthy.

Blumenberg anchors the perception of "the absolutism of reality" to the human being's biological lack of a securing niche in his/her world. Biologically compelled to take note of everything in the vast reality he/she confronts, the historical person's partial accumulation of rational certainty—itself achieved on borrowed time from the relentless force of myths—is incapable of accounting for "the absolutism," the overabundance of reality, that makes the world. Secular ideologies, with their claim on the "scientific" validity of their socialist or liberal claim on the historical person's credulity, are then no match for such concerted mythologies as "the Islamic Ideology." Such ideologies seek and succeed in explaining everything that exists in this and every other world. If, as Blumenberg insists,[7] there is a constitutional deficiency of instinct in man's biology to cope with "the absolutism of reality," then there is no limiting the range and duration of myth having a central significance in man's making the world bearable and meaningful.[8] Cultures and religions are specific orchestrations of concurrent mythologies collectively devised to help the historical person make sense of an otherwise senseless heap of relentless facticities.[9] Whether routinized or revolutionary, life needs explaining. The Islamic Revolution and its concurrent art of persuasion explains the world. Communal participation in a given explanation is as much comforting to the excited senses of anxiety as it is obligating to sacrifice everything dear to the participants. Enchanted by the rising calls of a new interpretative illusion about the world, the mobilized masses unknowingly celebrate a momentary coming to terms with an otherwise interminable "absolutism of reality."

No degree of "advancement" or "modernization" can make a political culture immune to recourse to mythical perceptions of reality. The "Islamic" Revolution of Iran is a perfect example of this. Here "primitive" and "advanced" political cultures, or conservative and revolutionary ideologies, share a more or less identical propensity towards myth-making. The 2,500th anniversary of the Persian monarchy is as much a colossal orchestration of historical myth and fantasy as the reconstruction of an Islamic Golden Age when all Muslims supposedly lived in peace and harmony. The ideological thrusts and

2.3 Mythologization through the routine activities of daily life.

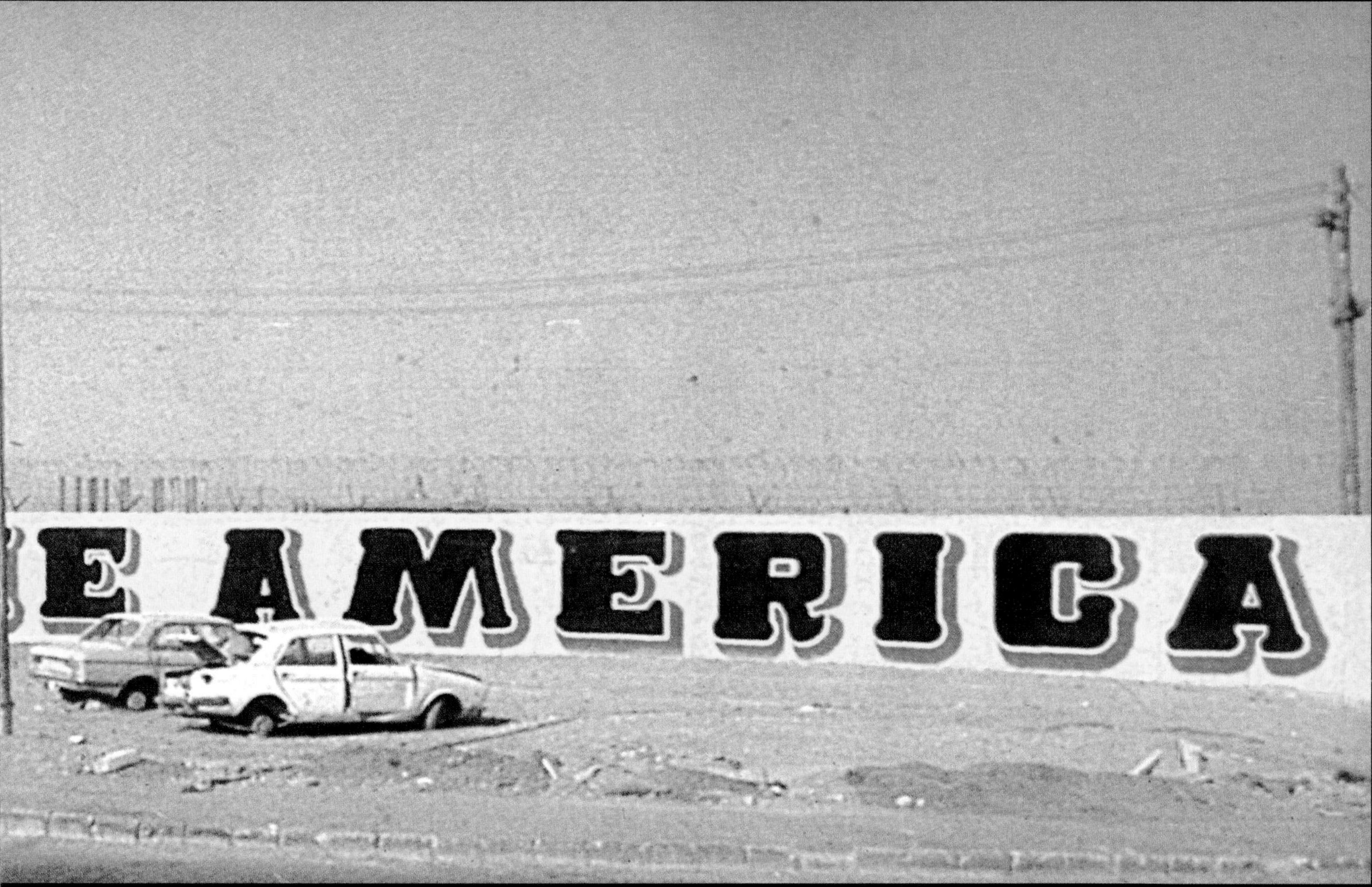
E AMERICA

political uses of myth are variable, but its inevitable seeking after collective membership and loyalty is constant. That membership is an invitation to security. To hide behind an image is the most natural refuge in the face of anxiety-provoking confusion of choice. Here, perhaps the most compelling icon of the Islamic Revolution was the bearded and turbaned image of Ayatollah Khomeini. The image epitomized for millions of his followers the safest and most secure haven from the sea of troubles that seemed to have flooded their disturbed imagination. Confession of obedience and trust in that image explained the world and made it, once again, trustworthy. Khomeini's image thus became the key mythological register, immediately activating a constellation of hidden and apparent symbolics. Refusal to take refuge behind that image meant relentless confrontation with a vast realm of perpetual possibilities and thus anxieties. A mere acknowledgment of its saving authority provided the security and sanctity of having an otherwise inexplicable and threatening world explained and made trustworthy.

The efflorescence of mythological constructs in the modern Islamic art of persuasion renders any teleological conception of history in which political cultures surpass their mythological imperatives and engage in logical fabrication of their identity highly dubitable. Man, in Blumenberg's ground-breaking anthropology, has made himself an *animal symbolicum* not through an involuntary accident in nature but by trying to compose an

2.5 Muharram banner. Black represents mourning; Red, blood sacrifice and on another level, enemy. White represents the colour of the shroud which Muslims are buried in and therefore martyrdom. Green is the colour of the family of the Prophet.

answer to his most fundamental problem, which is "the absolutism of reality."[10] Unfolding itself into unfathomable horizons of possibilities, this "absolutism of reality" perpetually necessitates the active legitimacy of compelling stories that make (apparently) permanent sense of the world and the historical person's location in it. Whenever that permanence is shaken, through whatever historical coincidence, terms of a new enchantment are created to compose yet another mythological explanation of the world. While any particular enchantment is active and valid, its mythological components make life meaningful and trustworthy, even as they exact a heavy toll of commitment and sacrifice from their individual believers. What makes that commitment possible, indeed inevitable, is a rhetoric of revolutionary expectation that links the most mundane realities of a people to their most distant ideals, all mitigated through their most enduring sensibilities. The mobilization of those sensibilities is the active agenda of the revolutionary leader. In Khomeini's revolutionary rhetoric, realities are raised obediently to meet the myth:

As for the oil, they have given all our oil to foreigners, Americans and others. They gave that all to the Americans, and what did they get in return? In return they received arms in order to establish military bases for Mr America. We gave them both oil and military bases. America played a trick on us. And this man [the Shah] was its accomplice. With this trick, America took our oil and in return constructed military bases for itself. It brought [such sophisticated] arms here that our own army cannot use them. Their own advisers have to be present. Their own advisers will have to be here. And that is all for the oil. If, God forbid, he had continued to rule he would have depleted all our oil reserves. He had already destroyed all our agriculture. This nation was in complete bankruptcy and it would have to engage in menial jobs for foreigners. That is why we cry out that we have had enough, and enough is enough. That is why the blood of our youth has been shed. Because we want freedom. It is for fifty years now that we have lived under suffocating tyranny. We had neither [a righteous] newspaper, nor good radio or television. Neither could the religious orators speak [their mind] or deliver sermons from the pulpit. Neither could the religious authorities carry out their duties freely, nor could any other group perform their responsibilities. In his [the Shah's] time too, suffocating tyranny has continued more adamantly. Even now that his half-dead body goes on living, so does the half-dead body of tyranny. We say that he is illegal, so is his government, his parliament. These are all illegal. Should the representatives continue in their positions, they will be held accountable. They will have to be tried. And we will put them on trial. I will appoint the government. I will slap the existing government in the face. I will appoint a government. On behalf of this people, I will appoint a government. I, because this people believe in me.[11]

In that "I" dwells the historical expectation of an age, agitated and defined by realities that yield obediently to myths. From a rhetoric of revolutionary expectation emerges a reconstruction of reality, and from that the enduring elements of a semiology of conviction. The semiology of the revolutionary images that were actively employed in the course of the Islamic movement in Iran constitutes perhaps the most significant of our systematic attempts to unravel the nature and organization, the narrative and rhetoric, of this cataclysmic event. Reading these signs and interpreting these symbols provide us with a unique opportunity to observe the act and the process of signification that became instrumental in the course of the revolutionary event. Operative in the context of illiterate masses, the functional significance of these images in the revolutionary mobilization can hardly be exaggerated. The act of ideological and political propaganda even in a fully literate society rests on a minimum of linguistic, as opposed to a maximum of pictorial, apparatus. The necessity of transmitting the most cogent political message with a minimum number of words, and in such simple words that register effectively with the lowest common denominator, requires an exceedingly simple semiotic machinery. That necessity is translated into pictorial imagery that under pressing revolutionary circumstances can immediately register with and thus mobilize a leviathan of public convictions. Pictures and signs, with the minimum of or even no accompanying words, are constitutional to revolutionary mobilization among illiterate masses.

2.6 A narrative painting, commemorating the sacrosanct events in Shiᶜi history and memory.

Any analogical representation, any system of signs brought together in the space of a revolutionary poster, a stamp, a banknote, or a mural, is a constructed reality. The constellation of signs and symbols is put together in order to make a statement. There is nothing "accidental" about such concentrations of imageries. They are brought together to inform, to convene, to commit, to move, to mobilize. How is this mobilization actually achieved? The communicative power of any symbolic constellation of imageries derives its energy from the common repertoire of the collective cultural memory. The memory is both active and acquisitive. From the scattered parts of dormant memories active ingredients of an exuberant recollection may be reconstituted. Images and pictorial rhetorics speak the language of these memories—sentimental, affective, mobilizing. The dialogue these pictorial imageries invite unfolds a self-sustaining narrative that can proceed until the full realization of its specific ideological and political objectives.

These pictorial constellations, whether on the small space of a stamp or on the vast span of a mural, are open invitations asking, indeed leading, their observers to participate in a feast of collective construction of sympathy, apathy, or a range of oscillating sentiments that fall in between. The observer, the observed, and the act of observation become one, through a process the Shi'i scholastic philosophers have long since recognized as "the unification of the thinker, the thought, and the thinking." The pictorial object of thinking (recollecting, identifying, sympathizing, etc.) draws those who pause, however inattentively or inadvertently, to think and reflect themselves into a relentless process of *rapprochement* with the constructed objects of deliberation. A representation of the figure of Imam Hussein, a suggestion of the color red, and a mere hint that "Verily! Life is belief and fighting [for that belief]" are enough to create a universe of relentless signification that in every minutiae of its detail recreates the macrocosm of Shi'i historical self-consciousness. As an image may appear resistant to meaning when observed outside its circumstantial charges, it acquires multiple and simultaneous layers of signification when looked at in its historical immediacies. Even the conjunction of explicit words with the obscure implicity of colors and shapes cannot render the image meaningful outside its cultural, always historically anchored, context. An image is a pictorial invitation to interpretation. To interpret the image outside of its historical immediacy, one has to think oneself into the collective mind of the receiving audience, on a march towards its revolutionary goals. It is in the charged vicinity of the ideological statement, on the sharp edges of the political event, that a pictorial image speaks the deepest aspirations of a collective imagination. Once the cultural and historical network centered around the symbolic image is spread and charted out, its multiple and simultaneous meanings, and more important the possibilities of its meaningfulness, become self-evident.

The communicative power of an image ought to be seen not on any set of linguistic parameters, that is, digital units of conceptual abstractions, but on its offering a pale or vivid text of imagination which sets a train of interpretations in motion. Linguistic communication, whether aural or textual, carries its own power of interpretability. The textual accompaniment of words often determines the range of interpretability that an otherwise almost open-ended image may contain. There are also the possibilities of verbal accompaniments, such as in *pardeh-khani* in traditional Iranian commiseration of the Karbala event. Standing, walking, motioning, narrating, and signing the events of Karbala in front of a spread-out "curtain" of images, the *naqqal* (literally, the narrator) or *morshed* (literally, he who leads to the right path) corresponds his words with the projected images, his conceptions with his audience's imagination, and moves towards a fluid construction of emotionally charged meaning between the Karbala's universe of imagination and the Shi'i audience. The occasional presence of a *bacheh-morshed*, a novice who accompanies the master narrator, creates a possibility of leading a dialogue in front of the curtain. At strategically significant moments, the *bacheh-morshed* interjects a crucial question or two and thus gives the master narrator added momentum and recharged energy to pursue the rest of the narrative. A similar strategy of concurrent aural narrative was adopted when the silent movie was first introduced in Iran. The functional equivalent of a *naqqal* would stand, walk, and motion on stage and in front of the silver screen, explaining and interpreting the implied narrative of the moving pictures. The interjected written passages, meant to inform the original English-speaking audience, were of no particular consequence or importance to the Iranian audience. The Persian narrative of the updated *naqqal* would have its own independent logic, almost *sui generis*, only tangentially related to the specifics of the moving images.

Quite independent of the aural or textual accompaniment, and equally independent of any picture-less aural or textual narrative, the image has a "language," the possibility of communication, of its own. Depending on the specifics of its composition and construction, an image, consciously and deliberately made (with all the powers of the subconscious that become operative at these moments), carries a limited range of interpretation, from a rudimentary level of instruction ('No left turn') to a complicated system of imaginal narratives (as in the *pardeh* of the Karbala event). It is the inherited or adopted universe of discourse engulfing the constructed images and the particulars of its rejuvenated energies in immediate historicity of the event that determines the range of possibilities constitutional to a constructed image. As there is a close, almost metamorphic, relationship between image and imagination, so there is an ineluctable reciprocity between the message(s) inherent in the pictorial representation of some reality and the universe of sensibilities that renders that reality truthful.

As we begin to read the images of the Islamic Revolution in Iran, one question should control all dimensions of our interpretation. How much "intention" determines the origin and destination of those pictoral images? The question of intentionality is central to the construction of any image. What are images made for? As the famous encounter between Hamlet and Polonius vividly shows, the natural (or better yet, accidental) lack of intentionality can make a mockery of all free-floating interpretations. To Hamlet's mocking suggestion, "Do you see yonder cloud that's almost in shape of a camel?" Polonius submissively agrees that "By th' mass, and 'tis like a camel indeed."[12] Hamlet can instantly offer a counter-reading of the innocent cloud, "Methinks it is like a weasel." Polonius can modify his reading accordingly, "It is backed like a weasel." "Or like a whale," Hamlet charges. "Very like a whale," Polonius updates and conforms his submissive readings. Hamlet's subsequential "Then I will come to my mother by and by" is as ludicrous in conclusion of such conflicting premises as those presumed premises themselves. Save the inherent meteorological forces of nature, of whose "intentions" we are unaware, there is no shape or purpose to the mass of a cloud. Readings can be as varied and contradictory as Hamlet wants, or as Polonius is willing to submit. But contrary to the shape of the cloud, pictorial representations of reality have every instance of intentionality in them. To be sure, there are instances where the natural and physical objects are subsumed under the disguise and rubric of intentionality. Early in the course of the revolutionary movement, a religious authority was reported to have actually seen, as an omen of divine approval, Khomeini's face on the face of the moon. It is of course possible to make believe to see Khomeini's face on the moon, as it was possible to depict Jackie Gleason's face on the rising moon of the title passage of the television series "The Honeymooners." But in both cases we have the intentional imposition of meaning and significance on an otherwise innocent natural object. In Khomeini's case it is the full power of the Persian and Shiʿi symbolic signification of the moon that informs the reception of the message; and in Jackie Gleason's case it is the rising face of Ralph Cramden over the panorama of Manhattan and the correspondence between the "happy moon" and "The Honeymooners," that announces half an hour of fun and joy in a particular geography and history.

Both these cases are examples of a specific kind of intentionality imposed on the physical innocence of a natural object. Beyond this imposition of a system of meaning and significance onto an otherwise mute object, we have the almost

infinite possibility of constructing intentional images for specific, in our case revolutionary, purposes. Whether it is a mere pictorial representation of a sound or of a red tulip, or the image accompanied by a few words, the constructed image has been put together intentionally, and it is precisely because of this intentionality that the pictorial representation contains what Roland Barthes has called "a veritable ontology of the process of signification."[13] As with the advertising image, which Barthes describes as "frank," "full," "emphatic," and "formed with a view to the optimum reading,"[14] so the revolutionary images are launched with a full range of intended propaganda built into them. The "art" of persuasion is precisely in this masterful coordination of the stated and hidden agenda of revolutionary conviction and mobilization, on the one hand, and the range of culturally mandated symbolics at the disposal of the artist, on the other. The story of the Islamic Revolution in Iran is the story of carefully and

deliberately constructed images, drawn from the depth of Persian historical memory, orchestrated towards specific political ends.

But as we begin to trace the "history" of these images, we realize that the element of intentionality has its inherent limitations. Beyond the textual intentionality of the symbolic construction of images, we have the multiple possibilities of readings, from the mere pictorial representation that this is a sword (as opposed to a gun), or that is a red tulip (as opposed to a rose), to what a sword or a red tulip signifies, means, indicates, as symbolized in a particular pictorial culture. That culture, in all instances, is instrumental in a public's reading of the pictoral text. There is no reading a semiotic construction, verbal or iconic, without the necessary cultural context that at once informs that construction and makes its deciphering possible. The semiotic ensemble brings together into the common space of the artifact a collection of shared symbolics that raises its audience beyond its immediate material surroundings and into the realm of their collective fantasy. In terms of that collective fantasy, the mundane realities of the recipient crowd are reinterpreted anew and thus an untapped well of energy is excavated in their deepest sensibilities.

Those sensibilities are always culture-specific in all their acts of symbolic signification, and yet universal in their claim to authority and obedience. The color symbolisms of these revolutionary pictures we are about to read ought to be "Islamic," "Shiʿi," or "Iranian" in some significant sense, and yet perfectly

2.7 Martyrdom represented by red tulips, an identification deeply rooted in Iranian literary and epic imagination.

2.8 Khomeni portrayed within the tradition of the ascension of the Prophet in classical Persian minature painting.

literate person from his/her received cultural artifacts, is doubly intensive by virtue of the inherent opaqueness of image *and* because of the transitory nature of Iranian society in the fourth quarter of the twentieth century, when the youthful revolutionary crowd could not have been assumed as fully participating in the pictorial representations of an ideological imagery, the iconic heritage of their immediate and distant ancestry.

The crucial distinction between pictorial and verbal communication in the context of the Iranian symbolic culture is best represented in the specifics of the *Shahnameh*, the "national epic" that has increasingly assumed an iconic significance of its own. There are various levels of participation in the stories and episodes of the "national epic," making it conducive to all projects of nation-building. First, there are those who can read Ferdowsi's account of these stories and thus gain certain access to the specifics of the epic. This group constitutes a relatively small proportion of the collective participation in the comm-unal construction of this "national epic." Second, there are those whose participation in the same "national epic" is merely pictorial. Although the first group, too, can enjoy the accompanying miniature paintings, whether in the aristocratic exclusivity of yore or in the modern printed versions, the pictorial representations, particularly in the popular form of *Naqqashi-ye Qahvehkhaneh* (coffeehouse painting), appeal in parti-cular to the unlettered observers. Third, there are those who find their way into their "national epic" through the dramatic narrative of the *naqqal* (narrator) in the same coffeehouses, or occasionally in other communal sites such as the mausoleum of a saint, a graveyard, a caravan of pilgrims, or just on a crossroads in any old town. The dramaturgical effects of the latter case are particularly congenial to the epical nature of the *Shahnameh* narrative. One can argue that these three major groups (there are subdivisions, such as a movie or a modern theatrical rendition of a *Shahnameh* story, which can be ignored for the moment) have three relatively different conceptions of what they collectively call their "national epic," the *Shahnameh*. But at the specific moment of political agitation, as we shall demonstrate repeatedly in the course of this study, all levels of reading and interpretation convene to mobilize a specific audience. The same range of possibilities become operative when a revolutionary poster, or a postage stamp, or a Friday sermon is mounted, mailed, or delivered. Participation in the revolutionary mobilization can be instigated through verbal, visual, and aural agencies, or any combination thereof.

Let us briefly consider the verbal aspect of such revolution-ary mobilizations. Khomeini's speeches, declarations, and edicts

universal in the range of meanings they intend to invoke. The particular construction of the image and/or word, which involves two simultaneous withdrawings from two distinct universes of discourse, is of immediate concern to us in this book. A semi-literate society can be taken as half-literate, half-illiterate, with the exact statistics of that "half" of no particular significance here. When the picture of a sword or of a red tulip is raised with certain words written above, below, or on either side of it, the recipient individual can either see and read both the image and the words or only see and read the image and only see but not read the words. Consequently, for this particular crowd the constructed image can operate at two independent levels: there are those who can see and read both, and there are those who can see and read one but not the other. The latter possibility itself falls into two subcategories: those who can see and read the picture but not the words, and those who can see and read the words but (precisely because of their verbal literacy) the picture remains mute to them. The latter possibility, made plausible by a range of cultural alienations that distance a are the archetypal epitome of the verbal mode in the art of persuasion. The wide circulation of his declarations made them massively available in print and on tape. They appealed to the most sacred sentiments and the most cherished memories of the Shiʿi constituency. Here is an example:

I am perplexed as to whom I should express my condolences for this tragedy, this profound tragedy [of some demonstrators being killed early in 1978]. Should I express my condolences to the most noble Prophet, God's salutations and greetings be upon him, to the infallible Imams, peace be upon them, to His Holiness the Hidden Imam, God's greetings be upon him? Or should I offer my condolences to the Islamic community, to Muslims, to all the oppressed people in the four corners of the world, or just to the poor people of Iran, the suffering people of Qom, or to parents who have lost a loved one, or to centers of religious learning and the noble men of knowledge? To whom should one express one's condolences, to whom one's congratulations, with these calamities that occur to Islam while this awakened nation puts up such resistance against them, getting killed voluntarily, getting insulted? They have machine-gunned people without any excuse. Although the reports are different, some news organizations report seventy [people killed], others say 100, most report to us from 100 to 250. Some telegrams from Europe and the United States report up to 300, and still it is not clear. The number of casualties is not clear here. Perhaps later, if at all possible. If as on 10 June [1963] they would not drop people into the Howz Sultan Lake, if [indeed reliable] statistics are possible, [more accurate] numbers will be reported. It is reported, and this has been confirmed, that people have gone to hospitals and volunteered to donate their blood to these people who need blood. And yet they have been incarcerated. Some of those who needed blood have died. They have not given [the bodies of] those killed to their relatives. If their relatives insisted, they have asked for 500 tuman for having killed the man. Whom should we thank for all these? To whom should we express our condolences?[15]

The emotional reach of such rhetorical exclamations, powerful precisely because they originate from reality and then take rhetorical flight, is hard to exaggerate. The reach of Khomeini's rhetoric, from his intonations to his use of very simple words, transcended all social and cultural groupings.

The revolutionary posters are the best examples of the visual mode in the art of persuasion. These posters appeared in all massive demonstrations and invariably invited the Shiʿi crowd to sacrifice their mortal and transitory life for what was more enduring in the world to come. The visual impact of these iconic representations of sacrifice and worship cut deep into the most enduring memories and sensibilities of the revolutionary crowd. These posters are carefully constructed orchestrations of shapes, colors, and memories. They draw their revolutionary zeal and energy from the very depths of Iranian visual history.

The Friday sermons are the most compelling mode of mobilization in the aural art of persuasion. The soccer field of the Tehran University campus was instantly redefined as the sacrosanct center of the Muslim gathering: the mosque, representing the mosque of the Prophet in Medina, an extension of the House of God Almighty Himself, the Kaʿbah. In the redefined soccer field were delivered the highest oratory of the revolutionary mobilization. The Friday sermons were delivered to tens of thousands who were present and to millions who participated *in absentia*. The verbal, visual, and aural forces of persuasion thus worked separately and together to prepare and whip up their audience into an absolute and final state of mental and emotional readiness—the cultural and ideological foregrounding of the Revolution itself, in all its material force and presence.[16]

1 THIS PASSAGE IS TAKEN FROM AN EYEWITNESS ACCOUNT OF THE ISLAMIC REVOLUTION BY AKBAR KHALILI, GAM BAH GAM BA INQILAB (TEHRAN, 1981). ALL TRANSLATIONS FROM ORIGINAL SOURCES, UNLESS OTHERWISE INDICATED, ARE OURS. 2 TERRY EAGLETON, THE IDEOLOGY OF THE AESTHETICS (LONDON, 1990). 3 TALCOTT PARSONS' INFLUENTIAL ESSAY ON PROPAGANDA, "PROPAGANDA AND SOCIAL CONTROL," APPEARED IN HIS ESSAYS IN SOCIOLOGICAL THEORY: PURE AND APPLIED (GLENCOE, ILL., 1949), PP. 275-309. 4 IBID., PP. 275-6. 5 ERNST CASSIRER, THE PHILOSOPHY OF SYMBOLIC FORMS, 3 VOLS. (LONDON AND NEW HAVEN, 1955). 6 HANS BLUMENBERG, WORK ON MYTH (CAMBRIDGE, MASS., 1985). 7 IBID., PP. 3-33. 8 FOR AN ELABORATION OF THIS POINT, SEE PHILIP RIEFF, "BY WHAT AUTHORITY: POST-FREUDIAN REFLECTIONS ON THE REPRESSION OF THE REPRESSIVE AND MODERN CULTURE," IN JOHN P. DIGGINS AND MARK E. KANN (EDS.), THE PROBLEM OF AUTHORITY IN AMERICA (PHILADELPHIA, 1981), PP. 225-55. 9 ON THIS POINT, SEE MAX WEBER, THE SOCIOLOGY OF RELIGION (BOSTON, 1922), PARTICULARLY PP. 58-9. 10 BLUMENBERG, WORK ON MYTH, PP. 9-11. 11 THIS PASSAGE IS TAKEN FROM A SPEECH OF KHOMEINI'S. SEE THE COLLECTION OF HIS SPEECHES, SAHIFAH-YE NUR (TEHRAN, 1982), VOL. 4: 284-5. 12 HAMLET, ACT 3, SCENE 2. 13 SEE ROLAND BARTHES, "RHETORIC OF THE IMAGE," IN ROBERT E. INNIS (ED.), SEMIOTICS: AN INTRODUCTORY ANTHOLOGY (BLOOMINGTON, IND., 1985), PP. 192-205. 14 IBID., P. 193. 15 KHOMEINI, SAHIFAH-YE NUR, VOL. 2: 1. 16 FOR AN EXCELLENT STUDY OF THE REVOLUTIONARY USES OF EMOTIONAL CHANGES IN SHIʿI RITUALS, SEE H. G. AZADANLOO, "PERFORMATIVE ELEMENTS OF SHIʿITE RITUAL AND MASS MOBILIZATION: THE CASE OF IRAN," CRITIQUE, FALL 1993, PP. 35-54.

theimaginativeset-up: NARRATIVE PAINTING

andpaintingrecitationin iranian shiism

IN ORDER TO APPROACH THE EFFLORESCENCE OF REVOLUTIONARY ART
THAT EXPLODED ONTO POSTERS, MURALS, BANKNOTES, AND STAMPS IN
THE WAKE OF THE ISLAMIC REVOLUTION, WE OUGHT TO START FROM
CERTAIN POWERFUL PICTORAL NARRATIVES CONSTITUTIONAL TO THE
IRANIAN AESTHETIC TRADITIONS. ALTHOUGH THE ROOTS OF THESE
TRADITIONS MAY BE TRACED BACK TO PRE-MODERN HIS-
TORY, THE ART OF THE QAJAR PERIOD (1779-1925) IS OF
IMMEDIATE SIGNIFICANCE. ARTISTIC TRADITIONS AND
NARRATIVES ORIGINATING IN THIS PERIOD WERE USED
AND MASTERFULLY MANIPULATED IN THE COURSE OF
THE REVOLUTIONARY MOMENTUM IN ORDER TO DEFINE
THAT CATACLYSMIC HISTORICAL EVENT AS AN "ISLAMIC
REVOLUTION." IT IS IMPOSSIBLE TO APPRECIATE MANY
CRUCIAL ASPECTS OF THE REVOLUTIONARY MOMENT THAT
LED TO THE ESTABLISHMENT OF THE ISLAMIC REPUBLIC
IN IRAN WITHOUT UNDERSTANDING THE RENARRATING
POTENTIALS CONSTITUTIONAL TO VARIOUS PERFORMING
ARTS ASSOCIATED WITH THE KARBALA EVENT. THE KARBALA EVENT, AS
A DEFINING MASTER NARRATIVE, HAS REMAINED AT THE HEART OF
SHIᶜI COLLECTIVE CONSCIOUSNESS, TO BE REINVENTED FOR ANY
NUMBER OF IMMEDIATE POLITICAL ENDS.[1]

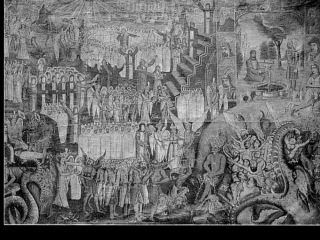

3.1 Muhammad Modaber:
The Last Judgement.
Marco Gregorian Collection.

The revolutionary ideologues, the new prophetic voices of
the "Islamic" enchantment, needed to proclaim themselves. In a
classical and useful definition of "propaganda," Talcott Parsons
identified the process as "one kind of attempt to influence
attitudes, and hence directly or in-
directly the actions of people, by linguistic stimuli, by the written or
spoken word."[2] Two modifications are
necessary, as we begin to trace a

crucial artistic tradition resuscitated for "the Islamic Revolution" in
this definition. First, the necessary and functional stimuli are not

3.2 Muhammad Modaber: The Karbala Battle.

3.3 The first Imam of the Shi'is 'Ali.

عاشورا

3.4 Muhammad Mudaber: ᶜAshura. Marco Gregorian Collection.

limited to the written or spoken word. Pictorial images—movies, pictures, posters, murals, stamps, banknotes, etc.—are equally, if not more, powerful in the art of mobilization for a common revolutionary purpose. Such orchestrations of visual stimuli are particularly important in a political culture that, by necessity, works through non-literate rather than literate modes of persuasion. Second, any such orchestrated mobilization of attitudes and actions does not stop at the artificial doorstep of a mere temporary conviction. It carries, if successful, the process of persuasion far and long enough to achieve an actual, for all practical purposes, transmutation of the revolutionary person. The art of persuasion, the aesthetics of revolt, is a culture-building, memory-making, and character-shaping act of enduring significance.

Where are the imaginative and historical roots of the culture-building enterprise? The large-scale paintings on wall and on canvas

that depict mainly religious martyrology and are now referred to as naive, primitive, folk, or coffeehouse paintings were first produced in Qajar times, and not, as is often argued by certain scholars, at the end of the Safavid period (1501-1736). They are, however, the result of some 1,100 years of gradual evolution and development in Shiᶜi mourning rituals. In Iranian art and culture various social groupings and the court have always lived in close proximity, but when mainstream art moved from the rustic and tribal to the urban and courtly, in the final product of this amalgam the folk aspects were usually overlaid by courtly appearances. In the case of the paintings we shall consider here, however, the situation was reversed. It was the folk mourning rituals and related arts that were encouraged and supported by the court and the landed or merchant elite, after Shiᶜism became the state religion of Iran during the Safavid period. The Karbala mourning rituals proved to be an

3.5 After B. Vereschquine, *Voyage Dans Les Provinces Du Caucase*, (1869).

effective means for spreading Shiᶜism across the land, and they retained their popular features and appeal. Only during the time of Nader Shah (1736-47), for sectarian reasons, and the Pahlavis (1926-79), for modernizing ones, was this not the case.

Since modern scholarship on Islamic art has by and large been devoted to so-called *Hochkunst*, these folk paintings have not been much studied. Even the few art historians who were interested in them ignored their iconographic and artistic value until Samuel Peterson's dissertation in 1981.[3] But not until the Islamic Revolution of 1978-9 did the full potential of these artistic forms become apparent in a very radical and dramatic way. Although this art lacks the refinement and the delicate touch of the miniature paintings of the Timurid and Safavid periods, which were intended for a small group of *cognoscenti* and are now favored by academia, it is a vibrant reflection of the aspirations and the *Weltanschauung* of a considerable segment of the Iranian people. While certain set artistic sensitivities may be offended by the often "crude and clumsy" brush-strokes of the *taᶜziyeh* painters, their work should be studied, if for nothing else, for their flouting of radically powerful Islamic taboos and restrictions concerning figural representation of the holy personalities, and for bringing Iran into an extremely significant pan-Asiatic painting recitation tradition.

The folkloric basis of this art is of particular significance here because it was on that basis that later revolutionaries made use of its mass appeal. The metarhetorical, iconic forces of this art should be kept in mind as it is being transformed into an art of persuasion. In the light of Parsons' contrasting of propaganda with "rational enlightenment," let us examine the precise mode of operation through which the act of persuasion achieves its ends. What turns the act of propaganda into the art of persuasion is precisely the

3.6 ᶜAshura in Mehriz, 1977.

3.7 After B. Vereschquine, *Voyage Dans Les Provinces Du Caucase*, (1869).

mythological—or what every generation likes to call "traditional"—components operative in that act. No political culture, no matter how "primitive" or "advanced" on some imaginary scale of comparison, is immune to the active, or reactivated, operation of mythos in claiming any minor territory temporarily lost to logos. In understanding the act and art of propaganda, then, we are compelled to investigate the specific operation of myth and symbol in a political culture. Signs and their systemizations into a collective ideological statement are essential to any art of persuasion, making a community of revolutionary interpreters do what they were otherwise unable to do. At the moment of revolutionary agitation, the community of interpreters assumes full, leading control of the images. Thus at the revolutionary turn of events every constellation of meaning and signification is suspended, awaiting a momentous redefinition. Signs need not be picturesque. Words, as Vygotsky has said, are paradigmatic "semiotic objects."[4] "A word is a microcosm of human consciousness."[5] In the stable and revolutionary phases of this consciousness, reconstructed images of past, present, and future become cooperative in giving the historical person an enduring sense of identity. There is no politically consequential social act without a culturally determined constellation of meaning linking that act to a larger frame of universal significance. Here, as elsewhere, the symbolic language does not merely represent reality; it makes it, it *is* reality. Thus entering every revolutionary semiosis are the historical person's constitutional forces of culture-building symbols.

How does the historical person redefine a living culture? Let us look at narrative painting closely. Painting religious personalities for the masses was a major development in Islamic art. To understand its meaning, purpose, iconography, and technique we must look to Shiʿi martyrology and its related rituals. In 680 CE a battle took place in the desert of Karbala in what is now Iraq. There the ritual and myth of Imam Hussein, which persist in all the Shiʿi communities, originated. Hussein, the champion of the Shiʿites, the son of Ali and the grandson of the Prophet Muhammad, was, according to tradition, on his way to join the community at Kufa when he, his band of seventy-two followers, and his entire family were overtaken by the hordes of the Sunni caliph Yazid (reigned 680-3 CE) and killed in a bloody battle in that arid desert on the day of ʿAshura, the 10th of the month of Muharram. All Shiʿites, but particularly the Shiʿites of Iran, congregate each Muharram and the following month of Safar in a passionate re-enactment of the Karbala scene. There they merge past with present in the firm belief that suffering all the agonies of Hussein will facilitate their own salvation on Judgment Day. The routine, regular, and periodic re-enactment of the Karbala event is the most significant mode of transhistorical identification that has for centuries held together generations of Iranians affiliated with the Shiʿi branch of Islam.

In the course of thirteen centuries the myths and legends that have grown up around this episode of martyrdom have found expression in processions of mourners who wail, weep, strike their heads, and otherwise mortify themselves to demonstrate their grief for the martyrs of Karbala. This ambulatory ritual in the main streets and squares of towns and villages in Iran has by now grown into an extraordinary pageant. The re-enactment of the Karbala event is one of the most compelling aspects of Persian performing arts. The account of Salmons and van Goch in 1737 describes the procession as follows:

Triumphal arches here and there display victory and honor with their decorations showing Hussein's every attribute. Outstanding in the large public processions are the big theatrically arranged wagons showing scenes of his life, his deeds, his battles, and his death. These wagons are often pulled about accompanied by people in armor, flags, and emblems of war and victory, depicting some of Hussein's deeds. For example, a wagon representing the death of Hussein has a deck-like cover coated with sand to represent the arid battlefield. Underneath people are lying thrusting their heads, arms, and hands through holes in the cover so they will lie on the sand above to appear as dismembered limbs, sprinkled with blood or red paint and colored with a deathly pallor so as to look most natural. Hussein, pallid and bloody, is lying on another wagon. Several living doves sit on his body, while others are nesting in his blood. After a while, the men under the cover release their bonds, two at a time, so that they can "fly to Medina" to announce Hussein's death to his sister. Wherever this wagon passes, the people set up such wailing to show their grief in so many ways and with such conviction, imitation, and naturalistic representations that one wonders at their capacity to give vent to such appropriate signs of suffering so realistically. Their spirit shows through plainly in these impersonations, nor do they spare their bodies: in zeal or desperation, they shed their blood, wound themselves, or are wounded in fights with others; they carry out these intentions with such zeal that it sometimes leads to their own death. It is not possible to tell the difference between feigned dizziness, fainting, and the real thing. One must consider what the stricken people on these tragic wagons endure while presenting their limbs, decapitated heads, hands, and legs in such an uncomfortable position, while lying there as if they were dead themselves. [They do this] in all kinds of weather during the processions. Still they suffer rather than move or do something which would disturb the verisimilitude which might be lost. [On the fringes of the procession] men in armor fight with each other or wound themselves and shed their blood in honor of the Holy One. Others lie down in the street and pretend to be the dying Hussein, looking so miserable that they seem to be *in extremis*. It is remarkable how they imitate the thirst Hussein is supposed to have suffered in the arid desert and in battle. Their tongues protrude, and they sigh and groan with such baleful looks and appear so weak that they really look as if they were pining for a drop of water. If it is offered, however, they refuse it so as to imitate the Holy One's restraint. About him there is a

3.8 Hussein Qullar Agassi: Siavash, The Iranian legendary hero victoriously endures the fire test. Marco Gregorian Collection. The greatly admired brave deeds and noble qualities of the heroes of the Iranian national epic, *The Shahnameh*, became in time the deeds and qualities of the revered Shiʿi martyrs.

3.9 Tekiyeh Muᶜaven al-Mulk, Kermanshah, tile painting representing the *rowzeh-khani*.

legend that when the angel offered him a cup of water, he refused it, saying, "Since it is determined that I must die, I must do it; otherwise I would only have to stick my finger in the earth and a fresh spring of water would issue forth. Indeed, I could produce a whole stream of water for myself." An armored man fends off help in the same way as Hussein would have done when, it is said, a legion of angels wished to stand by him against his enemies. Meanwhile they call out, "Hussein, Hussein," to the passers-by in a failing voice. Some are naked and paint themselves with blood or blood-colored paint. Others are painted black, in mourning for Hussein. Some really wound themselves and bleed. Still others bury themselves in the earth and dust with only their heads sticking out, with a pot or jar covering it; a second man stands by to remove the jug and show the passer-by the head of Hussein and to collect alms. Some rush down with pitiful cries and expressions, others with enraged screams of revenge.[6]

The Karbala tragedy had a great impact on the literature of the Islamic world, especially on a genre known as *maqatil*.[7] The *maqatil* in turn gave birth to a stationary Karbala ritual known by various names. In Iran it is called *rowzeh-khani*. The origin of this name goes back to the title of a Persian-language masterpiece of *maqatil* called *Rowzat al-Shuhada*.[8] This ritual of public recitation and chanting of elegies which recount the suffering of Hussein and other Shiᶜi martyrs takes place in public squares, under a tent or awning, in private residences, caravanserais, and in buildings especially erected for the purpose. Despite the fact that the *rowzeh-khani* is usually contained by the walls of a building, a courtyard, or

a tent, the emotions run as high as they do in the processions. The *rowzeh-khan*, the man who runs the show, can manipulate the mood and emotions of the audience, through voice modulation, chanting, crying, and gesture according to the content of the story. The function of the *rowzeh-khan* can hardly be exaggerated in the recreation and engendering of the Karbala narrative. That narrative draws its energy from an extremely powerful act of imagination that must wed the history of the present to the immediacy of the past. Somewhere between romanticism and rationality, every constellation of the mythical view of life finds its own particular niche. In this niche, Karbala paradigm presenting itself for active interpretation, truth is neither exaggerated nor categorized, simply represented. The mythical view of the world always begins, contrary to its appearing otherwise, with the most concrete, the most material miseries and expectations, and sublimates them into the most sacred and universal. Every act of persuasion, as a crescendo of rejuvenated pictures and images, links the most common denominator of a shared cause of suffering, actual or imaginative, to some universal term of explanation. This link, and that explanation, are either subservient to the ruling regime or else subversive to it. Under revolutionary circumstances, the subversive forces take over in the mythical explanation of the *status quo*, thus mobilizing every received and concocted image of persuasion to reach for an immediate political goal, as articulated in a distant ideological objective, the ideals of that representation of truth. Thus the *rowzeh-khan* becomes the effective truth-teller.

Around the middle of the eighteenth century the ambulatory and the stationary rituals fused together, giving birth to

54

the only indigenous drama in the world of Islam—*taʿziyeh-khani*, known also as *shabih-khani*. The story lines of *rowzeh-khani* were converted into the dramatic texts of the *taʿziyeh*. The movement of the parade was changed into the motions of the actors; the parade costumes became stage costumes. In the beginning the passion play was nothing more than a short playlet integrated into the procession and performed at street corners. Soon, however, it was separated from the parade and became an independent event performed in the open, in the courtyards of caravanserais, private houses, and special buildings called *tekiyeh* or *husseiniyeh*. It may share the space with the *rowzeh-khani*. In the second half of the nineteenth century these buildings became a major feature in Iranian towns. European travelers of the time tell us that structures for the purpose were being erected in every neighborhood. *Tekiyeh* and *husseiniyeh* were built mainly by the well-to-do as a pious act and public service. Some could seat thousands of spectators, but most accommodated only a few hundred. Many were temporary structures erected especially for the Muharram observances.[9]

In the Qajar period, and especially during the reign of Naser al-Din Shah (1848-96), *taʿziyeh* were turned out in abundance. No one knows how many there are, but the Cerulli collection has 1,055 from all over Iran, representing some 200 to 250 story plots.[10] These stories, all revolving around the central tragedy at Karbala, carry the dramatic potential of the Shiʿi creed to the farthest corners of Persian sensibilities. Although the Karbala massacre took place on the 10th day of Muharram (ʿAshura), in the dramatic representations each of the major characters in the event has his or her own play, and the series is performed in succession during the first ten days of that month. As the repertory grew and incorporated Qurʾanic stories and legends, the plays were performed all year round. Gradually, the annual commemoration of the Karbala event came to demonstrate seasonal changes of emotions in the Shiʿi collective imagination.

Originally, large paintings on canvas illustrating the dramatic scenes of the *taʿziyeh* productions would separate or group them into various events. According to Peterson, "Once it was publicly accepted, to the general dismay of the orthodox, that the roles of the martyrs and their adversaries were enacted by devout Muslims, the step toward the public's acceptance of paintings depicting the same narratives was not a major one. To illustrate that the Qajar genre of Karbala painting was essentially a translation of *taʿziya* productions into the visual arts, one need only compare the

paintings with productions and texts of the drama.[11] These portable paintings are called *sha-mayel* or *pardeh*. The ritual accompanying their use is called *shamayel-gardani* or *pardeh-dari*. This ritual of visual and verbal narrative is a one-man show with a backdrop painting depicting the scenes of the battle of Karbala, from left to right, painted in cartoon style. There is a haphazard sequence of events of the battle. On the right side of the painting are

3.10 and 3.11 Husseiniyeh Mushir, Shiraz, 1976.

scenes of the hereafter, which represent the fate of Hussein's supporters in the beautiful vista of paradise, while his opponents are tortured in hell. This oil painting is generally 3.5 x 1.5 meters, on canvas, and is easily rolled up for transportation. The parda-dar (storyteller) goes from one locality to another, hangs the paintings, and sings and recites the story, using a pointer to elucidate the scenes.[12]

Parviz Mamnoun, in his book *Taʿzija...*, describes the painting-recitation scene as he remembers it from his childhood:

55

...a cloth, called *shamayel* (picture), was nailed to a wall in an open space by the storyteller (*pardeh-dar*). In front of this [wall] a crowd of observers gathered, some squatting on the ground, others standing behind them... The story of the *pardeh-dar* proceeded somewhat in this fashion: he first sang in praise of the Prophet and his family. Thereafter he invited the public to send a salutation to the Prophet Muhammad. In this fashion he created a dramatic bridge between his song and the story. In the introduction to an episode he presented the characters [who would appear in the story] and then he would point to various people [in the painting] with his stick as he hoarsely described the battle on the painting. Naturally, the *pardeh-dar* utilized the tricks of the declamation while he told the story. He knows the importance of changes in tonality, in his speech, of imitation,

People from the upper classes became interested in the narrative paintings and commissioned them to decorate their residences. The nineteenth-century painting by ᶜAbdallah Musavar can serve as an example of this courtly *pardeh*-like style of painting. It differs from paintings used for the painting recitation, which are simpler both in color scheme and in the overcrowded placement of various scenes. In the courtly *pardeh* both coloring and mood are less violent, and the scenes are more subdued, the protagonists more princely and stately. As demonstrated in these pictures, the protagonist on a white horse is the central figure in the foreground; later an attempt was made to show scenes taking place in the background as well. In either case, however, the hereafter is always placed on the right side of the panel, with heaven above and hell below.

Samuel R. Peterson

3.12 and 3.13 The ritual of visual and verbal narrative of the Karbala tragedy.

and of gestures. During the following battle scenes he described the proceedings with a rough voice and a much faster rhythm. In order to stir up his public to the tragic fate of the Hussein family, he would march up and down clapping his hands and twirling his stick in the air. If it was necessary he would even weep.[13]

* Taᶜziyeh* were usually performed in towns and required elaborate preparations and considerable expense: therefore the outlying villages in the countryside could not participate.[14] Consequently the *pardeh-dari* ritual came into being for their benefit. To the traditional storyteller or *rowzeh-khan*, a visual element was added—an itinerant painting narrator, or painting singer, or painting reciter with a pointer followed the story on the painting from start to finish as it was recited and sung. Subsequently, narrative paintings were utilized in *husseiniyeh* and *tekiyeh* as decorative wall hangings. Even in the Tekiyeh Dawlat, the famous royal theater built by Naser al-Din Shah, these canvas paintings were utilized to increase the splendor and dramatic setting of the theater.[15]

The next step in the development of narrative painting was to paint the scenes directly on the walls, thus making the first religious murals, forecasting the later revolutionary uses, in the Islamic tradition. An example is the Imam Zadeh Shah Zaid in Isfahan, painted in the second half of the nineteenth century. Salmons and van Goch's elaborate and detailed description of the Muharram rituals in the year 1737 tells us that theatricals were not yet performed at that time. Although Parviz Mamnoun tries to prove that the wagons described by Salmons and van Goch that were pulled in the procession should be considered a theatrical performance,[16] there was no dialogue. Salmons and van Goch describe the people's passion for re-enacting the scenes of Karbala and representing the dead Hussein, but the result was closer to pantomime than to drama.

Yedda A. Godard, in "L'Imamzadé Zaid d'Isfahan," says, "The frescoes that decorated this little sanctuary form a rare collection of

3.14 Imamzadeh Shah Zaid painting final act of Karbala.

Muslim religious pictures. They illustrate the Shi'ite Passion rather like theatrical representations in showing various episodes in succession."[17] In this passage Godard is saying that the murals of the Imam Zadeh Shah Zaid of Isfahan illustrating a theatrical representation of the passion plays of Imam Hussein and his followers are in fact a translation of the ta'ziyeh productions into visual art. Iconographic analysis confirms that these murals should be attributed to the late Qajar period. The costumes are reproductions of the standard ta'ziyeh performances of the time, and the foreigners are dressed in the style of the late nineteenth or early twentieth century. It was customary for the ta'ziyeh actors to borrow clothing from the foreign residents who were in town at the time of the performance.

Several things indicate that these paintings illustrate ta'ziyeh productions. Many of the characters in the paintings are labeled *shabih* (impersonator, or likeness of), a term which refers to an actor playing a role in which he will be designated "*shabih* of so and so" to ensure that he does not pretend to be the character but only the role-player. Certain devices are repetitive: the major protagonists wear shrouds over their armor, as in *ta'ziyeh*, to show readiness for self-sacrifice. In this fashion, the actor can bring the audience to tears twice, once when he puts the shroud on and the second time when he is killed in front of the audience. As in the plays, so in the paintings all women have covered faces. This is a stage device, as all female roles are played by men. Peterson says:

A more general effect the *ta'ziyeh* had on religious paintings is demonstrated by the use of the veil. During the late

3.15 Imamzadeh Shah Zaid wall painting, Imam Hussein's last battle.

3.16 Imamzadeh Shah Zaid wall painting, Ali Akbar fights the numerous enemy.

Timurid period when it was in several instances an attribute of prophets, and then frequently in the Safavid period of the prophet Muhammad and the imams, it was not used to cover the faces of women... No longer used consistently as the sacred symbol it formerly had been, the veil in Qajar religious painting is ascribed only somewhat arbitrarily to holy figures: thus faces of Shi^cite imams and also prophets appear veiled and unveiled.[18] In ta^cziyeh the only obligatory use for veils, aside from covering women's faces, is in representing ghosts. The correspondences between ta^cziyeh and these Qajar paintings are specific historical examples of cross-fertilization in various forms of Shi^ci art. Such cross-fertilization became extremely significant in the course of the Islamic Revolution.

The paintings around the interior of this shrine follow the major events of the Muharram Karbala tragedy from the time Hussein and his followers were trapped in the desert and cut off from their water supply until the time when the women and the severed heads of the martyrs were taken to Damascus. This sequence follows the ta^cziyeh repertory. Despite the fact that all the male followers of Hussein except Zain al-Abedin, Hussein's son who was ill and in the women's tents, were killed in one battle, the pictures are painted as individual encounters and episodes. We therefore see Qassem, Hussein's nephew, bravely charging a whole detachment of the enemy. In the same fashion, Ali Akbar, the eldest son of Hussein, is fighting, armored and on horse-back. This is followed by a scene in which Hussein comforts the dying Ali Akbar. There is a panel in which the mounted ^cAbbas, Hussein's standard-bearer, is besought by women and children begging for water. He wears a white shroud over his armor (on this expedition to the Euphrates he was killed), and carries a waterskin on his lance. There is also a painting of Hussein on horseback holding up the infant Ali Asqhar, dying of thirst, to show the enemy how urgently water was needed. Instead of water, the enemy sent an arrow that pierced the infant's throat. Then Hussein readies himself for battle and is met by foreigners and an army of genii who offer him help (which he refuses because he knows he is fated to die). In the next painting, Hussein, riddled with arrows, is astride his horse. Below is the assisting friendly lion. In the final scene of this battle Hussein's head is severed by Shemr, and the lion is standing guard over the mutilated bodies of the martyrs. Finally Hussein's female relatives on camelback and his only surviving son are taken as prisoners to Damascus. The severed heads of Hussein and his men are carried on top of lances by the soldiers of Yazid's army.

In the case of a *husseiniyeh* or a *tekiyeh* designed for participation by many people in the Muharram rituals inside the walls, the paintings serve as backdrops for the *rowzeh-khani*, *sineh-zani* (breast-beating), and as a reflection of *ta^cziyeh* dramas. While the preacher tells the story, the people can see it taking place, and can therefore more easily express their grief and shed tears. In *ta^cziyeh* plays, the paintings serve as a permanent reflection of the *ta^cziyeh* performance. This reflection can well be seen in the pediment of the Husseiniyeh Mushir in Shiraz, where the paintings have been created on tiles, which are considered to be some of the best made in the nineteenth century. This *husseiniyeh* was erected as an act of piety and service by a wealthy philanthropist, Mirza Abdulhasan Khan Mushir al-Mulk, in 1876. The pediment overlooks the courtyard in which *ta^cziyeh* plays and other Muharram rituals are performed, and is immediately above the box on the north

William Shpall

3.17 Ta^cziyeh play. Imam Hussein puts the shroud on. Husseiniyeh Mushir, Shiraz, 1976.

side of the courtyard where the important spectators sit.

The scenes depicted are approximately those of the *pardeh,* except that the hereafter is divided not vertically but horizontally, and is separated from the lower band of pictures by a frieze of eight cartouches,[19] which contain a poem about Hussein and Karbala, written in fine calligraphy in white letters on a blue background. They differ from the *pardeh* in that there is no large central protagonist on a white horse. The Last Judgment is the centerpiece of the upper register. On the lower register, from left to right, the commander of the enemy surrounded by his soldiers admires the bravery and gallantry of Hussein and his followers. The admiration by the commander, on horseback under a parasol, is indicated by his index finger in his mouth, a device used since antiquity in Iranian art.

59

In the next scene, numberless spears and trumpets emphasize the magnitude of the enemy forces opposing ᶜAbbas, who is charging them on horseback; he still carries a goatskin waterbag as he kills the enemy with his sword. In the foreground is the water of the Euphrates, filled with fish. The decapitated heads and bodies of the enemy surround the horse's hooves. Just to the right of center, Hussein is preparing himself for the final attack and his own death. He too is on horseback carrying a lance, and is surrounded by angels. Genii, Gabriel dressed as a dervish, and an Arab emissary are unsuccessfully trying to assist him. In the two small vignettes which follow, one above the other, Hussein is seen comforting Qassem his nephew and Ali Akbar his son, both mortally wounded. The last scene of the lower register shows Hussein with a shroud over his armor, riding in front of the women's tents, bidding the women farewell. The infant Ali Asqhar is held in his right arm. Seven angels fly around his halo.

In the upper lunette-shaped half of the panel is a scene of hell on the left, over which the *sirat* bridge spans the distance between the Last Judgment and the hereafter. As they traverse it some souls fall to hell, others go to heaven. Heaven is depicted in allegorical terms, showing the cleansing waters of Kausar and a Tuba tree. The Prophet Muhammad sits above Imam Ali on the steps of the *minbar*. Angels with wings of green—the color of Islam—fly about the Prophet's huge golden halo. Behind and to the left of the pulpit stand a group of ancient prophets. In front and to the right of the pulpit stand the decapitated bodies of the Karbala martyrs, some of whom are holding their own heads, and the women of Karbala, who demand justice for the atrocities inflicted upon them. Beneath their feet are three rows of malefactors contained by a low wall of angels in red and blue gowns and wearing golden crowns. Between these standing angels and the wall of hell on the left a crowned and winged angel holds a pair of justice scale-pans. An astonished sun

3.18 This is veiled Imam Hussein demanding water from the enemy for his youngest son Ali Asghar. Instead of water the enemy sent an arrow.

watches over the entire proceeding.[20] As we shall see in the course of our study of the revolutionary art, these motifs are borrowed and heavily re-loaded with new ideological messages.

The presence of Karbala motifs in the Iranian aesthetic imagination was not limited to any specific social group. From the remotest villages to urban centers, Karbala motifs animated every aspect of pious imagination. The best examples of rustic Karbala wall paintings are to be found in the northern province of Gilan, where the most important building in many villages is the one devoted to the tragedy of Karbala. It is typically a medium-sized rectangular edifice called the buq‘a, which was erected toward the end of the Qajar period. A portico usually surrounds these buildings and protects the outer walls. Both the outer and the inner walls are painted. Some of the paintings are in their original state, others have been restored or repainted. Sima Kuban, who has studied more than thirty of these buildings in Gilan, writes: "It is almost a rule that one wall is devoted to Ali Akbar, one to Qassem, and one to ‘Abbas. Their bravery, struggle, and active fight are close to the class struggle of the simple people of Gilan... The features of protagonists in the paintings are not gloomy, but full of vigor and hope, they are vibrant and powerful."[21] In the area of Bidpish alone there are more than forty of these structures. Every village has one and it also functions as the communal center of the village. All the villagers share in its upkeep, and it is a matter of pride for them to have an impressive structure. Peripatetic painters attend to the paintings in the whole neighborhood, and the villagers supply them with eggs and other materials for the purpose. They are entertained every night by a different household in the village.

The teahouses—in fact inns, and traditionally called "coffee-houses" in Iran because tea was not grown there until the second half of the nineteenth century—also serve as the locus for many activities and rituals, both secular and religious. Naqqali, or story-telling, has for centuries been performed in coffeehouses. When pardeh painting was popular in Iran, they served as the ateliers of the painters. The pardeh painter was housed and fed by the owner of the inn who also supplied him with painting materials, canvases, and pocket money. The painter was commissioned either by the same hotelier or by outsiders. The name of the commissioner appears on the pardeh painting to immortalize his pious act. Surrounded in the coffeehouses by storytelling and religious rituals, the painters began to paint scenes from Karbala, from Qur'anic stories (which had entered the repertory of ta‘ziyeh drama by the first half of the nineteenth century) and from the national epic Shahnameh. The genre of the painting remained the same, and so it came to be known as coffeehouse painting.[22] A painting commissioned by the ‘Abbas Tekiyeh coffeehouse[23] showing Rustam killing Ashkabus is a typical example. Rustam's standard is inscribed with a Qur'anic quotation (61:13), which reads, "Help from God and a speedy victory," a motto generally found on flags in the ta‘ziyeh performances and used many times in the course of the Islamic Revolution. To this painter, influenced by Shi‘i religious performances and paintings, it did not matter that the legendary hero Rustam lived many centuries before Islam. In another painting in the same manner, Rustam is again seen, this time comforting his dying son Sohrab, just as Hussein cradles the dying Ali Akbar in other paintings, and in a photograph of a 1976 ta‘ziyeh performance of a play called The Martyrdom of Ali Akbar, at the Husseiniyeh Mushir in Shiraz.

The coffeehouse tradition persisted into the 1960s, when Muhammad Modabber, the last great painter of the genre, died. His painting of ‘Ashura shows certain modifications of the style of painting, but the subject-matter remains the same. In the same decade, an interesting development took place among the painters of the modern generation who were trained both in Iran and in the academies abroad and called themselves the Saqqakhaneh school. A saqqakhaneh is a small water-dispenser located in the alley of the bazaar and in the streets in the old quarter of an Iranian town. It is always dedicated to Hussein's half-brother and standard-bearer, ‘Abbas, and usually placed in a tiled niche decorated with pictures relating to Karbala.[24] The painters of the rather modern school named after these fountains did not really continue the coffeehouse tradition, but they did make use of the symbolism related to the Karbala tragedy and its rituals.

The imprint of the coffeehouse tradition is unmistakable in the graphic art of the revolutionary period. William L. Hanaway, Jr., in his article on "The Symbolism of Persian Revolutionary Posters," gives excellent examples of contemporary posters that are executed in the coffeehouse style.[25] This continuity points to the vast repertoire of religious symbolism at the disposal of the revolutionary artists when they began their pictorial narrative of the Islamic Revolution in Iran. It is clear that a certain dynamic lay behind the development of large-scale paintings deriving from the theatrical

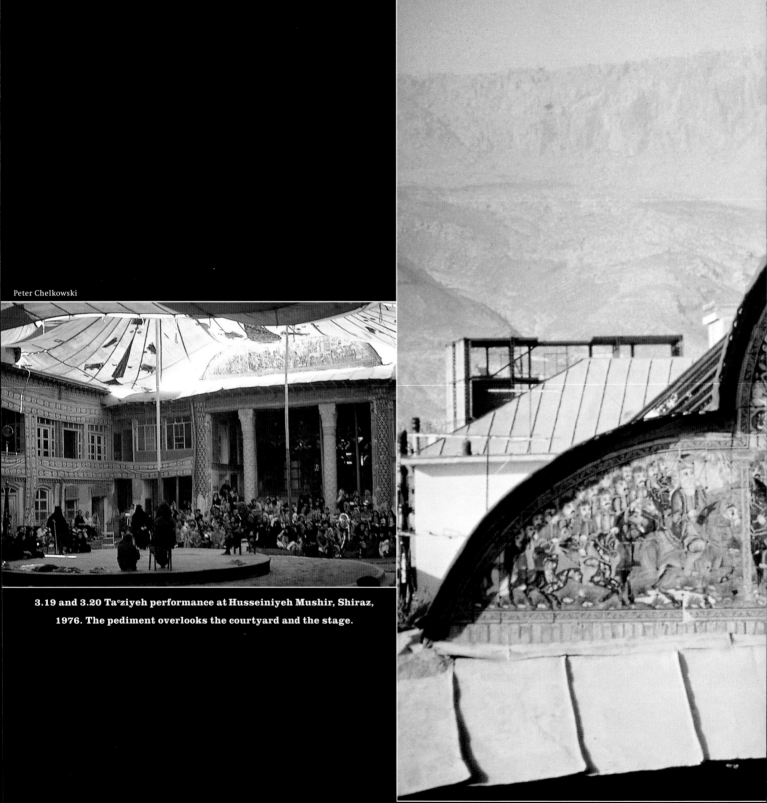

Peter Chelkowski

3.19 and 3.20 Ta‘ziyeh performance at Husseiniyeh Mushir, Shiraz, 1976. The pediment overlooks the courtyard and the stage.

3.22 (right) Hussein Qullar Agassi; Rustam comforting his dying son Sohrab. Marco Gregorian collection.

3.21 (left) Imam Hussein comforting his dying son Ali Akbar. Husseiniyeh Mushir, Shiraz, 1976.

productions of *ta'ziyeh* in the Qajar period. *Ta'ziyeh* inspired the narrative paintings on canvas, which became the backdrop for a one-man show called *pardeh-dari*. Paintings were also hung on the walls of buildings serving the Karbala rituals as well as in private residences. In time, instead of hanging a painting on the wall, it became customary to paint directly on the wall. Small paintings on glass also became popular. Whatever the medium, however, the subject was always the Shi'i martyrology, at least until Qur'anic stories and pre-Islamic themes were introduced, and even they reflected the *ta'ziyeh* tradition. The highly developed artistic tradition then went through major thematic and stylistic changes, reflecting the Iranian urban and rural settings. During the Pahlavi era, these traditions were overshadowed by a relentless process of "modernization." In the wake of the Iranian Revolution of 1978-9, when the religious ideologues were relentlessly at work to paint the cataclysmic event as an "Islamic Revolution," the latent motifs of *ta'ziyeh* and Karbala painting resurfaced like a volcanic eruption from the depth of an artificially placid lake.

As Blumenberg has argued, the centrality of myth in human existential self-understanding should not be considered in terms of its predating the advancement of the age of Enlightenment. Myth ought to be explained *terminus a quo*, in terms of its point of departure, and not *terminus ad quem*, its point of conclusion. The project of modernity did not, to any significant degree, subvert the human propensity for myth-making. Contrary to Cassirer's frame of reference, Blumenberg wished to understand what the funda-mental problem was to which myth gave a convincing answer. Avoiding an anachronistic projection of the spirit of the age of rationalization back into the time when myth operated convinc-ingly, Blumenberg postulates the problematic of what he calls "the absolutism of reality," to which homo sapiens is forced to provide an answer. "The absolutism of reality," the unbearable vastness of man's vertical observation of the horizontal universe, leads the historical person to the creation of "rational" myths of natural forces, by way of bringing them under a degree of control. Without this attempted control, the historical person is frightened by the unbearable angst of facing an infinite world. Myth is man's way of coming to terms with the vast uncertainties of his universe.

But while Blumenberg has postulated this theory of myth for an unspecified primordial time in man's historical self-consciousness, we can well extend this to any other period of deep and pervasive anxiety when uncertainties of life and this world create a new need for convincing mythologies to give a renewed measure of signification to things. There is no limiting the historical person's myth-making necessity, in response to ever-changing parameters of anxiety. At every revolutionary turn of a communal life, enough anxiety is created, by virtue of the infinite number of possibilities that are opened up, to necessitate new mythological god-terms. "The absolutism of reality" and the potential appearance of losing control over private and public existence are the most compelling conditions that make the historical person susceptible to the outburst of mythological measures. Cast into a revolutionary course of uninterrupted action, the historical person momentarily loses his/her received sense of security and significance. Under such circumstances, the anxiety-provoking uncertainties of private and public identities necessitate prolonged and recharged mythological proportions to circumspect life and its active fluency in the world. In response to the vast and anxiety-provoking possibilities open to the historical person, cultures—or specific constellations of symbolics of authority—chart the range of impossibilities which make being in the world meaningful and trustworthy. Without the cultural constructions of reality, the vast and mute expansion of the physical world would render the historical person inoperative by the sheer exhaustion of wasted energy. From a Zoroastrian to a Manichaean cosmology, from Islamic theology to Persian miniature or coffeehouse painting, there is a relentless engagement with bringing the vast universe of shapeless and endless possibilities to metaphysical or aesthetic order. Only within that order, metaphysical or aesthetic, is understanding—and through understanding the historical person's self-positioning in the world—made possible. The Islamic Revolution of 1978-9 was such a grand historical moment of self-reunderstanding.

1 PARTS OF THIS CHAPTER ARE TAKEN DIRECTLY FROM PETER CHELKOWSKI, "NARRATIVE PAINTING AND PAINTING RECITATION IN QAJAR IRAN," MUQARNAS 6 (1989), PP. 98-111. FOR A DISCUSSION OF THE SIGNIFICANCE OF THE KARBALA EVENT IN THE MODERN IRANIAN POLITICAL CULTURE, SEE MICHAEL FISCHER, IRAN: FROM RELIGIOUS DISPUTE TO REVOLUTION (CAMBRIDGE, MASS., 1980). 2 "PROPAGANDA AND SOCIAL CONTROL," IN ESSAYS IN SOCIOLOGICAL THEORY: PURE AND APPLIED (GLENCOE, ILL., 1949), P. 275. 3 SAMUEL R. PETERSON, "SHIcISM AND LATE IRANIAN ARTS," PH.D. DISS., NEW YORK UNIVERSITY, 1981. 4 QUOTED IN ROBERT E. INNIS, "INTRODUCTION" TO HIS EDITED VOLUME, SEMIOTICS: AN INTRODUCTORY ANTHOLOGY (BLOOMINGTON, IND., 1985), P. VII. 5 IBID., P. VIII. 6 SALMONS AND VAN GOCH, DIE HEUTIGE HISTORIE UND GEOGRAPHIE: ODER DER GEGENWARTIGE STAAT VOM KÖNIGREICH PERSIEN (FLENSBURG AND ALTONA, 1739), PP. 249-53. 7 SEE PETER CHELKOWSKI, "FROM MAQATIL LITERATURE TO DRAMA," IN ALSERAT (LONDON, 1986), VOL. 12: 227-64. 8 THE COMPOSITION OF THIS MAQTAL BY HUSSEIN WAcEZ KASHEFI COINCIDED WITH THE SAFAVIDS COMING TO POWER IN THE YEAR 1501. SEE PETER CHELKOWSKI, "POPULAR SHIcI MOURNING RITUALS," IN ALSERAT, VOL. 12: 209-26. 9 SEE JEAN CALMARD, "LE MÉCÉNAT DES REPRÉSENTATIONS DE TAcZIYA," IN LE MONDE IRANIEN ET L'ISLAM 2 (1974), PP. 73-126, AND 4 (1976-7), PP. 133-62. 10 ETTORE ROSSI AND ALESSIO BOMBACI, ELENCO DI DRAMMI RELIGIOSI PERSIANI (VATICAN CITY, 1969). 11 PETERSON, "SHIcISM AND LATE IRANIAN ARTS," PP. 111-12. SIR LEWIS PELLY, TRANSLATOR OF THIRTY-SEVEN TAcZIYEH PLAYS INTO ENGLISH, WRITES: "A PERSIAN ARTIST AT SHIRAZ PAINTED FOR ME IN OILS, SIX PICTURES, EIGHT FEET BY FOUR, ILLUSTRATIVE OF IN-CIDENTS DESCRIBED IN THE PLAY. THESE PAINTINGS ARE FULL OF QUAINT INTEREST" (THE MIRACLE PLAY OF HASAN AND HUSAIN (LONDON, 1879), P. 5). SINCE PELLY LEFT HIS POST IN IRAN IN 1873, THE PAINTINGS MUST HAVE BEEN PAINTED BEFORE THAT DATE. cABBAS BULIKIFAR, ONE OF THE LAST PAINTERS IN THE COFFEEHOUSE TRADITION, BELIEVES THAT THIS GENRE ORIGINATED IN TAcZIYEH PRODUCTION (SADEQ HOMAYUNI, TAcZIYEH VA TAcZIYEH-KHANI, FESTIVAL OF THE ARTS (TEHRAN, N.D.), P. 28). 12 CHELKOWSKI, "POPULAR SHIcI MOURNING RITUALS," PP. 218-19. 13 PARVIZ MAMNOUN, TAcZIJA SCHICITISCH-PERSISCHES PASSIONSPIEL (VIENNA, 1967), PP. 19-21. 14 EVEN TODAY, NON-PROFESSIONAL COMMUNITY MUHARRAM TAcZIYEH PERFORMANCES TAKE PLACE IN THE MOST REMOTE VILLAGES OF THE COUNTRY. 15 YAHYA ZOKA, TARIKHCHEH-YE SAKHTEMANHA-YE ARK-E SALTANATI-YE TEHRAN (TEHRAN, S. 1349), P. 294. 16 TAcZIJA SCHICITISCH-PERSISCHES PASSIONSPIEL, P. 24. 17 YEDDA A. GODARD, "L'IMAMZADÉ ZAID D'ISFAHAN, UN EDIFICE DECORÈ DE PEINTURES RELIGIEUSES MUSULMANES," IN ATHAR-E IRAN 2 (1937), PT. 2, P. 341. (THOUGH GODARD USES THE TERM "FRESCO," IT IS MISLEADING, SINCE THE PAINT IS APPLIED ONLY TO THE SURFACE OF THE WALL.) 18 PETERSON, "SHIcISM AND LATE IRANIAN ARTS," P. 118. 19 SEE SADEQ HOMAYUNI, HUSSEINIYEH MUSHIR, FESTIVAL OF THE ARTS (TEHRAN, S. 1355), P. 40. 20 FOR DETAILS, SEE IBID., PP. 18, 24, 41-9. 21 SIMA KUBAN, "NAMUNE'I AZ BAZTAB-E MUBAREZAT-E TABAQATI DAR HUNAR-E NAQQASHI" (TEHRAN, JULY—AUGUST 1360/1981), PP. 14-17. WE HAVE ONLY A PHOTOCOPY OF THIS ARTICLE AND DO NOT KNOW WHERE IT WAS ORIGINALLY PUBLISHED. ANOTHER INTERESTING ARTICLE FROM THE SAME AUTHOR HAS THE TITLE "SHAKHAH'I NASHENAKHTEH AZ HUNAR-E MARDUMI" AND WAS PUBLISHED IN THE SECOND VOLUME OF A JOURNAL CALLED BUSTAN. ITS PLACE AND DATE OF PUBLICATION ARE ALSO UNKNOWN TO US. WE PRESUME THAT IT WAS PUBLISHED IN TEHRAN SOME TIME BETWEEN 1979 AND 1982. ONE OF THESE MURALS FROM THE NORTH OF IRAN IS REPRODUCED IN THE NATIONAL GEOGRAPHIC MAGAZINE OF APRIL 1921. ON PAGE 379 UNDER A BLACK-AND-WHITE PHOTOGRAPH IS WRITTEN: "THE MURAL DECORATIONS, DONE IN VIVID COLOR, REPRESENT SCENES OF HOSEIN'S ILL-FATED ATTEMPT TO GAIN THE CALIPHATE." 22 SEE LES PEINTRES POPULAIRES DE LA LEGENDE PERSANE. THIS IS A CATALOGUE PUBLISHED FOR AN EXHIBITION OF COFFEEHOUSE PAINTINGS AT THE MAISON DE L'IRAN IN PARIS (N.D.). 23 cABBAS TEKIYEH WAS A FAMOUS TEAHOUSE IN TEHRAN IN THE 1950S. ITS NAME INDICATES THAT THE OWNER HAD A GREAT REVERENCE FOR THE HEROES OF KARBALA. MARCO GREGORIAN, A FAMOUS CONTEMPORARY IRANIAN PAINTER WHO NOW LIVES IN THE UNITED STATES, SPONSORED MANY OF THE ARTISTS WHO WERE ASSOCIATED WITH THE cABBAS TEKIYEH. GREGORIAN'S COLLECTION OF COFFEEHOUSE PAINTINGS FORMED THE CORE OF THE PARIS EXHIBITION. LATER THIS COLLECTION WAS PURCHASED BY THE NAGARESTAN MUSEUM IN TEHRAN. 24 SEE CHELKOWSKI, "POPULAR SHIcI MOURNING RITUALS," PP. 21314. 25 WILLIAM L. HANAWAY, JR., "THE SYMBOLISM OF PERSIAN REVOLUTIONARY POSTERS," IN BARRY M. ROSEN (ED.), IRAN SINCE THE REVOLUTION (BOULDER, COLO., 1985).

...the divine law

is different from the secular laws. In secular laws not more than one or two aspects can be considered, and even those are limited to this world. As limited as these laws are to this world, they still cannot foresee all its potential aspects and devise a regulation accordingly. The divine law, on the contrary, commences from the moment of an infant's conception, from the parents' marriage, and even before that, as to what sorts of people are necessary to produce a healthy and virtuous child. What sort of husband should be chosen for a woman, and what sort of wife for a man. And there are laws governing the marriage, all intended for the good of the fruit which is to grow. There are rules and regulations for that very moment when the fetus is to be conceived. All of this is to generate an innate growth in man. When the mother is pregnant, and the child is in the mother's womb, that too has rules and regulations.

AYATOLLAH KHOMEINI

how God

has exercised vengeance on all those who devote themselves to cruelty, to rapine, and to other extortions; and, next how he has punished lecheries and other infections when they have flourished too much; and then how he has punished perjuries; and that he has not been able to endure the pride of men. When we consider all that, should it not serve us well also today? Let us remember well this lesson, that since, from the creation of the world, God has not ceased to warn us that he is judge of the world, we should learn to fear him, and to walk carefully, and that the punishments that he has inflicted on the wicked should be to us many mirrors and so many bridles to restrain us. – JOHN CALVIN

the revolution

Part Two

Four **from mourning to revolu**

...tionary mobilization

In the preceding three chapters we discussed some of the salient forces in the Iranian historical, aesthetic, and folk imagination that were conducive to the revolutionary outburst of the late 1970s. What we plan to do in this, the second, part of the book is to identify some of the chief operative forces that colluded in the actual making of "the Islamic Revolution." Our purpose here is to see what immediate sources of creative imagination came into play once the "Islamicization" of the Revolution became one of the primary objectives of its successful leaders.

In this chapter we shall see how the annual ritual of the Muharram procession was turned into the most powerful mode of political mobilization during the Revolution. The "Revolution" itself was in effect the ultimate outcome of a series of successfully organized and staged demonstrations. These demonstrations, in which a wide range of ideological and political sensibilities and groupings participated, increasingly assumed the modality and processional power of religious rituals practiced to perfection by generations of Shiʿi Iranians. We need to understand the emotional charge as well as the historical significance of Muharram mourning processions before we can grasp the mode of operation in the series of political demonstrations which led to the downfall of the Pahlavi monarchy and the establishment of the Islamic Republic.

4.2 A political demonstration, symbolically assimilated into a Cosmic order.

Kamran Bayegan

Despite rapid social changes, despite the fact that the new middle class tried to distance itself from the Muharram observances, and despite the constant attempts of the Pahlavi government to contain and restrict them, regular observance of the Muharram ceremonies has continued to be part and parcel of growing up in Iran, especially among the disenfranchised. They still eagerly anticipate the coming of Muharram with its plethora of colorful activities. Central to Muharram is the cortège of the Mourners (*dasteh*), which goes through a town as the high point of a dignified carnival procession, at once sorrowful and jubilant. Those who participate in this event see themselves as center-stage in a

4.1 A Muharram procession.

Sa'id Sadeghi

mobile drama. Those who come to watch the procession are in fact equally present in the event. The people know the route of the procession days in advance. The question everyone faces is whether to join the procession or simply to walk along the way to see the main protagonists and to commiserate with them. As they try to make up their minds, the people are reminded of their childhood when similar processions annually marked the passage of the year; sometimes in summer, sometimes in winter, autumn, or spring. The lunar calendar rotating through the solar, along with its punctuation of sacred holidays, charted their childhood and youth through their adulthood, their coming of age, their becoming a man, a woman, a Muslim. Muharram and Ramadan stood out as the two most sacred months. Muharram was the more memorable, leaving more colorful pictures in their minds. Ramadan was more an occasion of solemnity. Muharram left them with aftertastes of innocent memories and muted anger, the anger of injustice inseparable from the martyrdom of Hussein, the most cherished hero of their young imaginations. During the revolutionary upheaval of 1978-9, as far as its participants were concerned, every month was Muharram; every procession became a demonstration; everywhere in Iran was Karbala. Rhythmically beating their breasts with their hands, large and small, the demonstrators, more than a million strong, marched along the main avenues of the capital.

4.3 Hands that beat the chests during a Muharram procession are easily raised in defiance during a political rally.

Those in the lead, dressed in white shrouds, chanted episodes from the story. A story common to all, collectively narrated, in procession. The story of the mutilation and massacre of the Prophet's beloved grandson, Hussein, his family, and companions. The number seventy-two — the number of followers, friends, and relatives who chose to die with Hussein — has a sacred hold on the people's imagination. The army of the accursed caliph Yazid massacred Hussein and his seventy-two followers on the 10th of Muharram, in the year 680 CE. As they sang and chanted and moved in procession, the flood of demonstrators would intersperse its litany with a list of wrongs suffered by the people under the Shah Muhammad Reza Pahlavi, the Yazid of the time, as they called him.

In 1978-9, as in Muharram, the distinction between those on the sidelines and those in the center of the procession no longer applied. Religion and politics, the litany of passion and power, absorbed everything into a collective narrative of resurrection from annihilation, of granting and denial of legitimacy. The hands ceased striking chests, clenched into fists; and time contracted from the seventh to the twentieth century, from a distant memory to the

4.4 Sacrificing blood is a major leitmotiv of the Karbala event.

William Shpall

**4.5 and 4.6 Scenes from
the taᶜziyeh performances,
Shiraz, 1976.**

blood and sweat of the present reality. The mournful groan "Hussein is dead, Hussein has been killed" changed in the same breath to an angry shout, "Down with the Shah!" Was it at a signal? Was it mass suggestion? Was it premeditated, or all at once? The procession, more than a crowd, a sentient moving force perhaps, propelled itself through the wide boulevards, possessed by Shiᶜi history. Time and again, the demonstrators were transported from Karbala back to Tehran, Isfahan, Tabriz; back from the whizzing of arrows and the clash of sabres to the rattle of machine-gun fire. The crowd would scatter, only to regroup in moments as soon as they saw the white shrouds spattered with blood as victims fell on the streets. Ducking the bullets, the men would pause to dip their hands in the blood on the pavements. To the foreign reporters, photographers, and cameramen on the scene, these were irresistible pictures of a revolution. And the procession continued, confused and yet collected. Now the clenched fists opened, the bloody palms were raised. Red palms over black heads. Banners of still-hot blood over the moving crowd. Filled with hatred, voices trembling with anger, the shouting became piercing, roaring, horrific. A revolution was in the making.

The martyrdom of Hussein is to Shiᶜites what the crucifixion of Christ is to Christians: the seminal event of the faith, always there to be read and reread into the changing reality of the communal anxieties. In Iran, where Shiᶜi Islam is the faith of more than 90 percent of the population, public mourning rituals for the fallen Hussein can generate desire as intense as those that moved early Christian martyrs to allow their bodies to be broken on the rack or burned at the stake. The urge for utter bodily annihilation seems to be concurrent with the equally strong desire for spiritual identification with the fallen Imam.

Processions like the ones that precipitated the fall of the Shah, rites of redemptive self-flagellation, dramatic recitations, and spectacular passion plays all possess a potent repertory of symbols,

Peter Chelkowski

a relentless cascade of collective memory that gives meaning and significance to the individual participants. To understand these symbols and the enormous wellspring of emotions they tap is to understand, at least in part, not only how the Revolution came about, but also the vehemence of the Iranian desire to punish the Shah and his protective ally, the United States. Identification of the Shah and the United States, and, at a later stage of the Revolution, Saddam Hussein with demonic forces in Iranian (Shiʿi) mythology elevated mundane political forces to cosmic proportions, demanding and thus extracting a hyperbolic demonstration of anger and anxiety.

The Aristotelian insight that the purpose of play is "for the sake of re-creation," and Gadamer's articulation of the specific mode of relationship between play and "seriousness," take us a considerable distance in explaining how *taʿziyeh* functions as a collectively re-created drama. The verbal script of *taʿziyeh* is comparatively superfluous. The drama emerges from the deepest layers of collective convictions that hold the players, the play, and the audience together, seamless parts of a relentless rhetorical re-creation of dramatic reality. Play, as Gadamer has noted, "contains its own, even sacred, seriousness."[1] This seriousness is integral to the situation of the play; it is not a dependent variable of the players' subjectivity. This is why there is no excelling in a particular role in *taʿziyeh*. One may be famous as a "good Imam Hussein" or as a "particularly nasty Shemr," ("That son-of-a-bitch is nothing short of Shemr himself" is the highest compliment); but that is quite different from a particular actor dominating the dramatic experience as a whole. The sacredness of the *taʿziyeh*, in effect, prevents a Laurence Olivier from entering with deliberate pronouncement, whether as Othello or as Hamlet. It is Imam Hussein or ʿAbbas who enters, not Hasan Aqa the butcher or Akbar Aqa the baker. The re-creation of the dramatic event thus becomes a simultaneous re-enactment of a cosmic reality in comparison with whose "seriousness" every other mundane reality and purpose fades. In fact, the periodic re-enactments of these archetypal symbolics of good and evil provide and sustain the most enduring measures of self- and other-perceptions. The goodness or badness of particular individuals are invariably measured, and thus experienced, in terms of their proximity to or distance from the ever-present archetypal memories of Imam Hussein and Shemr. Under revolutionary circumstances, when subliminal tensions and heightened anxieties give free reign to the deepest of all elements in the collective subconscious, these compelling forces of thought- and attitude-formation are immediately behind a variety of public demonstrations. They always compel the present to remember the past.

Collective participations in taʿziyeh, whether as actors or as spectators, also provides the most immediately accessible set of communal indexical expressions. The mere dropping of a name, Imam Hussein or Shemr, the mere suggestion of a color, green or red, can almost immediately register a universe of meaning and significance. In the national referendum, to vote "yes" for the Islamic Republic, all a pious Muslim had to do was identify with the green color of Imam Hussein on the ballot. The color red, that of Shemr, was reserved for those who wanted to say "no" to the Islamic Republic. Thus, to vote "yes" for the Islamic Republic was tantamount to, indeed identical with, fighting alongside the Imam Hussein, something all pious Shiʿites had always wanted to do but had never had the opportunity. Conversely, to vote "no" to the

4.7 Processional taʿziyeh performance Mehriz 1977.

Islamic Republic was, *horribile dictum*, the same as fighting in the army of Shemr against Imam Hussein: an impossibility, a total negation of identity to any remotely Shiʿi state of mind. Here, green ennobles; red debases. This is the power of symbol, the mere suggestion of a color, the enduring possibility of a sacred memory projecting its own unfolding future. Thus in effect the Islamic Revolution of 1978-9 fulfilled, however symbolically, the Shiʿi Iranians' ahistorical wish to fight (and die) for Imam Hussein: fighting for Khomeini in 1978-9 became tantamount finally to being able to fight for Imam Hussein in 680 CE.

The events leading to Hussein's martyrdom began with the division of Islam into Sunni and Shiʿi branches upon the death of

the Prophet in the seventh century (the first century of the Muslim era). When Muhammad died in 632 CE, his religious community, which was also the first Islamic state, faced a constitutional crisis: how was his successor to be chosen? One faction, later to be known as the Sunnites, who derived their name from the Arabic word meaning "tradition," argued that a caliph should be chosen the way Arab chiefs customarily are, through election. They were opposed by the Shiʿites, or "partisans of Ali," the cousin and son-in-law of Muhammad. The Shiʿites argued that Muhammad had been so extraordinary that his successors should come from his bloodlines, and, as they gradually formed into a self-conscious community, they thought that Ali was a perfect man, immune from sin and error in both spiritual and temporal matters.[2]

For a while, the dispute seemed to have been settled in favor of the traditionalists. But when Ali himself was assassinated in 661 CE, after becoming the fourth elected caliph, trouble broke out anew. Of Ali's two sons, one, Hasan, was poisoned; the other, Hussein, was invited by the Shiʿites of Kufa (near present-day Baghdad in Iraq) to become their leader. Hussein set out for Kufa, but spies informed his political and religious opponent, the caliph Yazid, who sent a large military force to intercept him on the sun-scorched plain of Karbala. Hussein's small band was encircled before it could reach the Euphrates to get needed water. Yazid's military commander tried to force Hussein to pay homage to the caliph; Hussein refused, since, according to Shiʿi doctrine, the caliphate should by rights have been his. After a ten-day siege, on the 10th day of Muharram, 680 CE, Hussein, all his male next-of-kin, and their supporters were shot with arrows and cut to pieces by the swords of the enemy. Their dismembered bodies were trampled into the desert under the hooves of horses, and their severed heads brought to Yazid in Damascus, together with Hussein's female relatives in chains. In these vivid portrayals, the Shiʿi memory persists, and upon these memories rests the cultivation of all updated revolutionary agenda.

No other historical event has captured the enduring contention of the Shiʿi faith as the battle of Karbala. Over the centuries, Hussein's martyrdom has come to be regarded by the Shiʿi community as the supreme self-sacrifice, and his suffering is relived in the annual mourning for him. During Muharram, what happened thirteen centuries ago on the plain of Karbala is perceived as if it were happening here and now. Shiʿites atone for their failure to rescue Hussein from his entrapment by donning shrouds, inflicting bodily pain on themselves, and even, as happened during the Islamic Revolution, giving their lives. The faithful believe that Hussein will act as intercessor at the Last Judgment, and that they may enter paradise if they commemorate the tragic events of Karbala each year. But the driving force of the Muharram self-flagellation is an innate passion to re-create and thus share the agonies of the patristic generation of the Shiʿi faith.

4.8 Self-flagellation in a Muharram procession.

Successive generations of the faithful have been increasingly distanced from the actual events of the archetypal martyrdom. Substituting for that historical distance is a relentless passion to remember the *condito sine qua non* of the faith: giving one's life for what one believes in. "Verily! Life is belief and fighting [for that belief]" has since become the rallying cry of the Shiʿi faith.

Hussein is the central figure of revolutionary contention as he is remembered in modern Shiʿi martyrology. The Shiʿites believe that his righteous claim to political authority over the early Muslim community was usurped by Yazid. The belief has become paradigmatic to Shiʿi doctrines; so much so that any act of contemporary political (de)legitimation appeals to that transhistorical reference. The drama of Karbala is full of passionate intensity, filled with heroic and treacherous characters: Muslim Ibn Aqil, a devotee of Hussein, who willingly sacrificed himself for his beloved master; Hur who, along with his brother, left the camp of Yazid and joined the righteous cause of Hussein; ʿUbaydullah Ibn Ziyad, one of the chief villains, who cut off the flow of water to Hussein's camp. The Shiʿi martyrological tradition, as best captured in Mulla Hussein Vaʿez Kashefi's *Rawzat al-Shuhada* (The Garden of Martyrs), is emphatic in numbering the enemy soldiers in thousands and those of Hussein in tens. The disequilibrium serves well in creating an atmosphere of drama and tragedy, elements which are in turn translated into highly emotional forces for contemporary political use. But more than anything else, it is the dramatic powers of the Karbala tragedy that have persistently engaged the Shiʿi collective memory.

One of the earliest descriptions of Shiʿi Muharram rituals is in a tenth-century account from Baghdad, which tells how the bazaars would close and people with faces painted black and hair disheveled would move around beating their chests and moaning songs of lamentation for Hussein. Muharram mourning rituals were not central to Iranian Shiʿism, however, until the sixteenth century, when the Safavid dynasty (1501–1736) assumed power. Under the Safavids, the country was sandwiched between two aggressive Sunni adversaries, the Ottoman Turks to the west and the Uzbeks to the east. Having begun as a political movement, Shiʿi Islam was now, in another politically inspired act, established by the Safavids as the state religion, and Muharram observances received royal encouragement and patronage.

In the annual mourning for Hussein's encirclement and destruction by the army of the wicked Sunni caliph, sixteenth- and seventeenth-century Iranians must have found much that was poignantly parallel to their own hazardous position, surrounded by Sunni enemies. Indeed, European visitors to Iran in the seventeenth century have handed down detailed descriptions of the depressed mood during Muharram and of the elaborate processions that took place in that month. Characters dressed in colorful costumes to represent the martyrs of Karbala rode on horses and camels, depicting the events of the tragedy. Mounted on wheeled platforms were living tableaux of butchered martyrs stained with blood, their bodies showing simulated amputations. Marchers engaged in various forms of self-punishment — letting swords and knives drop on their foreheads until blood gushed out, and repeatedly swinging sharp-edged chains against their bodies. Some walked with spikes through their flesh. The entire pageant was accompanied by funeral music. Weeping, breast-beating spectators lined the streets. It was as if Christians, instead of walking through the Stations of the Cross, were to stand still and watch scenes of Christ's ordeal passing before them. For the proceeding Shiᶜites, passionate identification with their martyred master, reminiscent of that of Christians with Christ, became the public manifestation of redemptive suffering — a suffering that assimilated the bodies and conditions of every generation to the patristic ideals of the originating martyrs, the material authority of the initiating myths.

A principal feature of these myths is the power of conviction and sacrifice over physical and material hardship. Potential and actual revolutionaries had much to learn from the sacrifices that Hussein, his family, and friends had to endure in order to prove the veracity of their cause. With only two options, sacrificing his family and friends or subjecting them to harsh and unbearable circumstances, Hussein remained steadfast in his revolutionary ideals. It was the appeal of this powerful story that constantly remained with Iranian revolutionaries as they rose to change the

course of their history. In modern renditions of Karbala events, Iranian historians took care to identify not only themselves but also their ancestors with the just cause of Hussein. "It is perfectly evident," one modern Iranian historian writes, "that not a single person among the evil-doers in Karbala was either Iranian or of Iranian extraction. Quite to the contrary, some of the Shiᶜi groups who gathered around Mukhtar-e Thaqafi to revenge the [crimes against] the family of Ali were some [Shiᶜites] of Iranian extraction who were born in Kufa and received their religious upbringing there."[3] In the course of the Islamic Revolution, Iranians took full advantage of such reconstructed sensibilities.

In Shiᶜi parades, straw effigies of ᶜUmar, the caliph who the Shiᶜites believe unjustly thwarted Ali's claim to the caliphate and who was also responsible for the military conquest of Iran, were carried about, spat upon, and burned. Condemnation of the evil characters was concomitant with the celebration of the heroes of justice. During Muharram, the Shiᶜites held dramatic narrations of the lives, deeds, and sufferings of Hussein and other martyrs before and after him taken from the book *The Garden of Martyrs*. These recitations, called *rowzeh-khani*, which were referred to in Chapter 3, were one-man shows with the narrator, seated on a podium, delivering the lines so expressively that the audience would be moved to tears. Using the language and metaphors of *The Garden of*

(after C.J. Willis, In the Land of the Lion and the Sun, London, 1891)

4.9 and 4.10 Scenes from the aural and visual commemoration of the Karbala event.

Martyrs, he might also make allusions to the contemporary situation, emphasizing the suffering of the deprived and the wrongdoing of current rulers and administrators. *Rowzeh-khani* thus became the historical vehicle of renarrating the events of Karbala to conform with the actual exigencies of the time. Every generation of believers was entitled to, and thus created, its successive mobilization of sentiments to re-create the events of Karbala, and with and through them give a vivid account of its own particular anxieties. Remembrance of things past, reconstruction of realities long since faded into time, became the enduring stronghold of coming to terms with realities demanding immediate recognition. Just like political rallies, the *rowzeh-khani* recitations served to mobilize the crowd, to provoke marches, sit-ins, and the chanting of slogans. Converted to religious political action, these meetings could prepare the crowd to go out into the streets to express its discontent and anger over grievances. The lingering memory of the Karbala event thus becomes the spring of relentless emotions through the agency of which contemporary politics is made. In the pre-modern state of any Shi'i collective memory, there is scarcely any recognition of reality unless mediated by such enduring sentiments.

The particular "history" of these sentiments is traced to selected dramatic epochs. As we indicated earlier, in the middle of the eighteenth century, the processions and the narrations gave birth to *ta'ziyeh*, a compelling form of mourning ritual and Islam's only indigenous drama. To understand the emotional change of the Muharram processionals, we need to remember their connections to *ta'ziyeh* proper. *Ta'ziyeh* fed upon a rich body of legends. Entire plays focused not only on Hussein himself but also on individual followers and members of his family, and on martyrs before and after Karbala. But each martyrdom was depicted as deriving its significance from the sacrifice of Hussein. The drama was at first staged at street intersections, then in caravanserais and mosque courtyards, and still later in specially built arena theaters provided by the rich as a religious and public service. The protagonists, who sang their parts, were dressed in green, the color of Islam, while the evil characters, who recited their lines, wore red. In the ritual theater of *ta'ziyeh,* there were no barriers between archetype and human, sophisticated and simple, rich and poor. The wealthy brought crystal, lamps, china, and tapestry to decorate the theater; the poor lent humbler objects with religious devotion. Children of the well-to-do served water and refreshments to all spectators, regardless of class, and the poor could sit in the boxes of the rich if there was space. Above all, there were no barriers between actor and spectator. The audience sat around a central stage, and when a scene was changed, the actor simply jumped off the stage,

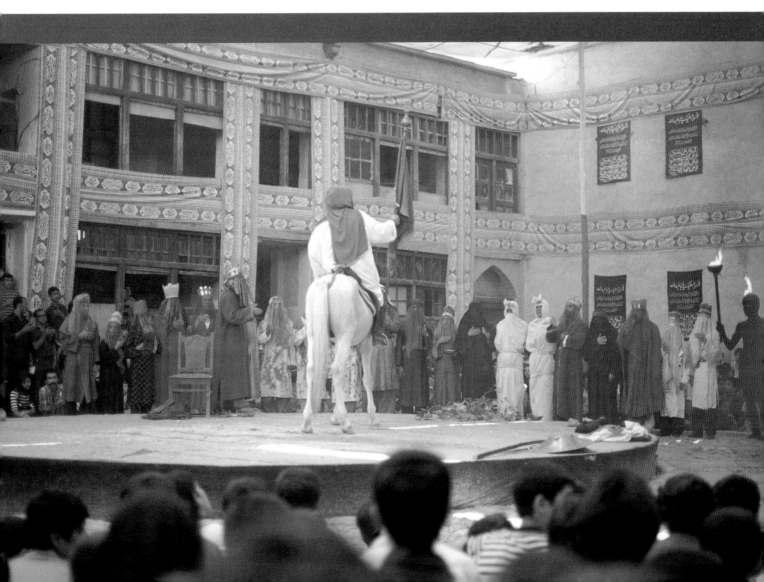

4.11 Poster using the original photograph of Khomeini's speech in the month of Muharram, 1963.

circumambulated it, and jumped back on. Some action took place on smaller stages extending into the audience pit, and duels and skirmishes were enacted in areas beyond the circle of the audience, with actors sometimes plunging through the audience to reach the central stage. By thus bringing the actors and the spectators together, taʿziyeh became the theatrical epiphany of the event it symbolized. Through the acting and observing the symbol and the symbolized, the representing and the represented, became one and the same. Both the actors and the spectators entered the dramatic scene as the scattered souls of separated individuals and they exited as the united consciousness of history remembered, of collectively feeling they had actually been there. The mutually induced feeling of having been there was then successively re-created and thus sustained, always ready at the threshold of whatever extratextual use, political or otherwise, it might be put to.

While Muharram processions and rowzeh-khani recitations have continued to the present day in much the same form as in the past, taʿziyeh lost its royal patronage towards the end of the nineteenth century and retreated to rural areas. It has not, however, lost its enduring power to erase the distance between the Karbala tragedy and the real or imagined calamities of the day. This relentless contraction of time and space, of actors and audience, is what impressed the famous theatrical innovator Peter Brook when he witnessed a performance in Iran. In a subsequent interview in *Parabola*, he said:

I saw in a remote Iranian village one of the strongest things I have seen in theater: a group of four hundred villagers, the entire population of the place, sitting under a tree and passing from roars of laughter to outright sobbing — although they all knew perfectly well the end of the story — as they saw Hussein in danger of being killed, and then fooling his enemies, and then being martyred. And when he was martyred, the theater became a truth — there was no difference between past and present. An event that was told as remembered happening in history 1,300 years ago, actually became a reality in that moment.[4]

The possibility of that reality being valid atemporally will have to be recognized as a particular modicum in a larger, more compelling, universe of discourse. According to Shiʿi belief, Ali and his sons Hasan and Hussein were the first three of eleven martyred Imams — righteous, divinely designated leaders. Their successor, the Twelfth

(Hidden) Imam, who lived in the ninth century, is said to have never died but to have gone into hiding, into a state of unseenness, from which he will one day return to rule the earth in justice. The future possibility of that justice makes the contemporary reality always contingent upon some recognition of the past. The (dis)appearance of the Hidden Imam makes all history, all eventualities, all realities, subject to the perpetual expectation of his return. That return is the enduring force of a memory that persists in rendering all historical reality meaningful, trustworthy. In every particular moment of remembering this event, all its historical and emotional changes come to life.

In the absence of the Hidden Imam, the Shiᶜi clergy have invariably looked upon themselves as interpreters of divine law and defenders of the oppressed, and regarded rulers as the preservers of temporal order. Early on, Shiᶜi Islam became a potent political force — a champion of the downtrodden and a threat to the power of the rulers. Although alternative moments of Shiᶜi supremacy did occur

sanctity of a religious duty. But the religious uprising was not to be controlled. On the day of ᶜAshura, the 10th of Muharram, thousands of demonstrators poured into the streets of Tehran, and their slogans condemned the Shah and recognized Khomeini as their leader.

But the center of action on this crucial Muharram was Qom. For days and nights before ᶜAshura, Khomeini went to various Qom neighborhoods and delivered fiery speeches. Tens of thousands poured into the street to greet, meet, and listen to him. Through the clerical network, tens of thousands of people were mobilized from the surrounding areas. The ᶜAshura of 1383 (3 June 1963) coincided with a hot summer day. The desert town of Qom was pregnant with expectation. Khomeini spoke, and someone in the audience thought:

The afternoon of ᶜAshura, reminiscent of Hussein's martyrdom, creates a particularly indescribable atmosphere in an Islamic society. Our sociologists have not yet had the opportunity

4.12 (left) Original photo of Khomeini's speech in the month of Muharram, 1963, used as a poster with excerpts of his speech in Persian. (right) Demonstration, Ashura 1963, in front of Tehran University.

in history, it was out of this enduring moment of distress that Ayatollah Khomeini came. As early as Muharram 1963, when he delivered the sermon at Madrasseh Fayziyyeh in Qom, Khomeini drew analogies between the martyrdom of Hussein and the plight of the Iranian people. Once he had activated the old hatred for the Sunni caliph Yazid, he had only to equate him with the Shah, and the Americans with his supporters, to arouse the people against them. Fearful of the approaching month of Muharram (of 1383 AH/May–June 1963 CE), the police warned the Shiᶜi mourners against politicizing the processions. Adamant as ever, Khomeini commanded his followers to charge full blast against "the illegal regime." Government officials warned the cleric to refrain from making any comment about three subjects: the monarch, the state of Israel, and that Islam was in danger. Khomeini, in response, declared that these were precisely the issues to be publicly discussed. In order to present himself as a devout Shiᶜite, the Shah publicly asserted that in his childhood he was blessed by a vision of the Twelfth Imam, and that his White Revolution had the

to analyze the society's psychological state on this day. Had they collected some data, and had they studied them carefully, they would have recognized that the condition of sacrifice and self-annihilation on this day is drastically different from those of other days. When a speech has divine support, its influence is hundreds of times more effective at this time. The crowd that had gathered in Qom in ᶜAshura of '83 [1963] was unprecedented. From every corner there was an insatiable appetite to hear Imam's speech.[5]

And what was Khomeini's speech?

I seek protection from the cursed Satan in the name of God the Merciful, the Compassionate. Now is the afternoon of ᶜAshura... Sometimes when I reflect on the events of ᶜAshura, I ask myself, if the Umayyads and Yazid Ibn Muᶜawiyah's regime were hostile to Hussein, then why did they treat defenseless women and innocent children so violently?! What had women and children done? What had the six-month-old baby of Hussein done? (People weep.) I think they were fundamentally opposed to

4.13 Khomeini as the supreme leader of the revolutionary event.

commerce and agriculture. It wants to control the wealth. Through its agents, it wants to annihilate those persons and things that are standing in their way, presenting [their actions]. The Qur'an is in their way. It has to be removed. The religious authorities are in the way. They ought to be crushed. The Fayziyyeh school and other centers of knowledge and learning are in the way. They must be demolished. The seminary students may later stand in the way. They ought to be killed. They must be thrown down from the roof-top. Their head and hands ought to be broken. In order for Israel to achieve its goals, the Iranian government, following the designs and intentions of Israel, continues to disgrace us...[6]

Following his speech, Khomeini was arrested. There were immediate riots in major cities all over Iran. Several hundred people were killed in Tehran alone. Expelled from the country in 1964, Khomeini went to Iraq, to Najaf (near Kufa and Karbala), where Ali is buried. From Najaf, one of the main centers of Shiʿi learning, where he both taught and wrote, Khomeini continued his attacks on the Shah.

These episodes, variations on the Muharram theme, were to be repeated in the course of the 1978-9 Revolution. Early in 1978, an article with derogatory references to Khomeini appeared in a semi-official newspaper in Tehran, and the people of Qom demonstrated in the streets in protest. They were met by the bullets of the riot police. Those who were killed were declared to be martyrs, and the Shiʿi martyrdom syndrome was once more re-activated. Just as Hussein is mourned not only on the 10th day of Muharram but also forty days thereafter, it is customary for Shiʿites to mourn the deceased forty days after their death. Those killed in the riots were mourned publicly forty days later by the multitudes in towns all over Iran. In Tabriz the riot police then fired on the mourners, creating new martyrs, and new cycles of remembrances forty days later. Four times this occurred, generating a chain reaction of mourning demonstrations and shootings, with more and more people participating every 40 days. That procession of events laid the ground for the final assault on the bastion of the Shah's regime.

One may wonder how it was possible to arrange such huge demonstrations in a country where the secret police prevented the formation of organized opposition. In each town, Muharram observance committees existed that could bring thousands of people into the street in an organized fashion. During the Revolution the Muharram procession tradition was instantly

them. The Umayyads and Yazid's government were the enemies of the Prophet's household. They did not want the Bani Hashem. Their intention was to uproot this most noble tree. The same question ought to be asked here, that if the tyrannical regime of Iran was fighting the ʿulama', if it was hostile to Islamic men of learning, what did they have to do with the Qur'an? What did they have to do with the Fayziyyeh? What did they have to do with the religious seminaries? What did they have to do with our 18-year-old Sayyid? (People weep.) What had our 18-year-old Sayyid done to the Shah? What had he done to the regime? What had he done to the tyrannical government? (People weep.) Then we reach the conclusion that they [too] are fundamentally opposed [to Islam]. They are fundamentally opposed to Islam and the ʿulama'. They fundamentally oppose us, old and young. Israel does not want Muslim ʿulama' in this country. Israel does not want men of knowledge in this country. Through its dark agents, Israel attacked Fayziyyeh, attacked us, attacked you. It wants to control your economy. It wants to destroy your converted into a cogent political weapon. When leaders of smaller units mixed Muharram slogans with political ones, they were repeated by the people who, nevertheless, remained orderly. Instead of inflicting wounds on their bodies in the traditional way, they stood ready to expose themselves to bayonets and bullets. Those in the vanguard, who were totally ready for martyrdom, would wear symbolic burial shrouds to show their willingness to sacrifice their lives. These revolutionary processions marked the martyrological calendar of the unfolding event. By the 10th day of Muharram in 1978, which fell on 11 December, millions of people were marching, and it was obvious that nothing could stop this Revolution. The religion and its ritual had become the mechanism for mass mobilization. Reenacting the Muharrams past became the revolutionary agency of anticipating those to come. In the process, the particular terms of the Revolution, the enduring illusions of its utopian coloring of the world, were articulated daily.

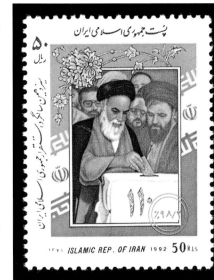

The traditional observance of Muharram mourning ends at a local cemetery. People go to the graves of their relatives and friends, or even of strangers. When Ayatollah Khomeini returned to Iran from Paris, where he had spent the last four months of his fourteen-year exile, his first stop was the Tehran cemetery where victims of the Revolution were buried. There he delivered his eulogy to the martyrs of the Islamic Revolution:

We have suffered calamities during all this time, huge calamities indeed. Some victories have also been achieved. They too were significant. The calamities of mothers who have lost their young children, men who have lost their children, infants who have lost their fathers. When I look at some of these people who have lost their children, I feel a heavy, unbearable burden on my shoulder. I cannot compensate for all these calamities that have befallen this people. I cannot [properly] thank this nation that has sacrificed everything it had for God. God Almighty and Exalted must repay them Himself. I express my condolences to mothers who have lost their children. I share their agony. I express my condolences to fathers who have lost their young children. To those young children who have lost their fathers, I express my condolences...[7]

With such eulogies, Khomeini wed the specifics of the Iranian Revolution of 1978-9 to the reconstructed history of Shiʿism. The enduring symbolics of the Shiʿi collective memory thus continued to be corresponded with the specific unfolding of the Islamic Revolution. In the spring 1979 referendum, in which the voters were to cast ballots for or against the Islamic Republic, the *taʿziyeh* symbolism of green and red played a significant role. In a society

where the majority of the population is illiterate, the pro-Islamic Republic cards were green, those against were red. Similarly colored ballots were used in the fall of 1979 during the voting for the Islamic constitution, which resulted — according to official reports — in an overwhelming victory for the green. The poster urging the people to vote for the Islamic Republic represented the hand of a young martyr sticking out of the grave and holding up a green ballot card. Underneath was written, "People — do not forget the martyrs for Islam." When the American Embassy was taken over by radical revolutionaries on 4 November 1979, Khomeini again orchestrated the Shiʿi ritual of martyrdom by telling President Carter that "as Shiʿites we welcome any opportunity for sacrifice." In an open letter to Pope John Paul II, Khomeini said: "Let me announce here that we are neither afraid of military interference nor are we afraid of economic siege, since we are Shiʿites and as Shiʿites we welcome any opportunity for sacrificing our blood. Our nation looks forward to an opportunity for self-sacrifice and martyrdom."[8] After the United States Navy was dispatched from the Indian Ocean and appeared at the mouth of the Persian Gulf, the commander-in-chief of the Iranian Navy appeared in public wearing a white burial shroud over his uniform. Following his lead, a throng of young people appeared in front of the besieged American Embassy wearing white shrouds on which was written, "We are ready to die. We are ready for martyrdom." [Fig. 4.15] Mobs at the Embassy also carried effigies of the Shah and President Carter, done in the style of the traditional ʿUmar effigies.

Completing the symbolism that linked the present to the past, Ayatollah Khomeini, from his return to Iran, began to be called Imam, a title that gave him an aura of infallibility. Some even suggested that he was the Twelfth Imam in his Second Coming. Although the suggestion was never fully realized and unfolded, still

Abbas

the mere appellation of Imam was strong enough to create a unique, unprecedented, and exclusive title of obedience for Khomeini. Terms of obedience were articulated from the deepest convictions of the Shiʿi populace. Within the strict confinements of a monotheistic theology there was nothing higher than the title Imam that the Shiʿi imagination could offer.

During the occupation of the American Embassy, the militants skillfully manipulated the symbolism of the Karbala tragedy for their own ends. Witness the first lines from the 101st statement by the militant captors in the form of an open letter to Imam Khomeini:

In the name of God most Gracious and most Merciful,
Salutations unto thee, O heir of Hussein!
Salutations unto thee, O heir to God's blood —
Blood which through the sword became victorious.
Salutations unto thee, O Imam.
Your message breathes spirit into the carcasses of
The dead. Salutations unto thee, O leader...

By cleverly employing the spirit of vengeance for Hussein's blood (and for the blood of the martyrs of the Revolution), and by painting the American government as the enemy of mankind, more especially of Islam, the militants succeeded in influencing Khomeini to side with them and block the United Nations commission from visiting the American hostages. Indeed, the motive of vengeance itself can be traced back to the Karbala tragedy. According to legend, there was one Sunni Muslim, Mukhtar, who was so incensed when he heard what had befallen Hussein that he converted to Shiʿi Islam and swore to avenge him. The wish for vengeance — a perfect fuel for any revolution — is deeply rooted in the legendary memory of Karbala. In the call for the return of the Shah and acknowledgment by the United States of its "crimes" against Iran, Mukhtar's revolt surfaced again. The historicity of Mukhtar is thus metaphoric — from a reconstructed past to an anxiety-provoking present to an uncertain future. What Mukhtar represents is the historical, this-worldly recognition of *justice*. Whereas Hussein personifies the cruel judgment of history whereby unjust rulers prevail and destroy their righteous opponents, Mukhtar is the sign of earthly salvation, the possibility of historical coming to terms with an essential notion of *justice*. Carried forward from the pre-Islamic into the Islamic period of Iranian political culture, *justice* has remained the most salient feature of Persian political culture. In and through the Karbala narrative, *justice* continues to be the key operative concept under which sweeping historical changes occur. Effectively translated from a remote historical event into a powerful universal myth, the Karbala story has the entire spectrum of modern and pre-modern history into which to narrate and attest itself.[9]

4.15 "We are ready for martyrdom!"

1 Hans Georg Gadamer, Truth and Method (New York, 1975), p. 102. **2** For further details of early divisions in the Islamic community, see Hamid Dabashi, Authority in Islam (New Brunswick, NJ, 1989). **3** Quoted in Sadeq Homayuni, Taʿziyeh dar Iran˘ (Tehran, 1989), pp. 34-5. **4** "Leaning on the Moment: A Conversation with Peter Brook," Parabola 4 (May 1979), p. 52. **5** Sayyid Jalal al-Din Madani, Ta'rikh-e Siyasi-ye Muʿasir-e Iran (Tehran, 1982), vol. 2: 37-8. **6** Ibid., pp. 38-9. **7** Ibid., pp. 335-6.**8** Khomeini, Sahifah-ye Nur (Tehran, 1982), vol. 10: 183. **9** Peter Chelkowski, "In Ritual and Revolution: The Image of the Transformation of Iranian Culture," Views: The Journal of Photography in New England 10, no. 3 (Spring 1989), pp. 7-11

Five

THE IDEOLOGY?

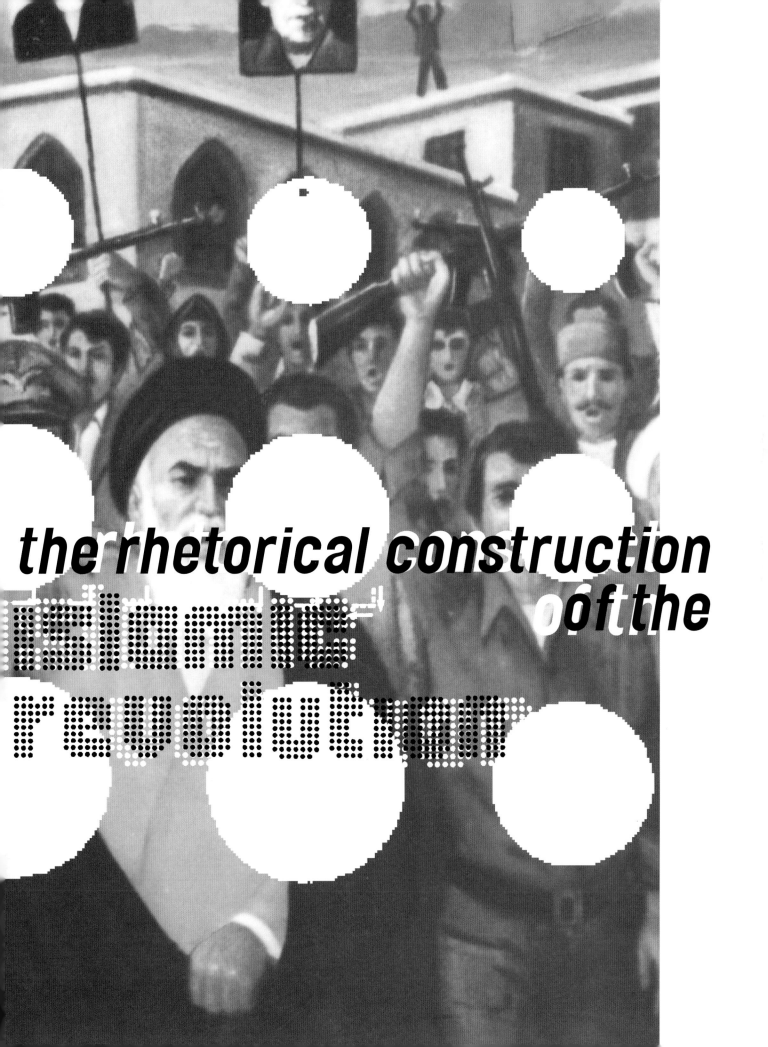

the rhetorical construction of the
of the
islamic
revolution

WHAT WAS IN THE MINDS OF THOSE WHO MASSIVELY PARTICIPATED IN THESE RITUAL PROCESSIONALS TURNED POLITICAL DEMONSTRATIONS? WHAT WERE THEIR HOPES, ASPIRATIONS, EXPECTATIONS, DEMANDS? IN THE PREVIOUS CHAPTER WE DESCRIBED THE RITUAL MACHINATION WHICH BECAME OPERATIVE IN THE WAKE OF THE REVOLUTION. THE MUHARRAM PROCESSION PROVIDED THE CHIEF RITUAL AND THE ICONIC FORCE NECESSARY FOR THE REVOLUTIONARY MACHINERY TO START MOVING. WHAT WE INTEND TO DO IN THIS CHAPTER IS GIVE A SYNOPTIC VIEW OF THE CHIEF IDEOLOGICAL DOCTRINES UPPERMOST IN THE MINDS OF THE REVOLUTIONARY LEADERS AND THEN IN TURN AMONG THEIR FOLLOWERS. WE NEED TO KNOW EXACTLY WHAT IDEOLOGICAL ASPIRATIONS ANIMATED AND MOBILIZED THESE REVOLUTIONARIES, AS THEY BEGAN TO LAUNCH THEIR REVOLUTION, AND AS THEY SUBSEQUENTLY SET THEMSELVES THE CRUCIAL TASK OF FURTHER PROPAGATING IT IN AN ART OF PERSUASION WHICH BECAME CONSTITUTIONAL TO THAT REVOLUTION.

5.1 Veiled women participated in the revolution from its earliest stages. Not all women were veiled from pious modesty; two centuries of active secularization had created a generation of Iranian women unaccustomed to the veil as part of their dress code. Instead, some politically active secular women veiled themselves as an outward show of solidarity in the revolutionary campaign against the Pahlavi regime. Soon after the revolution, however, posters began to propagate an "Islamic" code on the emerging vision of a revolutionary woman.

Ahmad Esmaili

Although the deeper roots of the ideology on the basis of which the Islamic Revolution was launched can be traced back to such crucial events as the Tobacco Revolt of the late nineteenth century and the Constitutional Revolution of the early twentieth century, the more immediate causes can be found soon after the establishment of the Pahlavi regime in 1926. The 1930s and 1940s were decades of Shiʿi polemical response to the rising power of secularism at large. Mirza Muhammad Hussein Na'ini (d. 1936), Shaykh Abd al-Karim Ha'iri (d. 1937), and Hajj Aqa Hussein Tabataba'i Qomi (d. 1947) were among the leading Shiʿi jurists of these decades, chiefly responsible for elevating Qom to a position of prominence in juridical studies, on the same level as Najaf, thus giving crucial political status to this holy city. It was the collective work of these leading jurists that paved the way for Hajj Aqa Hussein Tabataba'i Burujirdi (d. 1961), who enjoyed unprecedented power and prestige as a Shiʿi authority. The "political" agenda of the 1940s was chiefly characterized by the continued anger of the clerical establishment against the continued unfolding of secularism, whether sponsored by Reza Shah for his own political ends or as part of a general trend in urban centers throughout Iran. The enemy of the clerical authority now seemed to have extended from the tyrannical absolutism of the state to a widespread and hard-to-grasp presence of secular ideas and practices. Khalisi's treatise on "veiling in Islam,"[1] published in 1948, represents the dominant sentiment of the clerics in this period. In this treatise Khalisi tried to strike a balance between the radical traditionalists who denied women any social presence and status, and the rising secularism in which women were actively unveiled and socially present. The issue of women and their social status increasingly assumed a central role in the religious and political concerns of the Shiʿi clerics.

The two chief forces against which Shiʿi political thought responded actively in the 1940s were Baha'ism and communism. What the Shiʿi authorities considered to be the Baha'i apostasy and communist atheism were the principal forces against which the Shiʿites reacted in the 1950s. In 1951 Khalisi published *Bandits of Right and Truth, or, Those who Return to Barbarism and Ignorance* in

**5.2 Kazem Chalipa's "Everyday is Ashura"
depicts the active reconstruction of Shiᶜism
as a militant political ideology. The blank
face of the archetypical Shiᶜi martyr/hero
can be metaphorically configured by
believers wishing to substitute
themselves in that role.**

**5.3 The June 1963 uprising was
remembered after the 1979 revolution as
the immediate precursor of the movement
to topple the Pahlavi regime. The red
figure with the gun is depicted with a
crown, representing monarchy, and the
green figure with the flag of "God."**

response to the anti-religious tract published by the Tudeh Party, *Guardians of Magic and Myth*.[2] If the 1940s was the decade of socialism, then the 1950s gave rise to a re-emergence of nationalism in Iran, a movement chiefly identified with Muhammad Mosaddeq, the champion of the Iranian nationalist movement of the 1950s. And it was to nationalism that Shiᶜi political thought responded in the 1950s. Ali Akbar Tashayyud was chiefly responsible for an active coordination of Shiᶜi doctrines with the dominant themes of nationalism in the 1950s. While Tashayyud tried to assimilate nationalism into Shiᶜi political thought, Sayyid Mahmud Taleqani (1910-79) sought to provide an active rereading of key Shiᶜi figures such as Na'ini and Kharaqani by posing Shiᶜism as an alternative to nationalism.

As Said Amir Arjomand has noted, "the 1960s was a decade of fateful change in Shiᶜism."[3] The decade began with the death of Ayatollah Burujirdi as the last principally apolitical jurist in the tradition of Shaykh Abd al-Karim Ha'iri and Sayyid Abu al-Hasan Isfahani. Burujirdi's passive condoning of Muhammad Reza Shah, very much reminiscent of Ha'iri's passive acceptance of Reza Shah, had for long limited Shiᶜi political activism to an anti-secular, anti-Baha'i, anti-Tudeh Party agenda, some of which the Pahlavi regime in fact sympathized with. The death of Burujirdi, however, brought the whole question of supreme political authority in the Shiᶜi community to a new critical point.[4] Indicative of this critical moment was the commencement of a conference in Qom in which the leading Shiᶜi authorities gathered to ponder over the future of

5.4 Shari‘ati and Taleqani, two of the principal ideologues of the Islamic Revolution, are depicted with Khomeini as architects of the movement that rid Iran of the Pahlavi regime, represented here by the humiliated figure of the Shah seeking protection from the Americans.

Tabataba'i in Qom and those organized by Murteza Motahhari in Tehran added momentum and energy to Shi‘i political thought. Weekly and monthly journals such as *Maktab-e Tashayyu‘* and *Guftar-e Mah* propagated the ideas of the rising Shi‘i ideologues. Ultimately the Husseiniyeh Irshad, established in 1964 in Tehran, must be considered the most successful modern institution of radical Shi‘i thought. But by far the major event of the 1960s was the first revolutionary uprising by Ayatollah Khomeini. Khomeini had been active in Qom since the 1940s where he was busy pursuing his juridical studies under Shaykh Abd al-Karim Ha'iri. While such politically conscious and active clerics as Taleqani and Motahhari were busy beating about the bush of the Pahlavi (il)legitimacy, Khomeini seized the moment by going further than anyone and publicly calling for the ousting of the Shah. The June 1963 uprising was severely crushed and Khomeini was exiled.

As Amir Arjomand has noted,[5] Khomeini's 1963 uprising put all the ramblings of the clerical reform on hold and gave added momentum to the continued validity of the institution of the ‘ulama'. At least two high-ranking members of the ‘ulama', Hasan Farid Gulpaygani and Shaykh Ali Tehrani, carried forward the theoretical implications of Khomeini's 1963 uprising and in the 1970s wrote treatises in which ideas of supreme collective clerical rule for the Shi‘i ‘ulama' were expounded.[6] The result of Khomeini's radical politicization of the institution of the ‘ulama' is so drastic that one can indeed speak of "an ideological revolution in Shi‘ism."[7] The greatest and most effective challenge to the authority of the ‘ulama' as representative of an institution, however, came with

90

religious and political authority. The proceedings of this conference were subsequently published in a volume, *Bahthi dar Bareh-ye Marja‘iyyat va Ruhaniyyat*. Practically all the leading revolutionary ideologues of the late 1970s, with the notable exception of Khomeini, contributed to this volume, in which such issues as the range of the *marja‘-e taqlid's* religious and political authorities, the viability of the notion of following the most learned, the supervision of Sahm-e Imam revenue, etc. were openly discussed and debated. A major institutional development following the death of Burujirdi was the emergence of autonomous religious centers as Qur'anic commentary schools, such as the one established by Taleqani in Tehran. Muslim student associations on many university campuses and Muslim professional associations of engineers, physicians, teachers, lawyers, etc. were among voluntary associations that began to emerge in the 1960s. These organizations provided the institutional bases for the propagation of modern Shi‘i political thought. Informal gatherings, such as those organized by ‘Allamah

5.5 Fighting imperialism and aborting its designs on Iranian natural resources were major leitmotifs in Islamic ideology.

تداوم انقلاب ....تا
پایان غارتگری

حزب جمهوری اسلامی

overwhelming rhetorical power from Ali Shariᶜati (1933-77). In the 1960s and 1970s Shariᶜati single-handedly reimagined a whole new, radically active, spectrum for "Islam." In a series of effectively delivered public lectures and persuasively written essays he created an unprecedented energy and enthusiasm among his generation of politically committed intellectuals with a religious tendency in their characters. Educated in Mashhad and Paris, Shariᶜati mastered a powerful arsenal of rhetorical devices in Europe before returning to his homeland, wholly committed to transforming Shiᶜism into a full-fledged political ideology. He considered the entire institution of clerical establishment as fundamentally outdated and compromised, and sought to release the Shiᶜi sacred imaginations from their institutional hold under the authority of the ᶜulama'. With a barely concealed disdain for clerical quietism and irrelevant piety, Shariᶜati wed the sacrosanct memories of Shiᶜism to the most serious problems of his time: cultural colonialism, social injustice, political repression, and the worldwide domination of "Western imperialism." Combining his own brand of Sartrean existentialism and Fanonian Third Worldism, he opted for an autonomous and independent man fully in charge of his destiny. He equally reached for outdated figures of Shiᶜi collective history, and from such figures as Fatemeh, the Prophet's daughter and wife of the first Shiᶜi Imam, Ali, reconstructed the perfect, devoted revolutionary woman, to be

5.6 The Islamic Revolution was predicated on a century-old rhetoric of nativism, which sought to expel not only the political and economic apparatus of imperialism but also its cultural implications.

emulated by his contemporaries.[8] Shariᶜati redefined the role of the revolutionary intellectual, ridiculed and dismissed secular intellectuals, and made faith and belief once again acceptable, even fashionable, among young Shiᶜites. In his major work, *Islamshenasi* (1972), he took upon himself the stupendous task of redefining the whole wide domain of what it means to be a Muslim. He went back far into the most sacrosanct corners of Shiᶜi and Islamic memory and brought back to life what he thought was "the true Islam," an Islam which was all but forgotten, waiting to stir and mobilize its adherents to active, radical, and revolutionary commitment in life. He redefined "monotheism" in terms congenial to classless, repressionless, anti-tyrannical terms. He took a unique combination of existentialist, Marxist, and Fanonist lenses and through them read every major tenet of Islam. From ethics to politics, historiography to sociology, economics to culture, Shariᶜati swept through every niche and corner of contemporary moral and intellectual concerns and gave them a revolutionary Shiᶜi reading.

The person who had facilitated much of what Shariᶜati accomplished in his radical repoliticization of Shiᶜi Islam was Jalal Al-e Ahmad (1923-69), who, in such works as *Westoxication* and "On the Services and Treasons of Intellectuals," argued vociferously against what he called "Western" culture, including its revolutionary ideologies, and for a local, domestically viable, construction of a revolutionary ideology. Al-e Ahmad pointed towards recent Iranian and Iraqi history in which the only successful social mobilizations had occurred when the Shiᶜi clerics were involved. A disillusioned Marxist, he sought, as far as possible in his generation of frustrated revolutionaries, to rekindle a radical trait in Shiᶜism. What he had barely noticed and detected, Shariᶜati took to its fullest potential and persuasively argued for the revolutionary possibilities of the "Shiᶜi ideology."⁹

By far the most erudite, systematic, and relentless ideologue who carried the revolutionary potential of a repoliticized Shiᶜism to its logical conclusion was Murteza Motahhari (1920-79), although he disagreed with Shariᶜati on some fundamental issues, particularly the central role of the ᶜulama' in politics. Perhaps the unintended consequence of his ideas was the further consolidation of "the Islamic Ideology" as the most potent revolutionary machinery that preceded the events of 1978-9. Launching his revolutionary zeal from his solid place in the heart of the Shiᶜi clerical establishment, Motahhari mobilized his massive knowledge of Shiᶜi doctrines and institutions to argue against all other (Marxist-materialist and nationalist-liberal) revolutionary alternatives. "Islamic philosophy" was the principal weapon that he actively popularized in a deliberate attempt to dislodge historical materialism. He shifted his attention from a pervasive popularization of the extremely recondite language of Islamic philosophy to public lectures to various Muslim associations on a variety of issues, and even to renarration of popular religious stories. He severely criticized the clerical establishment for its abandonment of politics, and in such works as *Akhlaq-e Jensi dar Islam va Jahan-e Gharb, ᶜIlal-i Gioagish bih Maddi-Gari,* and *Islam va Muqtaziyat-e Zaman* he confronted practically all the ritual issues of his time, preaching to and preparing a massive audience that ultimately joined him and other clerics to topple the Pahlavi monarchy.¹⁰

Motahhari's philosophical preoccupation with historical

5.7 Through the collective efforts of Shiᶜi ideologues, a new revolutionary energy capable of mobilizing believers was created.

5.8 After his assassination, Murteza Motahhari was remembered as a principal architect of the Islamic Revolution.

materialism and his concerns with popularizing a more readily accessible and politically relevant "Islamic philosophy" was largely indebted to his close association with ᶜAllamah Sayyid Muhammad Hussein Tabataba'i (1903-81), a distinguished Shiᶜi scholar who was equally concerned with the erosion of Islamic doctrines and ideas. In his major philosophical contribution to the active engagement with Marxism and historical materialism, *Usul-e Falsafah va Ravish-e Realism* (1953-85), Tabataba'i took issue with every aspect of those pervasive ideas. His concern was primarily the seminary students in Qom who had apparently been drawn to radical, secular ideas. But Motahhari's extensive commentaries on these texts made them accessible to more secular students in Tehran University. Throughout his Qur'anic commentaries, and in his participation in questions of supreme juridical-political authority among the Shiᶜites and a host of other, related, issues, ᶜAllamah Tabataba'i actively took part in his generation of high-ranking clerics' concern with the rise of Marxism, historical materialism, secularism, and ultimately the future of the Shiᶜi faith and its social and political contexts.¹¹

To address the specifics of those social and political contexts in a language that bore the sacred authority of the Qur'an, another major political thinker of this period, Sayyid Mahmud Taleqani, used the discourse of Qur'anic commentary as his preferred narrative. Through a succession of Qur'anic commentaries, published later as *Partuvi az Qur'an* (1979-83), Taleqani read an actively revolutionary message into the Islamic holy text. In and out of prison for his political activities over an extended period of time, he preached his radical, revolutionary reading of the Qur'an, linking its sacrosanct message to the most immediate and compelling problems of his time. Taleqani felt equally compelled to battle Marxism, especially its economic theory. He wrote a book, *Islam and Ownership* (1953), in which he countered the Marxist conception of the economic basis of social structure, and then assimilated its principal terms and discourse in narrating an "Islamic" political economy.¹²

The economic aspect of "the Islamic Ideology," as the Shiᶜi ideologues now actively identified their rallying cry, was more extensively elaborated by Sayyid Abu al-Hasan Bani Sadr (b. 1933). Long before he attained the distinction of becoming the first President of the Islamic Republic of Iran, Bani Sadr actively participated in anti-Pahlavi movements and wrote extensively on the political economy of oil production in the Middle East in general and in Iran in particular. In such works as *Iqtisad-e Tawnidi* (1978) and *Naft va Sultah* (1977), he argued enthusiastically that the Pahlavi regime was plundering the Iranian natural resources and selling

But by far the most rhetorically successful revolutionary Shiʿite who ultimately engineered the downfall of the Persian monarchy was Ruhullah Musavi Khomeini (1902-89). Born in the small village of Khomein, near Tehran, Khomeini grew up in the immediate aftermath of the Constitutional Revolution of 1906-11, an event which, as exemplified by the execution of Shaykh Fazlullah Nuri in 1909, ushered in the rapid institutionalization of modernity in Iran. He received his early education in Khomein and Arak and then moved to Qom to pursue his higher scholastic studies, where he was further aggravated by the rise of Reza Shah to power and the even more rapid dissemination of politically mandated modernization. Having witnessed the brutal tyranny of Reza Shah (for whose secular modernism Khomeini had no patience), the abdication of Reza Shah in favor of his son Muhammad Reza Shah, the Allied occupation of Iran, the rise of the Tudeh Party, the nationalist movement

5.9 Years of political activism and imprisonment turned Sayyid Mahmud Taleqani into a veritable revolutionary.

5.10 Mahdi Bazargan and Muhammad Mosaddiq were assimilated into the ranks of revolutionaries who led the Iranians' to rid themselves of the Pahlavi monarchy.

them cheaply to the United States and Europe.[13]

A quiet revolutionary with a profound admiration for Mahatma Gandhi became the link between the revolutionary ideologues and their targeted audience. Long before he had the precarious distinction of becoming the first (transitional) prime minister after the fall of the Pahlavi regime in 1979, Mahdi Bazargan (*b.* 1907) had been actively involved in the political mobilization of the professional classes. Having received his engineering education in France (he was sent to Europe along with a group of other students by Reza Shah in 1929), Bazargan returned to his homeland determined to reawaken religious sensibilities against the rising tide of secularism and for active political mobilization to gain power. In 1961 he, Sayyid Mahmud Taleqani, and a number of other Muslim activists established the Freedom Movement of Iran.[14] Imprisoned for his political activities, Bazargan spent much of his time rewriting a history of the Indian independence movement as a way of expressing his own wishes for a similar revolutionary movement in his homeland. He used the occasion of his defense at the Pahlavi court to issue a strong condemnation of tyranny and injustice. After his release from prison, he wrote and gave public lectures on a variety of issues, all targeted at an active resuscitation of a religious sensitivity conducive to revolutionary changes in the *status quo.*

of Mosaddeq and the National Front, and ultimately the reinstitution of Muhammad Reza Shah by the CIA-engineered coup of 1953, Khomeini watched with visceral contempt the Shah's absolutist rule in the late 1950s and early 1960s. His 1963 uprising against the Shah was thus based on decades of resentful deliberation in religious and political terms. The increasing secularization of society, the aggressive unfolding of the projects of modernity, the rapid decline of Islamic doctrines and institutions, the widespread presence of Marxist and materialist conceptions of the history of the world, and ultimately the suffocating authoritarianism of the Shah (which went hand in hand with American domination of Iranian political, social, economic, and cultural life) were the principal points of contention that moved Khomeini to open revolt.

After the June 1963 uprising was severely crushed, he was forced into exile, first in Turkey and then in Iraq. After a short period of hesitation, Khomeini launched a major campaign against the legitimacy of the Pahlavi regime and of the monarch's authority. The principal text he produced in this period was *Velayat-e Faqih* (1970), in which he defined the principal doctrines of his "Islamic government."[15] The major thesis of *Velayat-e Faqih* is quite simple. The Islamic government established by Prophet Muhammad, and according to the Shiʿites continued *de jure* (if not *de facto*) by the Imams, was not meant to be a transitional government. In the absence of the Twelfth Imam, who is now in occultation, the world is plunging deeply into corruption and despair. The Shiʿites cannot know exactly when the Twelfth Imam is to appear. In the mean time, the responsibility of leading Muslim nations cannot be entrusted to corrupt and tyrannical rulers like the Shah. They simply aggravate the corrupt institution because they are deeply corrupt themselves. At this point, Khomeini cites a series of Qur'anic passages and prophetic traditions which he interprets to mean that the (Shiʿi) jurists are to assume power because, by virtue of having access to the specifics of the sacred law, they know how to regulate the daily affairs of Muslims in order to ensure their this-worldly and other-worldly salvation. Other than *Velayat-e Faqih,* Khomeini wrote letters incessantly to Muslim student associations in Iran, Europe, the United States, and Canada, inviting and encouraging them to unite and revolt against the Pahlavi regime. The rhetorical edge of these letters cut with precisely the same political and emotional edges as those more fully developed in Velayat-e Faqih. Khomeini wrote extensively on other issues — juridical, mystical, and philosophical in particular. Even some of his poetry has been published. But the main access to his political ideas remains in his letters, his proclamations, and *Velayat-e Faqih.*

The collective impact of these revolutionary changes in Shiʿi political thought, prompted as they were by historical changes in the social context of the faith, gradually led to an explosive situation in the late 1970s. By virtue of a charismatic authority, solidly based on a lifetime of struggle within the context of Shiʿi

clerical institutions, Ayatollah Khomeini emerged as the chief spokesman of the Revolution, which now became totally identified as "Islamic." In the next chapter, we shall turn our attention to the semiotic significance of some of the revolutionary banners that were used in the marches and demonstrations calling for the implementation of these ideas.

5.11 In his writings and speeches, Khomeini invoked doctrinal and historical sources of Shiʿi collective sentiments in order to mobilize a massive revolutionary force. One placard in this picture reads "We are not Kufans," a historical reference to the people of Kufah who had pledged, and then reneged on, their help to the third Shiʿi Imam, Hussein.

1 For a discussion, see Said Amir Arjomand (ed.), Authority and Political Culture in Shiʿism (Albany, NY, 1988), p. 188. **2** For a discussion, see ibid., pp. 188-9. **3** Ibid., p. 189. **4** For a discussion, see Hamid Dabashi, Theology of Discontent: The Ideological Foundations of the Islamic Revolution in Iran (New York, 1993), pp. 264-5. **5** Authority and Political Culture, p. 190. **6** See ibid., p. 191. **7** Ibid., p. 192. **8** For further reading on Shariʿati, see Dabashi, Theology of Discontent, ch. 2. **9** For further details on Al-e Ahmad's ideas, see ibid., ch. 1. **10** For further details, see ibid., ch. 3. **11** For further details, see ibid., ch. 5. **12** For further details, see ibid., ch. 4. **13** For further details, see ibid., ch. 7. **14** For further details on the Freedom Movement of Iran, see Houchang E. Chehabi, Iranian Politics and Religious Modernism: The Liberation Movement of Iran under the Shah and Khomeini (Ithaca, NY, 1990). **15** For a translation, see Hamid Algar (trans. and ed.), Islam and Revolution: Writings and Declarations of Imam Khomeini (Berkeley, Calif., 1981).

COLORFUL BANNERS
IN REVOLUTIONARY
PROCESSIONS

six

BANNERS, AND WHAT THEY PROCLAIMED, LED THIS REVOLUTION TO SUCCESS. IN THE PREVIOUS CHAPTER WE GAVE A SUMMARY OF THE REVOLUTIONARY IDEAS THAT GRADUALLY LED TO THE CATACLYSMIC EVENT. IN THIS CHAPTER, WE SHALL CONSIDER THE SEMIOTIC SIGNIFICANCE OF THE CALLIGRAPHIC BANNERS THAT LED THE REVOLUTIONARY PROCESSIONS. THE CENTRALITY OF QUR'ANIC PASSAGES IN THESE REVOLUTIONARY BANNERS REQUIRES THAT WE PAY CLOSE ATTENTION TO HOW PEOPLE READ A SACRED LANGUAGE WHICH IS NOT THEIR OWN.

6.1 Arabic script and language was used in many revolutionary banners to give an aura of sanctity to the revolution.

A central feature of publicity in the Iranian Revolution is the use of the Arabic language in posters, stamps, banners, and many other such agencies of constructing collective signification. The first thing to remember is that Iranians are not Arabs. The overwhelming majority of them do not speak, read, or understand Arabic, which is as familiar and yet as alien to them as Latin is to a Briton or an American. Arabic, however, is the sacred language of the Qur'an, of the prophetic and imami traditions, and of many other canonical sources in the Shiʿi doctrinal culture. The custodians of that culture are the Shiʿi clerics, the ʿulama', literally those who know, or claim to know, the Arabic language and all the canonical sources of Islam in it. The sheer repetition of Arabic phrases, from whatever canonical source, has the immediate impact of announcing the Islamicity of the revolutionary movement. This is particularly crucial in view of the contemporary (secular) ideological alternatives to the revolutionary movement. The symbolic signification of the Arabic semantic constructions is quite independent of their functional significance. The overwhelming majority of the revolutionary participants did not actually read or understand the meaning of the Arabic phrases, but the sheer semiotic impact of the Arabic construction, with its *naskh* calligraphy and its diacritical notes, has an aura of sanctity about it. That aura of sanctity was immediately translated into the visible Islamicity of the Revolution and thus competed effectively against all secular challenges to its monopolizing the event. On the most semiotically significant level, the Arabic language made the Iranian Revolution of 1978-9 "the Islamic Revolution." There is no underestimating the power of an alien sacred language. The very incomprehensibility of it carries authority. The dual aspect of Arabic phrases — one denotational, the other connotational — needs further consideration, especially in its correspondence with the iconic (or pictorial) message.

Looking at an advertisement with both verbal and iconic references, Barthes has identified three distinct, yet interrelated, modes of communication: "a linguistic message, a coded iconic message, and a non-coded iconic message."[1] This identification can function as a further point of departure in our observations here. Observing the Iranian revolutionary banners, among other things,

6.2 The Arabic verse from the Qur'an radically Islamicizes the blatantly Marxist image in this poster, put out by Mujahedin Organization, to celebrate May Day.

we notice four, not three, levels of operation. The linguistic message itself is divided into two sections, very much on the iconic model. First there is the immediate calligraphic level, and second the actual linguistic (or conceptual) message. Glancing at Arabic calligraphy, before any meaning is deciphered from it, reveals its exclusive range of sensibilities quite independent of what is actually being communicated through it. This is particularly true of Arabic phrases, with the stylistic features of the calligraphic representation, its diacritical notations, etc. For most Iranian recipients of this calligraphic event, the Arabic phrase, usually from the Qur'an or another canonical source, first and foremost creates a sense of awe and solemnity. It is only later, and mainly for the very few who can decipher the Arabic phrase, that its actual meaning can begin to exercise its independent linguistic effect. Thus, as in the iconic registration, there are two aspects to the verbal communication contained in the caption, a calligraphic and a linguistic. The result is the simultaneous formation of four levels of canonization: (1) calligraphic, (2) linguistic, (3) the denoted image, and (4) the connoted image. We can further argue that at the calligraphic level, the shape and contour of the Arabic phrase constitutes, in its own right, an iconic representation. For those who cannot read the Arabic phrase, what is the difference between the calligraphy and the supporting images? Thus the calligraphic representation may itself be taken as consisting of a denoted image and a connoted one. This gives us three divisions in the verbal part and two in the iconic, altogether five interrelated messages. But the last subdivision does not necessarily lead to deeper insight into the multiple constructions of the iconic or the linguistic. We can argue that, although distinctively different, the denoted and connoted aspects of the calligraphy and of the icon blend and fade into each other. That would lead us to further considerations about the dialectics of the linguistic and iconic interactions beyond the levels contemplated by Barthes. The importance of this unfolding dialectics between words and images is particularly pronounced in a semi-literate society. But such theoretical considerations will lead us astray from our immediate objectives here. For the sake of the present study, let us merely focus on our fourfold construction of (1) the calligraphic message, (2) the linguistic message, (3) the denoted image, and (4) the connoted image.

THE CALLIGRAPHIC MESSAGE

The calligraphic message is the most immediate registration that any particular constellation of words in a revolutionary caption entails. Whether in Persian or in Arabic, but with crucial differences that need not concern us here, the revolutionary message makes its first impression through the semiotic qualities of the calligraphy with which it is delivered. The Persian and Arabic messages are immediately recognized through their calligraphy. The Persian, ordinarily a revolutionary message, is usually in *nasta*ʿ*liq* and without the diacritical notes, while the Arabic, always a Qur'anic passage or from the prophetic or imami traditions, is almost invariably in *naskh* and with the diacritical notes. Since

6.3 In this poster, celebrating May Day by Mujahedin Organization, the four calligraphic, linguistic, denotational, and connotational formations are evident.

6.4 This mural, not far from the notorious Evin prison in Tehran, condemns the bloody massacre of Iranian pilgrims to Mecca in July 1987. It competes for attention with a commercial advertising radio and television services.

6.5 A calligraphic message appropriates May Day into an Islamic mold.

101

there is a doctrinal injunction against making a mistake in reading the Qur'an, all sacred statements are written in the more legible *naskh* and with the diacritical notes. The calligraphic message, thus constituted, is a sacred certitude that whatever is written in Arabic is the word of God, the Truth manifest. The Muslim observer encounters the calligraphic message with a sense of awe, respect, and humility, his guard dropped, his hands loose, his shoes taken off in a sign of utter devotion. Whatever is actually written in that Arabic cannot be but the Truth manifest. The maze of curves and movements, rotations and revolutions, the sudden stops, the abrupt movements, the restrictings and warnings of the diacritical notes,

the shapes and patterns, all create a sacred field of obedience and certitude into which the Muslim believer steps, ready to receive further signals and indications of what needs to be done.

THE LINGUISTIC MESSAGE

Beyond the imperatives of the calligraphic message, the linguistic message, registered in the few words of the caption, has a reality *sui generis*. It may or may not immediately correspond with the iconic image that it supports. It is conceivable that members of the younger literate generation would more immediately grasp the linguistic message than the iconic, or even the correspondence between the linguistic and the iconic. The caption could be a

Qur'anic phrase, a prophetic or imami tradition (saying), a line of Persian poetry, or simply a proclamation of a political or ideological stance. Beyond its calligraphic registration, the content of these captions has a profound and independent impact on its mobilized audience. The phrase "Verily! Life is belief and fighting [for that belief]," especially when customarily delivered in Arabic, demands obedience by its very matter-of-factness. There is no questioning its validity, truth, relevance, or contemporary authority. The phrase stands there in Arabic, with all the might and majesty of a conquering faith behind it. The phrase is Islam incarnate, the faith of the conquerors, the word of God Almighty. Centuries of historical validation and the eternities of metaphysical certitude stand behind it. There is no question of possible flaws, of its historicity, humanity, or probability, and no plausible faults. The Truth manifest, such Arabic phrases demand obedience by merely being there.

THE LINGUISTIC-ICONIC MESSAGE

Barthes has identified two modes of relationship between the linguistic message of the caption and the twofold iconic image: "anchorage" and "relay." The "anchorage" function of the linguistic message is crucial for the entire operation of the semiotic construction — verbal and iconic. Any representation of image, no matter how "primitive" in its visual construction, is a polysemous opening to almost infinite possibilities of readings. The signifiers in the image can lead, as Barthes puts it, to a "floating chain" of

signifieds. Left to its own open-ended vastness, the polysemous power of an image leads to a dysfunctional multiplicity of readings that can practically render the picture mute.

When the pictorial presence says too many things at the same time, there is no understanding anything. "Hence," Barthes argues, "in every society various techniques are developed intended to *fix* the floating chain of signifieds in such a way as to counter the terror of uncertain signs; the linguistic message is one of these techniques." Any representation of iconic images creates the immediate question of "What is it?" Among a range of almost inexhaustible possibilities, the caption limits the range of legitimate answers. Again in Barthes's words, the caption "helps me to choose the *correct level of perception*, permits me to focus not simply my gaze but also my understanding."[2] The linguistic message thus proceeds through a bifocal relationship with both the denoted image, which it helps to identify, and the connoted image, which it renders interpretable.

Sahat Loo

6.6 A linguistic message with only two words, "Ya Hussein" ("O Hussein"), but considerable symbolic energy.

6.7 An excellent example of a polysemous image with open-ended readings, were it not for its caption "22 Bahman," which refers to

6.9 A poster without an intra-textual linguistic message, either in "anchorage"
or in "relay." Only via an extra-textual caption, "The Nights of 'God is Great',"
does the dialogical delimitation of the hermeneutic field take place.

Techniques of "fixing" the intended meaning of a text are not monolithic or essentialist to a society. Changing historical circumstances lead to transfixation of renewed frames of signification. Perhaps the most crucial function of textual anchorage of the denoted and connoted image is its ideological use. "[T]he anchorage," Barthes tells us, "may be ideological and indeed this is its principal function; the text *directs* the reader through the signifieds of the image, causing him to avoid some and receive others; by means of an often subtle *dispatching*, it remote-controls him towards a meaning chosen in advance."[3] In practically all the iconic images considered in this book, the ideological function of the textual anchorage is high on the revolutionary agenda. The selection of the iconic, the linguistic, and their corresponding messages, is such that it would instantly create a maximum level of revolutionary fervor. A mere rising sun in red, over a dark horizon, would yield an anxiety-provoking range of multiple and conflicting readings. It is only when the caption reads, in Arabic, "Verily! Life is belief and fighting [for that belief]" that the red and the black, the shapes and the postures, begin to register their intended meanings. It is this combination of iconic and linguistic registrations that represents the deepest ideological forces operative in a revolutionary culture. The linguistic caption thus "remote controls" the sensibilities of the receiving audience in correspondence with the iconic constructions of the ideological message. The otherwise "projective power of pictures," as Barthes calls it,[4] is thus brought under specific ideological control, launched towards identifiable political ends.

The second aspect of the linguistic message is in what Barthes calls its relation of "relay" to the iconic representation. In a relation of "relay" the linguistic message complements the icon, carrying it, as it were, to a higher level of semiotic operation. While in the relation of "anchorage," the linguistic message has a delimiting function whereby the icon is circumscribed; in the "relay" the caption and the image enter into a complementary dialogue which advances the syntactical result to a shared level of discourse. Barthes gives the example of comic strips and movies, where the caption or dialogue is in complementary "relay" correspondence with the static or moving images. The linguistic message and the iconic image in this kind of relationship are, in Barthes's words, "fragments of a more general syntagm."[5] Thus in the "relay" relationship the linguistic message is more "costly" (while in "anchorage" it is "lazier"). The more general syntagm presumed by or generated through the complementary dialogue of the caption and the image is where the whole semiotic enterprise finds its destination and purpose. Under revolutionary circumstances, that higher syntagm is of course the ideological mobilization of the receiving audience. That mobilization, in turn, speaks, through the "relay" correspondence between the culture-specific caption and icon, the language of its historical vicinity. The audience stands at the cross-currents of the iconic and the linguistic signals, receiving, decoding, synthesizing, and interpreting them simultaneously.

6.10 The revolutionary audience stands where cross-currents of iconic and linguistic messages meet; they are carrying, embodying, receiving, decoding, synthesizing, and interpreting them to their rhetorical conclusions.

1 Roland Barthes, "Rhetoric of the Image," in Robert E. Innis (ed.), Semiotics: An Introductory Anthology (Bloomington, Ind., 1985), p. 196. **2** Ibid., p. 197. **3** Ibid., p. 198. **4** Ibid. **5** Ibid.

Seven

writings on the wall:
the graffiti in black and blood

THE TRADITIONAL IRANIAN DWELLING IS SURROUNDED BY A HIGH BRICK OR ADOBE WALL. THE SURFACE OF THE WALL IS OFTEN WHITEWASHED. IRAN, THEREFORE, PROVIDES ENDLESS SURFACE SPACE FOR GRAFFITI, MURALS, AND POSTERS. DURING THE REVOLUTION AND THE WAR AGAINST IRAQ THAT WALL SPACE WAS USED TO THE UTMOST. IN THIS CHAPTER WE SHALL LOOK AT SOME OF THESE REVOLUTIONARY GRAFFITI.

IN HIS INTRODUCTION TO PROFILES OF THE REVOLUTIONARY ART THE EDITOR WRITES:

Whether before or after the Islamic Revolution, these walls have been used as the arenas of expressing the people's dissatisfaction and anger against oppression through slogans, emotion-choked paintings, and caricature. Today these walls stand as valid documents of the people's communications, motives, and strivings. Even before the righteous cries of our ummat [Islamic community] brought down the walls of the oppressive ruler, the walls of our cities had gone to war against the walls of the oppressive regime, consequently weakening and shaking their very foundations.[1]

7.1

In the first stage of the Revolution the propaganda war was being fought on the surface of the walls. The revolutionaries would write their slogans on them; then the functionaries of the Shah's government and their supporters would try to whitewash them or cross them out, often writing their own counter-revolutionary slogans on top of them. Sometimes the walls were covered with layer upon layer of graffiti and counter-graffiti. The main technique employed by the opposing camps of graffiti artists was to cross out parts of a slogan and substitute new words. For example, if the supporters of the Shah wrote "Long live the Shah" the opponents would cross out "Long live" and scribble in "Death to." Very often the word "Shah" was written backwards or upside-down, suggesting the imminent downfall of the imperial regime. Many demonstrators who had been wounded by gunshots would write slogans on the walls in their blood; others would smear their hands in the spilled blood of their wounded and dead comrades and leave their bloody handprints on the walls. As the editor of Profiles of the Revolutionary Art writes, "The demonstrators recorded the crimes committed by the oppressive regime, and on the other hand they invoked the spirits of their compatriots in their continuation of the struggle against the oppressive regime."[2]

This wall covered with murals runs along Imam Khomeini Avenue in the southwestern town of Andimeshk. It is a good example of the art of persuasion in an urban environment. The first vignette reads "Our armor is Faith and Islam," signed Imam Khomeini. Next to this pronouncement, a young soldier in battle gear is visible holding and reading the Holy Qur'an. On the next vignette a text in a very fine calligraphy reads: "The martyr is the heart of history." Next to it is the logo of the Martyrs' Foundation. On the next vignette three flags—of the United States, of Israel, and the third is unclear—are on fire. In the middle of the picture is written "Death to Israel." [Fig. 7.1]

Kazem Chalipa

7.2

7.3

7.4

One of the most dramatic artistic reflections of the revolutionary struggle fought with paint, ink, and even blood on the walls of Iranian towns comes from the brush of a master poster-designer, Kazem Chalipa. This descriptive painting of the Black Friday Massacre is done in the style of Socialist Realism. It is like a photographic snapshot, capturing the most commonly used revolutionary slogans painted in red and black on the walls and the store shutters in Zhaleh Square. The graffiti on the left shutter reads: "Praise to Khomeini, death to the Shah." In order to belittle the monarch, the word "Shah" is written upside-down. The slogan in red on the center shutter reads: "Independence, Freedom, Islamic Republic." Beneath it is written in black "This American Shah must be put to death." The graffiti in black next to the stenciled portrait of Khomeini and the stenciled painted figure of an armed revolutionary reads: "God is Greatest, Khomeini is the leader," and beneath it is written "Neither East [communism] nor West [capitalism] but the Islamic Republic." The soles of the shoes of a fallen demonstrator are visible next to the shutter on the left, and the body of a woman next to the shutter on the right. A *pietá*-like figure of a woman holding the head and shoulders of a dying male

demonstrator takes up the center and foreground of the painting. The woman observes a strict Islamic dress code. Everything but her face is covered; her expression is one of sorrow and steely determination. The man's shirt and the bandage around his head are soaked with blood which drips onto the pavement. Minor attributes of a crushed demonstration — a fallen poster on a stick, a few loose bricks scattered on the pavement (the only weapon of the crowd against the modern weaponry of the assailants) — further underline the mood. [Fig. 7.2]

The same mood of sorrow and steely determination is conveyed through the graffiti written in blood on the nameplate of Galeh (Zhaleh) Square, renaming it "The Square of the Martyrs" and obliterating the old name with a bloody handprint. Underneath is written the date of the Black Friday Massacre, the 17th of Shahrivar, and a photograph of the leader of the Revolution, Ayatollah Khomeini, is stuck up beside the date. This image was so gripping that the Revolutionary Guards later made a poster from a photograph of it. [Fig. 7.3]

Bloodstained hands are connected emotionally with the Karbala tragedy; they symbolize the fight until the last drop of

7.5

blood. ʿAbbas, Hussein's half-brother and standard-bearer, lost both his arms in the battle, yet fought on. [Fig.7.4] A photograph taken in front of Tehran University of a young demonstrator holding his bloody hands defiantly aloft testifies to the revolutionary spirit driven by the Karbala paradigm. [Fig. 7.5] The theme of a bloody hand writing on the wall was taken up by the Islamic Republican Party of the city of Mashhad which in 1979 commissioned a poster commemorating the 15th of Khordad (5 June 1963) showing the date written in the blood of a dying martyr. Here the Revolution pays tribute to its forerunner, the uprising of 1963. [Fig. 7.6]

Typical wall graffiti from the Revolution were used in a poster by the Ministry of Culture and Higher Education of the Islamic Republic. In this way, revolutionary wall graffiti could be disseminated, thus strengthening the revolutionary zeal of thousands of viewers in thousands of places far away from the original site of the graffiti, at the same time as a record of it was kept for posterity. The wall shows several layers of posters and handbills that were scribbled over, crossed out, written over, and white-washed. The legible slogan in red paint denounces the United States, the Soviet Union, and China as the enemies of the Muslims. This slogan is flanked by two portraits: Ayatollah Khomeini on the right, and Ali Shariʿati, one of the principal ideologues of the Islamic Revolution, on the left. Someone has added "Israel" (in black ink) to the list of enemies. The same hand reminds passers-by that, according to Khomeini's instructions, they should maintain order:

7.7 An image of Khomeini presides over the palm of the hand, its outstretched fingers representing five holy personalities; in the Shi'i pantheon: Muhammad, Ali, Fatemeh, Hassan, Hussein.

110

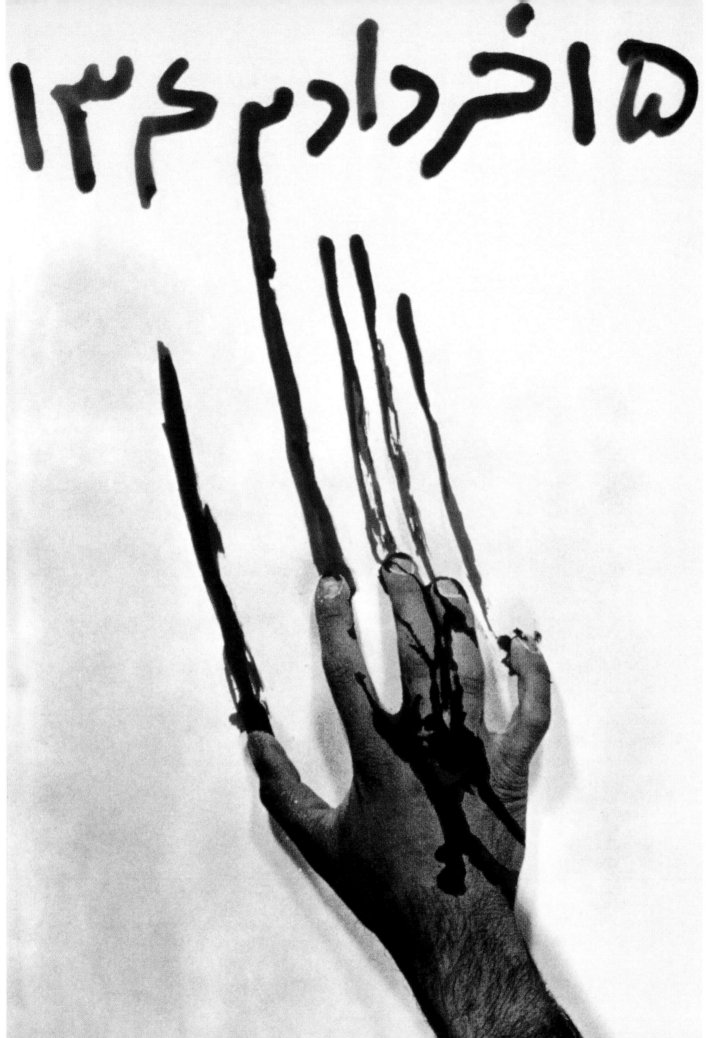

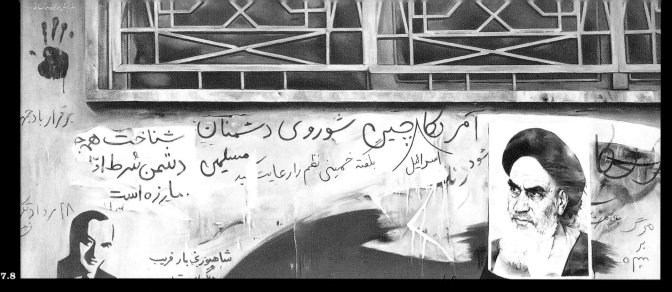

7.8

7.9

the Revolution is not being fomented by a mob; one can achieve victory only with discipline. Next to Khomeini's portrait is scribbled "Death to the Shah" ("Shah" being written upside-down), and in the upper left-hand corner is the imprint of a bloody hand. [Fig. 7.8]

It has been said that every Iranian is a poet, despite the fact that half the population is illiterate. This exaggeration is probably due to the fact that almost every Iranian is familiar with the great poetic tradition of his/her country to a degree that is rare among people of contemporary cultures. It is therefore not surprising that when the Shah, under the pressure of the growing Revolution, announced his willingness to leave the country in the middle of January 1979, and Ayatollah Khomeini declared his intention of returning to Iran from exile, a line from the great fourteenth-century Persian poet Hafez appeared on the walls of Tehran: *Div chun borun ravad fereshteh dar ayad* (When the demon departs the angel shall enter). This implicit statement taken from the work of one of the most revered lyrical poets of Iran had a far greater impact on Iranians than the most explicit statement would have had. That is why the supporters of the ancient regime tried to obliterate the slogans, as on this photograph. Though a good calligrapher, the writer of this slogan was not a connoisseur of Persian literature;

for the meter's sake, the word *chun* must be written *chu*. This line was taken out of its original context and used for political purpose. [Fig. 7.9]

With the taking of the hostages at the American Embassy in Tehran, the number of anti-American graffiti and murals shot up. This large one on a wall is based on a photograph of a crying child taken during the Vietnam War. The slogan in Persian is stronger than the one in English; it says "Death to America." [Fig. 7.10] The "Death to America" cry, rather than being a product of recent politics, is an extension of a 1,000-year-old tradition of cursing and vilifying enemies. This practice was already common during the rule of the Persian Shiʿites, the Buyid dynasty of the tenth century. At that time, the curses were directed at Abu Bakr, ʿUmar, and ʿUthman, the first three caliphs, as well as the Umayyad dynasty. Poets and minstrels known as *munaqebkhans* sang and recited condemnations of these enemies to the public. When Shah Ismail declared Shiʿi Islam the state religion of Iran in 1501, he ordered the congregants at the Friday Mosque in Tabriz (northwestern Iran) to curse the first three caliphs. Those unwilling to do so soon realized the danger in not following the official line. This ritual dissociation from the enemy was called *tabarra* and spread across the Safavid

realm, becoming an integral part of Iranian Shiᶜi practice. Each district in the country had its own official "curser," or *tabarraᶜin*. Other than the Umayyad caliph Yazid, who was responsible for the death of the Imam Hussein, the main target of vilification is the second caliph ᶜUmar (634-44). ᶜUmar is believed by the Shiᶜites to have blocked the election of Ali to the caliphate.

The cursing of the first three caliphs created a constant tension between Shiᶜi Iran and its Sunni neighbors, particularly the Ottomans. By the second half of the nineteenth century, this cursing was toned down in order to relieve political tension between Shiᶜites and Sunnites. It was at this time that all Muslims were trying to unite under the banner of pan-Islamism in order to fight against Western colonialism and further the goal of the pan-Islamic movement, which was urging unity in the struggle against Western colonialism. The cursing mechanism and its traditions survived up to the time of the Islamic Revolution. Ayatollah Khomeini, consciously promoting the export of his Islamic Revolution, managed to smooth out relations between Sunnites and Shiᶜites by substituting the Shah, the United States, Israel, the Soviet Union, and the internal opposition for the three first caliphs. From the very beginning of the Revolution (and to

a lesser extent now), a huge crowd could be found in any Iranian town cursing and vilifying the enemy of the day. These crowds were ambulatory, revolutionary hordes, their banners inscribed with *tawalla* (a proclamation of loyalty to the imams including Imam Khomeini) or with *tabarra*. The moving crowds, divided into choruses, would take their cue from the leaders and shout curses against those who were regarded as the threat of the day. During the eight-year war with Iraq, both the soldiers and citizens used to wear headbands proclaiming their devotion to God and the imams. Stationary crowds like those at Friday prayers, political rallies, or even academic conferences served as the perfect medium through which the day's *tabarraᶜin* could spread their curses. The *tabarraᶜin* would shout vilifying slogans in order to agitate the crowds and play upon their pent-up emotions. *Ta Khun dar rag-e mast Khomeini rahbar-e mast* (As long as there is blood in our veins, Khomeini is our leader) was often shouted by the crowds, inscribed on walls and banners, and served as a modern version of *tawalla*. *Marg ber America* (Death to America), on the other hand, is an example of a modern, persistent *tabarra*.

During the Iraq-Iran war, the number of graffiti damning Saddam Hussein and the "heathen" Baᶜath Party of Iraq reached

7.11

7.12

تنها ره سعادت

ایمان

جهـاد

شهــادت

7.14

115

tens of thousands. This mural from the city of Qazvin shows the head of Saddam about to be cut off by two bayonets. On his familiar green beret is prominently figured the Star of David, implying that he is in fact a pawn of Israel. [Fig. 7.11] "Death to Israel" was another popular slogan written on the walls. This mural was denouncing Israel's involvement in Lebanon in 1981-2, by showing Menachem Begin, the Israeli prime minister, as Dracula in his manifestation as a bat. [Fig. 7.12] The mural from the city of Gorgan depicts the Dome of the Rock in Jerusalem entangled in the coils of an unsightly pink serpent/dragon with a Star of David on it. The monster is being pierced by a sword, the hilt of which consists of the calligraphic inscription... "There is no deity but God." On the left-hand side of the mural is written Khomeini's fiat: "Israel Must Be Wiped Out!" Apparently the Iranian artists were influenced by an exhibit of Palestinian political art which was brought to Tehran from Beirut in 1979, [Fig. 7.13]

Inevitably, revolutions bring hectic and chaotic times reflected early on in the revolutionary slogans, manifestoes, and vilification of the enemy written in nervous haste on the walls of the cities and towns. Homemade posters are fixed on the walls, shutters, lampposts, and those who put them up are in danger of being shot at by the police and armed forces of the besieged regime. The situation changed dramatically when the revolution is victorious and the revolutionary regime controls the country and has all the mass media at its disposal. The propaganda has now become integral to self-preservation and a bulwark against counter-revolution, with the graphic artists in the vanguard.

7.15

7.16

7.17

the Revolutionary Guard's headband is written: "God is Supreme," and on his red armband is inscribed the Qur'anic line: "Help is from God and a speedy victory also." It is believed that this line was inscribed on Hussein's banner at Karbala. [Fig. 7.16]

Hussein and his followers rise from a phantasmic whirlpool, themselves like a ghostly cavalry, in another mural from Qazvin. Although the mural's inscription is partially obscured by a geranium plant, the sentiment is clear; Hussein's martyrdom is worthy of emulation. [Fig. 7.17]

The mural triptych from Gorgan expresses the apotheosis of sacrifice. The vibrant, dynamic, swirling crowds storm forward in a human torrent. In the center, the Revolutionaries have overwhelmed the Imperial regime, and the head of the Shah lies fallen from his hollow statue of bronze. On the right, Khomeini leads a charging crowd of old men, women and youngsters, all shouting at the top of their lungs fit to wake the dead, as if to drown out Saddam. On the left, the throng of sacrificers signifies death and rebirth. A coffin of a martyr is counterbalanced by a naked newborn babe presented by the chador-clad women who surge forward in their own human wave. Other women hold portraits of their martyrs or babies in swaddling cloths, and a man and woman carry huge bunches of tulips, the flower of sacrifice and a mirror. The whole triptych has an epic sweep which transcends barriers of Time and Place. [Figs 7.18; 7.19; 7.20]

The awesome sacrifice by the nation is acknowledged by its leader in an inscription bearing Imam Khomeini's signature in this mural from Hamadan, which reads, "I see that the nation has become godly." [7.21]

In Iran, as soon as the Islamic Republic was well entrenched, hundreds of miles of city, town, and even village walls were covered with colorful murals. The artists could now ply their skills without fear of being beaten up, arrested or shot. Various governmental and non-governmental bodies would supply them with the necessary materials and equipment as well as with payment for their work and directives concerning the subject matter of their art.

The permanent subject at hand during the 80s was, of course, the "Imposed War." The nation had to be willing, even eager, to sacrifice for the war effort with blood, sweat and tears. On this mural from the city of Qazvin is written: "The Sole Way to Heavenly Bliss; Faith, Struggle, and Martyrdom." The painting on the left-hand side of the mural is the pictorial reflection of these words. [Fig. 7.14]

This mural from Gorgan, with its portrayal of the aged and adolescent *basijis* (volunteers) at the front, a green banner invoking Imam Ali at their head, was originally a photograph by Sa'id Sadeqi, which was then made into a poster which then became the basis for the wall painting. [Fig.7.15]

The catalyst for the entire war effort was the Karbala paradigm. In this mural from Qazvin, the tomb of Imam Hussein forms the background, and the young Revolutionary Guard in the foreground is flanked by the gun turret of a tank and the red flag of martyrdom which corresponds to the red flag on top of the cupola of Hussein's tomb. The inscription on the martyrs' red flag reads: "There is no deity but God and Muhammad is His messenger." On

7.21

7.18

7.19

7.20

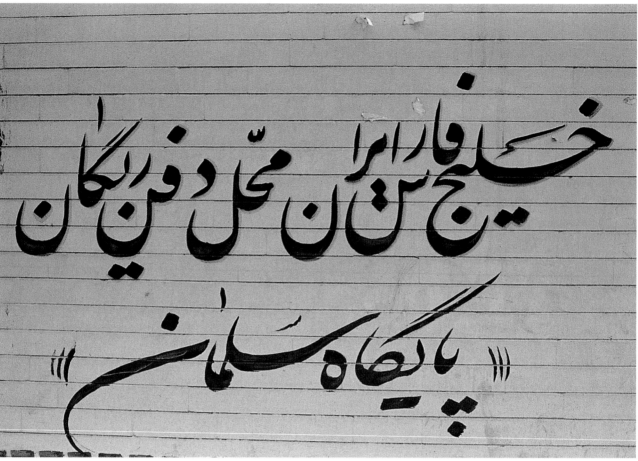

7.23

With the concentration of the U.S. Naval forces in the Persian Gulf, the muralists of Hamadan painted what was tantamount to a curse, depicting a sinking battleship and floating coffins draped with the American flag. The inscription on the side reads: "The Persian Gulf of Iran will become the graveyard of Reagan." [Fig. 7.22 and 7.23]

Heartily invoking "a plague on both your houses," that is on the Capitalist and Communist blocks alike, the muralist of Qazvin anticipate the total destruction of those feuding powers. The Kremlin, the Capitol and Wall Street collapse. The torch of the falling Statue of Liberty is literally going up in smoke. Along with Hitler, an unwieldy steel bug-eyed world-devouring monster straight from *The Thing From Outer Space* is annihilated by the Sword of Virtue. [Fig.7.24]

In sweeping calligraphy the graphic artist from Hamadan reminds the passers by that "Every day is ᶜAshura and the whole earth is Karbala." [Fig. 7.25]

Even in the snow-covered lanes of Borujerd, the Ayatollah Khomeini is present in mural form, along with a prayer to God to bless him with a long life until the Imam (Mehdi) reappears. [Fig 7.26]

It seems that since the end of the war against Iraq, and especially after the death of Ayatollah Khomeini, the use of graffiti and wall paintings has gone down in intensity. In August 1990, when Tariq Aziz, the Iraqi foreign minister, was scheduled to arrive in Tehran in the wake of the Iraqi occupation of Kuwait, hundreds of anti-Saddam graffiti, slogans, and murals on the route from Mehrabad Airport to the city had to be painted over or removed. In 1991 the mayor of Tehran ordered the final whitewashing of the already faded pictures and slogans; the mayors of other towns followed suit.

OBLITERATION AND LAUDATION: CHANGING THE NAMES ON THE MAP
Authoritarian regimes like to project themselves and their ideologies onto city maps. Streets, avenues, squares, parks, sports complexes, schools, hospitals, and other public facilities are therefore named after the main personalities of the regime, or after the ideologies they try to instill in the minds of the people. During the Pahlavi rule there was no town in Iran whose main artery was not called Pahlavi. The other main streets, avenues, and public places in Iranian towns were named after Reza Shah, his son Muhammad Reza Pahlavi, his consort Farah Pahlavi, and their son the Crown Prince Reza. When not named after a personage, public places were named after the Pahlavi monarchy's main goals and achievements, such as the White Revolution or the 28th of Mordad (the day in 1953 when the Shah returned to Iran after he had yielded to Mosaddeq's pressure and left the country).

With the establishment of the Islamic Republic, not only were all the names associated with the Pahlavi rule changed; even those names which could be associated with a monarchical system in general were altered. In order to reflect a new Islamic world-view, themes from Islamic history, as well as personalities and heroes

7.24

from the Islamic Revolution and the war against Iraq, lent their names to Iranian streets and public buildings. In Tehran alone, between the years 1979 and 1987, 302 avenues, forty-one squares, thirteen freeways, and seventeen parks had their names changed. The streets in Tehran that bear the names of *shuhada* — martyrs of the Islamic Revolution and the war against Iraq — number more than 1,400. Often, before their deaths, the "martyrs" used to live on the streets or in the quarters of the city named after them.

This changing of names was not done haphazardly but according to a well-thought-out plan. The transformation of names in the center of Tehran speaks for itself. Before the Revolution, one of the main east–west arteries in Tehran started on the east side at the Circle of Shahnaz, named after the daughter of the late Shah. (Earlier, the same square bore the name of Shahnaz's mother, Fuziyeh, sister of King Faruq of Egypt.) The Circle of Shahnaz was linked with the huge Circle of Shahyad in the west side by a broad ten-kilometer-long avenue divided into two almost equal parts, called Shah Reza and Eisenhower. Shah Reza was the founder of the Pahlavi dynasty. Eisenhower was one of three American presidents after whom main avenues in Tehran were named. This was a clear indication of the very close relations Pahlavi Iran had with the United States. The Shahyad (Shah's Memorial) is an impressive modern arch surrounded by an enormous circle of the same name. It was built in 1971 for the 2,500th anniversary of the Persian Empire. The western part of the Avenue of Shah Reza was often used as a ceremonial route along which visiting heads of state were driven in horse-drawn imperial carriages. During the Revolution, millions of anti-Shah demonstrators marched along this route, while the two circles at either end were used for rallies and mass assemblies. After the victory of the Revolution, the Circle of Shahnaz was renamed the Circle of Imam Hussein; the Avenue of Shah Reza became the Avenue of the Revolution (Enqelab); the Avenue of Eisenhower was renamed Azadi (Freedom); and the Circle of Shahyad is now called the Circle of Freedom. At the point where the Avenue of the Revolution joins the Avenue of Freedom, there is a large circle which was called the 24th of Esfand during the Pahlavi period; now it is called the Circle of the Revolution. Before the Revolution, this circle was popularly known as Mojasameh (Statue). In the middle of the circle was a huge bronze equestrian statue of Reza Shah atop a high pedestal decorated with a replica of the Royal Immortal Guards of Persepolis. The statue was pulled down during the Revolution. This symbolized for many the downfall of the Pahlavi and the end of monarchical rule in Iran; it was depicted on posters and even on postage stamps.

The Circle of Imam Hussein is linked to the south with the Circle of the Shuhada (Martyrs) by the avenue now called the 17th of Shahrivar. (All these new names evoke the Hussein-Karbala paradigm.) Before the Revolution the circle was called Galeh, and the avenue linking the two squares was called Shahbaz (Royal

Falcon). Both the circle and the avenue were witnesses to the Black Friday Massacre, and the new names pay tribute to that tragic day and its heroes. The avenue heading east from the Circle of the Martyrs is aptly called Victory (Piruzi) and the one heading west is called the Holy Fighters for Islam (Mujahedin-e Islam). The main parallel avenues of the Avenue of the Revolution are called the Avenue of the Islamic Republic and the Avenue of Imam Khomeini. The Avenue of Imam Khomeini originates at the Circle of Imam Khomeini; halfway to the west it crosses what is now known as the Circle of Horr. Horr was one of the commanders of Yazid's army at Karbala; he defected to the camp of Imam Hussein and died a martyr's death together with Hussein and his supporters. The Avenue of the 15th of Khordad lies to the south of the Avenue of Imam Khomeini. It skirts the Bazaar district, a clear indication that the merchant class of Iran was instrumental in the Khomeini uprising of 1963 and supported him all the way through the Revolution. The north–south avenues that cross these are the Martyr Mustafa Khomeini (the Ayatollah's son), the Avenue of Islamic Unity, and the avenue named after Navab-e Safavi, the leader of the Fada'ian-e Islam, the most militant underground Islamic group fighting against Pahlavi rule.

7.25

Some avenues had their names changed twice. Tehran's longest north–south avenue, which for seventeen kilometers spans Tajrish at the foot of the Elbors mountains with the railway station in downtown Tehran, was called Pahlavi. After the Revolution it was renamed Dr Mosaddeq in honor of that national hero. However, when relations between followers of the Islamic orientation and the National Front deteriorated, the name of the avenue was changed again, this time to Vali-ye Asr. Tajrish Circle was renamed the Circle of Qods (Jerusalem). Before the Revolution another north–south avenue that crosses the center of Tehran was called the 6th of Bahman to celebrate the victory by referendum of the Shah's White Revolution. After the victory of the Islamic Revolution it was renamed Kargar Avenue (Worker). No doubt this name was chosen by the leftist elements in the first post-revolutionary municipality of Tehran. However, even after the honeymoon was over between the leftists and Khomeini, the authorities did not feel the need to change its name again.

7.26

Since the Pahlavis had been emphasizing the Iran before Islam, street names such as Takht-e Jamshid (Persepolis) and Cyrus the Great were changed to Ayatollah Taleqani and Dr Ali Shariʿati, both major personalities in the Islamic revolutionary movement. The famous Husseiniyeh Irshad, where Dr Shariʿati preached and lectured and roused thousands of people in the early 1970s, is situated on the avenue that now bears his name. Another symbolic gesture by Tehran's municipal government was the changing of the

ای بخون خفتگان جمعهٔ سیاه ،

ای شهیدان ،

ای زندگان جاوید ،

ای مجاهدان حماسهٔ خونبار هفدهم شهریور ،

ای منادیان حکومت عدل اسلامی و

ای اسناد گویا و رسواگر شیطان بزرگ آمریکا ،

روانتان شاد و یادتان گرامی باد.

O' THOSE MARTYRS OF "THE BLACK FRIDAY",

O' MARTYRS ,

O' ETERNAL LIVING SOULS ,

O' MUJAHIDEEN , THE VICTIMS OF "THE BLOODY FRIDAY"
(SHAHRIVAR 17 th),

O' PIONEERS OF THE ISLAMIC JUSTICE STATE ,

O' MARTYRS , ELEQUENT WITNESSES OF CRUELTY OF
THE GREAT SATAN (AMERICA)

GOD BLESS YOUR SOULS AND
LONG LIVE YOUR MEMORY .

ministry of national guidance
ISLAMIC REPUBLIC OF IRAN
اداره کل تبلیغات وزارت ارشاد ملی جمهوری اسلامی ایران
(اداره کل تبلیغات و انتشارات)

7.27 Poster featuring a street map of the area of the circle
of Shuhada (Martyrs) and surrounding streets, over which

قبل از رسیدن به پل مسیر خود را
انتخاب فرمایید

7.28 Some old street names obliterated shortly after the revolution.

name of the Avenue and the Circle of Kakh (Palace) to Palestine. Before the Revolution, the headquarters of the Israeli Mission were on Kakh Avenue; after the Revolution, they were turned over to the Palestine Liberation Organization. The major avenues and freeways in the north of the city have been named after famous Ayatollahs such as Beheshti, Motahhari, Modarres, and Nuri. The names of these Ayatollahs are also the ones most often used to name schools, hospitals, parks, and stadiums. The cult and veneration of martyrs and martyrdom led the authorities in Tehran to name sixty-five elementary schools, thirty-nine preparatory schools, thirty-one high schools, and sixteen sports facilities with the names of the martyrs. Almost every other name for the schools is taken from the vocabulary of the Islamic Revolution: Independence, the 22nd of Bahman, the 15th of Khordad, the Prophetic Mission, Zeynab, Qods, etc.

Qods (the holy city of Jerusalem) is used to name streets, avenues, squares, and urban districts. The other cities and towns of Iran have undergone the same transformation in order to live up to the ideology preached by Tehran. Some towns have changed their name as well. Bandar-e Pahlavi on the Caspian Sea regained its old name of Bandar-e Enzeli. Bandar-e Shahpur on the Persian Gulf was renamed Bandar-e Imam Khomeini. Bandar-e Shah on the Caspian is now called Bandar-e Torkoman. The town of Shahr-e Reza regained the name Qomsheh. Rezayeh became Urmiyeh; Kermanshah became Bakhtaran. The port city of Khorramshahr has been renamed Khuninshahr (City of Blood). This change of name is a tribute to the thousands of the city's inhabitants and the thousands of Iranian soldiers who died there during the Iraq—Iran war. The battle for this city could be called the Iranian battle of Stalingrad.[3] In Isfahan the famous Meydan-e Shah and Masjid-e Shah (the Square and the Mosque of the Shah) are now called Meydan-e Imam and Masjid-e Imam.

An excellent example of how the naming of the city streets is dictated by the changing political climate is the Avenue of France in Tehran, which was renamed Neauple-le-Château when the first President of the Islamic Republic, Bani Sadr, fled the country and was granted political asylum in France. Neauphle-le-Château is a village situated some twenty miles (thirty kilometers) from Paris, where Ayatollah Khomeini spent the last sixteen weeks of his exile, before his triumphant return to Iran. This renaming was yet another signal to the French government that the granting of asylum to Khomeini was a correct action but the granting of it to Bani Sadr was not.

7.29 Handbill which shows 'Hypocrite Street' and a stamp over the top in Persian which says "void".

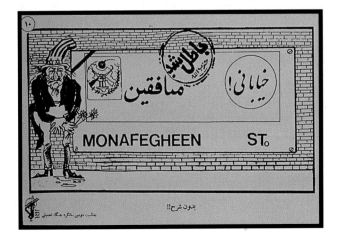

---

1 Profiles of the Revolutionary Art: The First Collection: War-Stricken Area (Qom, [1985]). **2** Ibid. **3** For further details, see Atlas-e Kamel-e Shahr-e Tehran (Tehran, 1364). See also Giorgio Rota, "L'Importanza delle scritte murali nell'Iran Rivoluzionario," Majmu'e-ye Bahariye (Rome, 1989), pp. 155-95; anon., Tasavir: Divarneveshteha-ye Inqelab (Tehran, 1361).

revolutionary literacy

textbook propaganda in the making of an islamic education

EIGHT

IRAN IS A VERY ANCIENT NATION WITH A VERY YOUNG POPULATION. THE CURRENT POPULATION GROWTH RATE PUTS IRAN AMONG THE FASTEST-GROWING COUNTRIES IN THE WORLD. THE DEMOGRAPHIC SURGE OF THE LAST THREE DECADES HAS BEEN ACCOMPANIED BY IMPROVEMENTS IN PUBLIC HEALTH, WHICH HAVE REDUCED THE RATE OF INFANT MORTALITY. AS A RESULT, MORE THAN 50 PERCENT OF IRAN'S POPULATION IS COMPRISED OF JUVENILES. OVER 14 MILLION IRANIANS ARE OF SCHOOL AGE. IN THIS CHAPTER WE SHALL CONSIDER SOME OF THE SPECIFIC EDUCA-TIONAL DEVICES THAT WERE USED BY THE ISLAMIC IDEOLOGUES TO CONVERT THE YOUTH TO ARDENT SOLDIERS OF THE REVOLUTION. FOR CENTURIES IRANIAN EDUCATION WAS, BY AND LARGE, IN THE HANDS OF THE SHI'I MUSLIM CLERGY. THOUGH THE EDUCATIONAL COUNCIL, ESTABLISHED IN 1897, DECIDED TO USE THE FRENCH EDUCATIONAL SYSTEM AS A MODEL, THE TRADITIONAL EDUCATIONAL SYSTEM CONTINUED UNTIL THE PAHLAVI DYNASTY'S RISE TO POWER IN 1926. REZA SHAH AND HIS SON ESTABLISHED A HIGHLY CENTRALIZED, FORMAL, MODERN SYSTEM OF EDUCATION. IN 1943 THE IRANIAN PARLIAMENT PASSED A LAW MAKING EDUCATION COMPULSORY FOR ALL CHILDREN BETWEEN THE AGES OF 6 AND 12. IN THIS CHAPTER WE ARE CONCERNED PRIMARILY WITH THE TEXTBOOKS DESIGNED FOR THIS AGE-GROUP.

8.1

شاه

هر یک از ما در خانه‌ای زندگی می‌کنیم. ما در خانهٔ خود به پدر احترام می‌گذاریم. و او را دوست داریم.

ما یک خانهٔ بزرگتر هم داریم. این خانهٔ بزرگ کشور ما ایران است. ما در این خانهٔ بزرگ مثل یک خانواده هستیم.

شاه مثل پدر این خانواده است. ما مثل فرزندان او هستیم.

شاه همهٔ ما را دوست دارد. ما شاهنشاه مهربان خود را مثل پدر خود دوست داریم. ما به شاهنشاه خود احترام می‌گذاریم.

۸۷

دا

خُدا خورشید و زمین و ستارگان را آفرید. خُدا ماه و ستارگان را آفرید.

خُدا گیاهان و جانوران را آفرید. خُدا ما را آفرید.

ای خدای مهربان که خورشید و زمین و ستارگان را آفریدی؛

ای خدای مهربان که گیاهان و جانوران را آفریدی؛

ای خدای مهربان که ما را آفریدی؛

ای خدای مهربان که برای ما همه چیز آفریدی؛

ما همیشه تو را می‌پرستیم.

۸

The secularization of Iranian education was another in a series of blows to the power of the Shi'i clerics. After the end of the Second World War, the United States gradually gained more influence in Iran than any of the other Western powers. From the mid-1960s, the Iranian educational system came under American influence more than that of any other Western nation. The Ministry of Education, together with the Imperial Organization for Social Services, was responsible for the composing, publishing, and nationwide distribution of textbooks. Every student in the country used the same textbooks, which were part of a national curriculum established to reflect the government's long-term goals, ideals, and beliefs. Textbooks for elementary schools, which serve the largest number of students, are the most interesting of the educational materials produced during the time of the Pahlavis' rule because of the transparent manner in which the authoritarian government's educational directives are implemented in these basic texts. First of all, the centrally directed educational system, with its Persian-language texts, was intended to provide a sense of national cohesiveness in a nation composed of many ethnic and linguistic groups. Such an educational system is aimed at creating a strong nationalist sentiment. Secondly, the system tried to instill in the students a feeling of pride in ancient pre-Islamic Iran, as well as in their modern, rapidly industrializing nation. Thirdly, it was intended to build students' confidence in a future under the monarchical system of government, represented by the Pahlavi dynasty. Fourthly, it portrayed Iran as one of the world's leading progressive nations, on the verge of joining the First World community by means of the White Revolution.

Each textbook published between 1965 and the Islamic Revolution bears on its cover the motto, taken from the great tenth/eleventh-century Persian epic poet Ferdowsi, "Knowledge is power." The first four pages of the textbooks are dedicated to the ruling Pahlavi family, with photographs of the Shah, the Empress, the Crown Prince, and the Shah's sister Princess Ashraf —head of the Imperial Organization for Social Services. The Pahlavi *Weltanschauung* projected in the textbooks was: God, Shah, Country. Towards the end of the first-grade textbook (for the students who have learned to read simple sentences), after a passage about God, there is a lesson dedicated to the Shah. Next to a picture of the Shah dressed in his bemedaled imperial uniform, dazzling in its colors to the eyes of the little children, the text reads: "Each of us lives at home. At home we love and respect our father. We also have a bigger house. This big house of ours is our country Iran. In this big house we are like one family. The Shah is like the father of this large family and we are like his children. The Shah loves all of us. We love our kind Shah like our own father. We respect our Shah." [Fig.8.1] Since the perpetuation of the political system is essential to the continued well-being of the rulers, especially in a monarchy, this lesson is followed immediately by a lesson about the Crown Prince. In the second-grade textbook a lesson about the Crown Prince follows lessons about the birthday of the Shah and the imperial coronation. From this lesson, which is accompanied by a full-page color photograph of the Crown Prince, we learn that the birthday of the Crown Prince is observed in Iran as "Children's Day," and that on that day special programs for children are organized throughout the country.[1]

The Islamic Republic of Iran has continued the authoritarian, centrally organized system of education with politically and ideologically oriented textbooks. The radical change from monarchical to Islamic ideology in the educational system is graphically reflected in the textbook illustrations. A comparison of the pictures that appear on the first page of Pahlavi and Islamic Republic textbooks is most telling. Both portray an elementary-school classroom. The illustration in the Pahlavi textbook shows children of both sexes sitting together and wearing Western-style clothing. Behind the desk stands a female teacher in profile. She wears a skirt and a short-sleeved, tight green sweater which accentuates her breasts. Her hair is cut short, in a modern style. A

girl standing at the blackboard is wearing a short blue dress, leaving her bare legs visible. The girl stands casually, with one hand in her pocket and the other pointing at a picture of a classroom, a reflection of the one she is standing in. Her head is not covered and her shoulder-length black hair is braided. Above the blackboard hangs a picture of the Shah. The blackboard spans the width of the classroom, which contains modern furniture.

The illustration on the first page of the Islamic Republic's textbook depicts a classroom segregated by sex. The female students are sitting at their desks, their heads covered by scarves so that no hair can be seen. They are wearing long-sleeved tunics. The teacher is standing behind a desk and in front of a contour map of Iran. She is wearing a headscarf and a long baggy brown dress with sleeves that cover her wrists. Her bosom is not accentuated. The girl at the blackboard wears loose navy-blue trouser-like pants and a long-sleeved blue tunic. Her hair is covered with a brown headscarf. She stands stiffly as she points to a picture of a landscape on the wall. Above the picture hangs a photograph of Ayatollah Khomeini, who is engaged in writing in the traditional manner, without a table, holding a pen in one hand and paper in the other. A framed sample of Persian calligraphy hangs above the blackboard which reads, "In the Name of God." Though the furniture in both illustrations is almost identical, that in the second picture seems more spartan. [Fig. 8.2]

A comparison of the two sets of elementary school textbooks shows that, according to the Islamic Republic texts, the Shah sold

8.2

8.3

Iran to the Western powers; therefore Western encroachment on Iran must be eliminated and the country purified by the reintroduction of Islamic values. Visually, that purification is represented by the traditional Islamic modes of dress, behavior, and furniture. [Figs. 8.3 and 8.4] This comparison also shows that less than half of the lessons from the Pahlavi texts of the 1970s have been retained, either intact or with minor revisions, in Islamic Republic texts printed in 1989. The new material in the Islamic Republic's textooks consists of lessons which stress the importance of an Islamic upbringing and criticize the reign of the Pahlavis. While the Shah is portrayed as a father-figure in the Pahlavi textbooks, he is portrayed by the Islamic Republic's texts as a brutal tyrant who ordered the murders of thousands before he fled the country.

In the penultimate lesson of the first-grade text, students read about the Islamic Revolution. The text is illustrated by two photographs: one is of a demonstrating revolutionary crowd with outstretched hands and clenched fists, the other is of the first public speech given by Ayatollah Khomeini, after his return to Iran, at the Behesht-e Zahra cemetery. The text reads: [Fig. 8.5]

It was the year 1357 [1978]. The Muslim people of Iran suffered under the oppression of the Shah. At that time Imam Khomeini was away from Iran. The people wanted Imam Khomeini to lead them in ousting the Shah from the country. They wanted Independence, Freedom, and an Islamic Republic. To reach that goal they demonstrated in the streets and at night they cried out *Allahu Akbar* **from the rooftops of their houses.**

The Shah wanted to crush the people. On the 17th of Shahrivar he gave the order to kill thousands of men, women, and children. But the resistance stiffened and all over Iran the people rose up in revolution. The Shah was forced to flee the country.

Several days after the Shah's flight, Imam Khomeini returned to Iran. The people were extremely happy. In groups, they came to Tehran from towns and villages to welcome Imam Khomeini. And Imam Khomeini addressed the people. On the 22nd

of the month of Bahman the Islamic Revolution was proclaimed victorious. Every year we celebrate this great day. The 22nd day of Bahman is the day of the triumph of the Islamic Revolution of Iran.

A more detailed description of the triumph of the Islamic Revolution is to be found in the second-grade textbook. In this book the children learn slogans such as *Ta khun dar rag-e mast Khomeini rahbar-e mast* (As long as there is blood in our veins, Khomeini is our leader).[2] From the first grade onward the students are introduced to the symbolic language of the Revolution: blood sacrifice, martyrdom, and the certain reward of heavenly bliss, all of which are represented by the red tulip.

The Islamicization of textbooks is not only found in the lessons on religion, which have increased fourfold, but in an eightfold decrease in the number of lessons about pre-Islamic Iran. Even the first names of the children in the textbooks are changed. Islamic names such as Amin, Akram, Javad, Majid, Tahereh, Fatemeh, Asghar, Jalal, Ahmad, Hasan, and Hussein replace ancient Persian names such as Dara, Parviz, Bizhan, Ziba, Zhaleh, Kiomarth, Iraj, Darioush, Manuchehr, and Fereydoun.[3] Islamic names that were used in the Pahlavi textbooks have been retained.

Since some of the pre-Islamic festivals such as Now Rouz[4] could not be eliminated, the textbooks of the Islamic Republic attempt to add an Islamic and revolutionary flavor to these observances. In the third-grade textbook is the passage: "Each year we celebrate the Spring of Freedom together with the Spring of Nature. Concurrent with Now Rouz, we celebrate the Day of the Islamic Republic. During Now Rouz, we Iranians go to the tombs of the martyrs and give praise to those who gave their lives for Islam and the freedom of Iran."[5] These sentiments are repeated in almost every new textbook at all levels. On the 10th and 11th days of the month of Farvardin in the year 1358 AH (1980 CE) the people of Iran cast their votes in the national referendum, and on the 12th of Farvardin the landslide victory of the Islamic Republic was announced: "Imam Khomeini, our beloved leader, named this day the Day of the Islamic Republic. He asked the nation to celebrate this day and to offer congratulations to each other for the victory of Islam and the Islamic Republic... From this year on we have celebrated Now Rouz and the Day of the Islamic Republic to be the most beautiful day since it is the day of freedom and the spirit of freedom..."[6]

All twelve of the Shi‛i Imams are subjects of lessons in the textbooks. It is, however, the exemplary nature of their lives that is stressed, and not the difference between Shi‛ites and Sunnites. Iran is projected as the leader of the Muslim world; for this reason, the textbooks contain many stories about the Palestinians. In the second-grade textbook is a "Letter from a Homeless Child" which reads:

Do you know me? I am your brother. I am Palestinian. We, the children of Palestine, are Muslims. The name of our country is Palestine. The name of your country is Iran. You live in your own country and in your own home. But we are homeless and live in the desert. The enemy has occupied our homes and the land of our birth. We live now in the plains and deserts and our days and nights are spent in camps under tents. The tents are also our schools. But even here, the enemy does not let us live in peace and sets fire to our dwellings. The enemy is cruel to both children and grown-ups. He even bombs our schools and our hospitals. Do you know why? Because we want to return to our homes and our country and to throw the enemy out of our homeland. From the day on which your Islamic Revolution triumphed under the leadership of Imam Khomeini, the enemy has been very scared. For that reason, he now persecutes and harms us more. Our enemy is Israel. Israel is our enemy and your enemy and the enemy of all free and noble human beings. We will fight Israel until our last breath. We know that you will help us. We will not give up and, with the help of God, we will be victorious. Then we shall return to our beloved homeland. There we shall live in freedom. In the hope of victory, goodbye.[7] The same letter, translated into English, appears in a little book called *Children of Revolution*, published in Tehran by the Institute for the Intellectual Development of Children and Young Adults.[8] [Fig. 8.6]

8.4

The themes of struggle, martyrdom, and victory occur frequently in the textbooks. Most are to be found in the lessons devoted to the Islamic Revolution or the "Imposed War." It must be remembered that many youngsters left school to go to the front and were killed in the war with Iraq. Often, in such cases, the students in the dead child's class would place a photograph and flowers on what was once the seat of their martyred classmate. The most celebrated young martyr of the Islamic Republic of Iran is Hussein Fahmideh, who is honored with a postage stamp and whose portrait appears in a watermark on Iranian banknotes. His story appears in the fourth-grade textbook under the title "The Children of Islam." [Figs. 8.7 and 8.8]

He had come from Qom, from the city of blood and insurrection. He knew very well why he had come. The enemy had invaded his homeland to inflict a death-blow to the Islamic Revolution. The enemy strafed the towns of his country with bullets. The enemy

tanks. From time to time he instinctively checked his belt, to which several more grenades were attached. Nobody knew what was in his heart. The deafening sound of mortars and machine-guns came from all sides, but he paid no attention to them. His eyes were fixed on the enemy tanks as the distance between them closed. The tank reached him and a tremendous explosion brought it to an instant halt. It jerked, jolted, and was enveloped by flames. Hussein Fahmideh had reached his goal. Hussein Fahmideh was a teenage boy who became a great legend. The people of Iran will never forget this brave young patriot. Imam Khomeini, the leader of the Islamic Revolution, said this about him: "Our leader is that 13-year-old youth who attached grenades to his body and threw himself under an enemy tank." The schoolchildren of today's Islamic Republic of Iran speak proudly of Hussein Fahmideh. In Tehran a large sports arena is named after him. The athletes exercising there hold him in their

اِنقلابِ اِسلامی ایران

سال هزار و سیصد و پنجاه و هفت بود. مردم مُسلمانِ ایران، از ظُلمِ شاه بسیار ناراحَت بودند. در آن زَمان، اِمام خُمینی از ایران دور بود. مردم می خواستند به رَهبریِ امام خمینی، شاه را از کشور بیرونْ کنند. آنها اِستقلال، آزادی، جُمهوریِ اسلامی می خواستند. برای رَسیدَن به این هَدَف، در خیابانها راه پیمایی می کردند. شبها هَم روی بامِ خانه ها اَللهُ اَکبَر می گفتند.

شاه می خواست مردم را سَرکوب کند. دُستور داد در روزِ ۱۷

شَهریوَر، هزاران نَفَر از مرد و زن و بچّه را به گُلوله بَستند. امّا مردم بیشتر خَشمگین شدند و در همه جایِ ایران انقلاب کردند. شاه هم مجبور شد از کشور فَرار کند.

چند روز پس از فرارِ شاه، امام خمینی به ایران بازگَشت. مردم بسیار خوشحال شدند. دسته دسته از شهرها و روستاها برایِ دیدنِ امام خمینی به تهران آمدند. امام خمینیُ برایِ مردم سخنرانی کرد. در روزِ ۲۲ بهمن ماه انقلابِ اسلامیِ ایران پیروز شد.

هر سال، ما این روزِ بزرگ را جشن می گیریم. روزِ ۲۲ بهمن، روزِ پیروزیِ انقلابِ اسلامیِ ایران است.

۱۰۹

8.5 After the revolution the penultimate pages of the Persian textbook, for the first grade, teach young children about the "Islamic Revolution of Iran."

killed his innocent brothers and sisters. Now he wanted to defend the Revolution. He wanted to throw the enemy out of his country. He wanted to fight him face to face. He was in a very agitated state of mind. His wounds were not yet completely healed. He had already been at the front, at battles including that of Khorramshahr — since known as Khuninshahr — the City of Blood. His youth was evident in his small stature. If the blood, smoke, and dust of the battlefield were washed away from his face, it would be clear that he could not be more than 13 years old. He remembered the time when he first wanted to join the fighters at the front, how he came here and persuaded the commander to accept him as a fighter, how he had attracted the attention of all by his ingenuity and bravery. These memories and moments flashed through his mind, but he did not have time to dwell on them, for he had to act. He had to show the enemy that Muslims are not afraid of artillery, tanks, or machine-guns. He was clutching a grenade as he crawled toward the enemy

memories as an example of Islamic heroism.[9] [see p.219 chapter 13]

On the back covers of the textbooks used for grades one through five is a picture of schoolchildren demonstrating on behalf of the Islamic Republic. Boys, as well as girls, are shown with clenched fists and outstretched arms. The girls, all but their faces covered with black veils, shout their support. The slogan inscribed in red ink over this image reads:

With faith in God, with purity and honor,

Accumulation of knowledge,

With hard work, self-sacrifice, and self-denial,

We stand guard over Independence, Freedom and the Islamic Republic.

The back covers of the Pahlavi textbooks bear no illustrations. They simply state that "In accordance with the blessed order of the Shahenshah Arya Mehr [king of kings, Sun of the Aryan Race,] this book has been prepared by the Ministry of Education and distributed by the Imperial Organization for Social Services."

8.6 A rally of schoolchildren holding a banner inscribed "Death to The Shah;"
this appears as an illustration in '*Children of the Revolution*' published by
The Institute for the Intellectual Development of Young Children and Adults.

The Institute for the Intellectual Development of Children and Young Adults was established in Tehran in 1965 to assist in reaching the goal of universal literacy in Iran. The aim of the Institute was the encouragement of literacy and artistic sensibilities among children and young adults by means of picture-books and illustrated storybooks. Like the government-sponsored film industry, the Institute's efforts rapidly won international recognition. Books composed and illustrated by Iranian authors and artists were soon winning international prizes. The Islamic Republic added the spreading of propaganda to the duties of the Institute. The books published by the Institute are directed at five age-groups: kindergarten, grades one through three, grades four and five, junior high school, and high school. The age-group of the targeted readership is indicated on the cover of each publication. These divisions seem meaningless since, as Deborah S. Maier aptly states, "One of the most compelling observations that one can make about many of the books for children published in Iran, then and now, is that they do not seem to be for children."[10]

Foreign influences can be found in the graphic arts, layout, printing, and publishing of the Institute in the time before the Revolution. Picture-books for children were a new development in Iranian publishing. For centuries the Iranians had been the masters of the art of the book, with their miniature painters, calligraphers, illuminators, and binders; but the technical skills for the mass production of children's books had to be acquired from the West. The children's books now published in Iran display Western techniques combined with characteristics that are distinctly Iranian.

Comparing the books published by the Institute before and after the Revolution requires no great effort, since books published before the Revolution are almost devoid of any ideological content dictated by the regime other than an optimistic trust in the future. It might even be said that some of the books published before the Revolution were, to a certain degree, anti-establishment. The best example is a celebrated book by Samad Behrangi, *The Little Black Fish*, which is full of

political allegories critical of the Shah's secret police and other governmental agencies. Out of the 128 books considered to be supplements to school texts at our disposal, and published by the Institute since the Revolution, thirty-four can be categorized as tools of ideological persuasion by the Islamic Republic. The art of persuasion can be found in both text and illustrations. These books are devoted to the Islamic Revolution, the Islamic Republic, the

8.8

mobilization against the "Imposed War," and the Islamic *umma*. The Institute has maintained its high artistic and production standards, as well as a high level of output. On average, a first printing runs to 30,000 copies and is followed by two or three more printings on a similar scale. These are some titles published after the Revolution: *Outcries in Pictures*, a collection of eighty-seven illustrations of the events of the Revolution drawn by children and young adults; *The Buds in Storm*, comprised of photographs of children in the revolutionary period and during the war against Iraq; *Children of Revolution*, also available in English-, Arabic-, and Turkish-language editions, a collection of writings and illustrations by children; *The Sprouts of Hope*, a compilation of poems written by children and young adults after the Revolution; *Kaboutar-e Par*, based on a child's game and describing martyrdom and the flight of the soul to paradise; *War Memories*, a five-volume set in which children and young adults tell their horrifying stories of the war.

My Name is Ali Asqhar is narrated by an Iranian boy. Every year during the month of Muharram, Hussein and his son Ali Asqhar play the roles of the martyred Imam Hussein and his martyred son. Upon the outbreak of war with Iraq, Hussein goes to the front and dies a martyr. Ali Asqhar then takes his father's place at the front. *Ascension* is a tale of the self-sacrifice and martyrdom of the young fighters who defend their faith and homeland. *Victory* concerns the Army of Good overcoming the Army of Evil. The theme of this book is taken from the Qur'an, which attests to the victory of a righteous people. In *The Masters of ʿAshura*, the reader becomes acquainted with the lives of the companions of Imam Hussein and their martyrdom. [8.9.] *The Immortals* is the story of the heroine of Shiʿi Islam, Zeynab, the sister of Imam Hussein who witnessed the tragedy of Karbala. *God's Blessed Day* is a collection of writings and illustrations by young adults who were winners of a contest held to celebrate the third anniversary of the creation of the Islamic Republic. *A Letter to the Imam* is a collection of twenty-nine out of 2,700 letters addressed to Imam Khomeini and sent to the Institute.

The story that follows, "Weeping of the Tree," is taken from *God's Blessed Day*. It was written by Mitra Khayyam, aged 14, from Rafsanjan. It is written in an allegorical style which is a time-honored tradition in Iran. [8.10.]

My name is the Tree of Revolution. I grow on blood. When it rained on the 17th of Shahrivar, I sprouted and grew. My roots became strong. From that day on and for a long time afterward my growth was incredible. The clouds would not blot out the sun, which was like a hugh blanket of warmth. They soon evaporated. In the heat of struggle, when thirst overpowered my whole being and my endurance was nearly exhausted, many youths gave their blood for my sustenance. Everything in me moved upward and outward in growth. But alas, this period did not last for ever. The enemy sent new clouds, called Disunity, to my homeland, clouds that blocked my lifeline to the sun. The eternal enemy came this time in the guise of an Iranian charcoal-maker and for a long time he hacked away daily at my soul and my body. Everybody

8.9 The war with Iraq is equated with the paradigmatic events in Karbala.

8.10 "Death to Saddam,"
"Death to America," proclaim
the children of the revolution
on "The Good Day of God."

wanted to get the biggest possible share of me to burn in their own ovens, to burn the fruit of so many martyrs' blood. The grief-stricken fathers and sorrowful mothers who had brought their children to the Revolution's sacrificial altar and the wounded and the crippled of the Revolution, all, all of them, seeing my growth stopped and my once-green leaves withered, became depressed and lost all hope. Have you ever, to this day, seen a tree shedding tears? My friends either left me alone, picked my unripe fruit, or went on about their own business. But that old enemy, who had profited from my friends neglecting me, continues to strike my body so that my whole being is nothing but pain. In time, my faithful friends ambushed the malicious charcoal-maker. They closed his house, which had been a nest of spies. They seized his servants. The people now recognized the charcoal-maker as a foreigner. Once again, I attracted the attention of all. Hearts began to beat for me. For me, they appointed guards [Pasdaran-e Enqelab]. This period made real for me the joyful air of the 22nd of Bahman. My guards, all of them young and full of zeal, had a message for the charcoal-maker: "Come, if you dare, and get what is due you for your actions!" He then pulled another trick. He appeared in a different form with different clothes. This time he was dressed as a friend. He said: "I am a botanist; take me to the tree so that I can heal its wounds." Some naive friends, caught off guard, were deceived by the disguise and brought him to me. He immediately began to strike me. Instead of healing me, he made me sicker than ever. Then he changed into a foreign reporter. He said: "I want to make this tree famous throughout the world, and…" Once again I screamed "Do not let them in — they are spies and they want to annihilate me!" Nobody listened. My vigilant friends even gave orders that they be prohibited from coming here, but it did not work. In the name of reporting, the eternal enemies poured in and wrote many things about me. All the things they wrote were absolute lies. After a short time, a vicious woodcutter appeared again in the guise of Saddam and violated my sacred place. This time he was unaware that my friends and supporters were alert. They smashed the enemy on the spot. The enemy axes will never again strike at my body. My friends have appointed new guardians to watch over me. They are the zealous youths who have been willing to lose their lives in order to preserve me. Yesterday, a small tulip, who watches over the grave of a martyr, told me how the boy's mother comes to see him every day. The little tulip said that the mother had whispered softly: "That I have lost my breadwinner and am all alone does not worry me so much. It is for the sake of the Revolution that I really worry.[11]

1 Farsi, dovvom-e dabestan (Tehran, S. 1350), p. 22. **2** Farsi, dovvom-e dabestan (Tehran, S. 1368), p. 172. **3** During the reign of Reza Shah the government tried to discourage parents from giving their children Arabic (i.e. Islamic) names. The Islamic Republic has continued this practice, but in reverse. It is very difficult to register and get identification papers for a child with a non-Islamic name. **4** Now Rouz, celebrated on the spring solstice, marks the beginning of the Persian solar year. **5** Farsi, sevvom-e dabestan (Tehran, S. 1368), p. 191. **6** Farsi, dovvom-e dabestan (Tehran, S. 1368), p. 174. **7** Ibid., pp. 68-70. **8** Children of Revolution (Tehran, n.d.). **9** Farsi, cheharom-e dabestan (Tehran, S. 1368), pp. 26-7. On the stamp issued in his honor, Hussein Fahmideh is referred to as being 12 years of age. On a poster representing the leave-taking of a young combatant going to the front, on which Hussein Fahmideh's story appears as a background, he is referred to as having been 12 years old. However, he is sometimes presented as having been a 13-year-old. **10** Deborah S. Maier, "Children's Literature in Iran," MA thesis, New York University, 1991, p. 3. **11** Ruz-e khub-e Khoda (Tehran, S. 1361), pp. 11-14.

8.11 *Iran Our Home*

Thou good and dear, thou beautiful Iran,
Be thou everlasting, O our home.
I love your cities and towns,
Your rivers and streams, Your mountains and plains.
God is Supreme! Once again
The Sun of Islam from within you has shone.
The blood of martyrs all over your land
Flows in an unceasing current, O the soil of my Homeland
Along thy streets and lanes and across thy plains
The tulips are in full bloom O land of my heart, may I be thy ransom!
Mustafa Rahmandust
(The first poem the first-grades learn in the Islamic Republic)

137

137

PICTURES THAT COMMAND:
revolutionary posters

THE SUCCESS OF POSTERS IN STIMULATING THE SPIRIT OF REVOLUTIONARY PREPAREDNESS AND SACRIFICE IN IRAN WAS SO GREAT THAT IT SEEMS TO HAVE OVERSHADOWED EVEN THE ROLE POSTERS PLAYED IN THE RUSSIAN REVOLUTION OF 1917. THIS IS FURTHER PROOF THAT POSTERS CONSTITUTE THE MOST

REVOLUTIONARY GENRE OF THE GRAPHIC ARTS. IN 1917 AND SUBSEQUENT YEARS, WHEN THE POSTER HELD A PARTICULAR PLACE IN THE REVOLUTION RAGING INSIDE IRAN'S NORTHERN NEIGHBOR, THE SOVIET UNION, THIS FORM OF COMMUNICATION WAS VIRTUALLY UNKNOWN IN IRAN. THE GRAPHIC ART OF THE POSTER CAME TO IRAN FROM THE SOVIET UNION SOME TWENTY-FIVE YEARS LATER DURING THE ALLIED OCCUPATION OF IRAN IN 1941. THE FIRST IRANIAN POSTERS CAN BE TRACED TO THE NORTHWESTERN CITY OF TABRIZ, WHERE THEY WERE USED TO ADVERTISE CULTURAL EVENTS. THEY WERE CALLED PLAKATS, A TERM BORROWED FROM THE RUSSIAN LANGUAGE, WHICH HAD INCORPORATED THIS GERMAN WORD INTO ITS OWN VOCABULARY. SINCE, HOW- EVER, FRENCH CULTURE WAS STILL THE DOMINANT FOREIGN CULTURE IN IRAN, AT LEAST UNTIL THE END OF THE SECOND

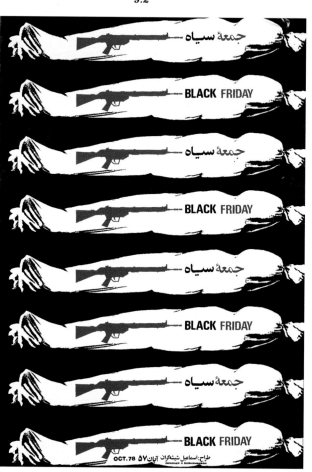

WORLD WAR, THE FRENCH WORD AFFICHE (PERSIAN AFISH) WAS MORE COMMONLY USED, UNTIL IT WAS SUPERSEDED BY THE ENGLISH WORD "POSTER." IN THIS CHAPTER WE SHALL EXAMINE THEIR SIGNIFICANCE DURING THE REVOLUTION AND THE WAR THAT SUCCEEDED IT.

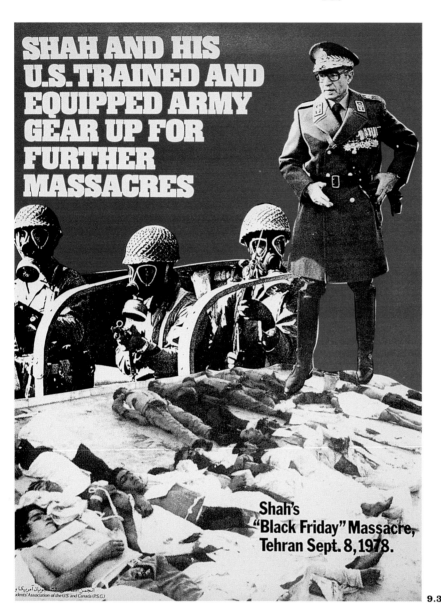

SHAH AND HIS U.S. TRAINED AND EQUIPPED ARMY GEAR UP FOR FURTHER MASSACRES

Shah's "Black Friday" Massacre, Tehran Sept. 8, 1978.

9.3

In the years between the Second World War and the Islamic Revolution posters in Iran were used for commercial purposes: to advertise domestic and foreign goods and products; to advertise cultural events such as movies, theatrical productions, concerts, exhibitions, and literary, artistic, and scientific international conferences; and in tourism. As time passed, they were increasingly used for political purposes: to commemorate historical events such as the 2,500th anniversary of the Persian Empire, fifty years of Pahlavi rule, and to sell to the public projects dear to the Shah, such as the White Revolution and the Rastakhiz (Resurrection Party). Posters featuring the Shah and members of the royal family, especially the Crown Prince and the Empress Farah, were ubiquitous in Iranian life. They were omnipresent in both public and commercial places. On the posters, the Shah appeared in the uniform of the commander-in-chief of the Imperial Iranian Navy, of the Air Force, or of the Army, or in gala regal uniform resplendent with glittering medals and decorations. He also appeared in a variety of civilian outfits, both formal and casual. Through these posters, the

9.4

poster artists—both photographers and graphic designers—tried to convey the message to the Iranian nation that as long as the Shah watched over the people Iran would remain stable, strong, prosperous, and confident in her bright future. [Fig. 9.1]

During the revolutionary upheavals in the fall and winter of 1978-9, the public burning and defacing of posters representing the Shah became a common crowd ritual in the streets of Iranian cities. At the same time clandestinely produced posters of the Ayatollah Khomeini were affixed to the walls along the streets and squares. One of the first revolutionary posters aside from the Ayatollah's portraits was produced soon after the Black Friday Massacre in Zhaleh Square on 8 September 1978. In its simplicity and directness, in its use of color and imagery, this is one of the greatest examples of political art in the twentieth century. Against a black background are laid out the bodies of eight demonstrators wrapped in their white shrouds. (In Iran, as in other Muslim countries, people are buried in their shrouds, not in coffins.) Each corpse is pierced by a red rifle, the red signifying blood; from the barrels of the rifles are fired the words "Black Friday/*Jomᶜeh-ye Siyah*." The designer was so courageous that he put his name on the bottom of the poster in both English and Persian, although it was only October 1978 and the outcome of the Revolution was still in the balance. [Fig. 9.2] Another, more standard-issue, political poster lays the blame for the Black Friday Massacre squarely on the Shah's shoulders. Put out by the Iranian Students' Association of the United States and Canada, this poster is a clearly designed black-and-white photomontage against a lurid red background. [Fig. 9.3]

The real explosion of poster art took place, however, after the Shah left the country on 16 January 1979. That very day, handmade posters appeared in thousands in the streets of Tehran bearing the simple but powerful message "The Shah is gone"—*Shah raft*. These handbills, written in bold calligraphic strokes in ink on cardboard measuring roughly two feet by one, were stuck under the windshield wipers of passing cars. Soon motorists realized that driving in the city without these posters could be dangerous, as they might be considered enemies of the Revolution. Until that time, the major thrust of revolutionary art was the graffiti on the walls. There were compelling technical reasons for that: the presses needed for the production of posters were either in the hands of the Shah's government functionaries or controlled by them. Once the Shah was gone, the revolutionary organizations, associations, and political parties of every shade of Islamic, leftist, or secular nationalist orientation rose to the surface from the underground, and many new ones mushroomed. In order to manifest their presence and to show their revolutionary zeal, they took to creating and producing posters, using artists of varying backgrounds and training, from the revolutionary art of Socialist Realism in the Soviet Union, Eastern Europe, and Cuba, or Parisian and other Western schools of art, to native Iranian traditions. Poster creativity and productivity in Iran was maintained at an unusually high degree throughout the 1980s. It could be said that since the

Revolution Iran has been plastered with posters inside and out, as posters have literally covered the exterior and interior walls of Iranian cities, towns, and even villages. Even in the countryside, where there are no walls, boards were erected to which posters were affixed. Many were glued to portable boards and carried by the hugh crowds either supporting the Islamic Revolution and the Islamic Republic or cursing and condemning their enemies.

Unlike postage stamps and banknotes, even when the production of posters was taken over by various government organizations and ministries, the art of the poster has been considered and projected as a spontaneous art of the people, and not that of an official agent of the state. Despite the fact that some of the graphic images designed for posters were transferred on to postage stamps, and even banknotes, and vice versa, there is a definite dividing-line between them. When it comes to personalities, only those who are dead can appear on stamps and banknotes; whereas the portrait of the Ayatollah Khomeini, for example, graced posters for ten years before his death. Through posters, one can study the development of the Revolution and the evolution of the Islamic Republic. They are the mirror of the struggle of the Islamic Republic against perceived internal and external enemies. The posters are the most powerful vehicle of the art of persuasion. Until about the middle of 1981, the posters subtly reflected the differences between the goals of the Islamic-oriented parties and organizations and those belonging to parties of other political persuasions. However, as soon as those who differed from the world-view of the Islamic Republic were eliminated or forced underground, the graphic art of posters became an unofficial spokes-art of the Islamic Republic. The production of posters and other graphic arts returned to the *status quo ante*, with the new government exercising its control.

Posters created in revolutionary Iran come in various sizes, from small ones measuring twelve by nine inches to gigantic ones which consist of many sheets assembled together and plastered on huge external walls or boards. Many posters are printed on fine glossy cardboard sturdy enough to be placed on shelves or in the traditional niches often found in Iranian houses. Many posters were also reproduced as postcards, and in textbooks of all kinds and illustrated periodicals.

A multimedia poster commemorating the Islamic Revolutionary Guards provides a good example of the poster as a hybrid art form through the use of various graphic schools and techniques. In the foreground we see a revolutionary fighter with a rifle in his left hand and a Molotov cocktail in his right. The movement and composition of the picture, and even the details of the young man's apparel are reminiscent of Robert Capa's photographs of the Spanish Civil War. The parallel is not coincidental, as the very bandolier with ammunition worn over the shoulder and across the chest of the young fighter belongs more to Spain in the 1930s than Iran in the 1970s. The bloodstained bandage around his head is yet another graphic reminder of the Spanish Civil War. [Fig. 9.4] On the

Habib Sadeqi

9.5

red brick wall in the background, black, thick graffiti declare *Allahu Akbar, Khomeini Rahbar* (God is Greatest, Khomeini is the leader). To the right, a photograph of Khomeini has been hastily affixed to the wall with masking-tape, further emphasizing the atmosphere of revolutionary spontaneity. The lower part of the poster is composed of a color photograph with some obvious retouching, specifically the flames coming from the Molotov cocktail. Although this image appears to have been staged for the photographer, its message remains clear, direct, and even reportorial. The painting which makes up the top portion of this poster is more complex. A fiery story is depicted from which the holy scripture of Islam, the Qur'an emerges, enveloped in a blue cloud. In addition, a black embroidered prayer mat, a rose (symbolizing beauty and love), and a string of beads (symbolizing the ninety-nine Beautiful Names of God) are painted next to the Qur'an. The lower part of the poster addresses the attributes of struggle; the upper, the attributes of faith. A quote from the Ayatollah Khomeini in the upper right-hand corner states, "Our objective is our ideology," further underlining the fact that Islam is triumphant as long as men fight for it.

The designer of this poster had obviously seen the world-famous photograph of the American Marines raising the American flag on Iwo Jima. Here in the center of the poster Iranian Muslim revolutionaries raise a green flag emblazoned with the words "There is no god but God." They are surrounded by the bodies of demonstrators mown down by the imperial tanks which are visible in the distance. In the background, the equestrian statue of the Shah is being pulled down. Still in exile, the Ayatollah Khomeini is very much present in spirit, as is indicated by his hovering over the crowd, fist clenched, inspiring them to fight on until victory is won. [Fig. 9.6] The raising of the Islamic flag drawn by children appears in the book entitled *Children of Revolution*. [Fig. 9.7]

On the evening of the 1st of Muharram 1399 AH (2 December 1978) thousands of people in Tehran took to their roof-tops and chanted *Allahu Akbar* (God is Greatest). Some who were particularly active in the Revolution, and wished to have a record of the event, actually took their tape-recorders to their roof-tops and made tapes of this nocturnal chorus of revolutionary outcries. The following day, Khomeini's message to the Muslim revolutionaries was circulated throughout the country. In this message Khomeini mourned the brutal suppression of the revolutionary movement by the Shah and the military. He warned that "the Islamic and Husseini slogans" of the Muslim revolutionaries were being confronted with bullets and tanks. "Our people," he declared, "are the followers of the greatest man in history [Imam Hussein] who with only a few followers launched the great ʿAshura movement and forever buried the Umayyad regime in the cemetery of history. God willing, Great that He is, the dear people [of Iran], the true followers of the Imam [Hussein], will sacrifice their blood, bury the satanic regime of Pahlavi in the cemetery of history, and raise the banner of Islam throughout this country, and maybe other countries." Khomeini encouraged the Iranian soldiers to abandon their posts and barricades. He told the parents of these soldiers to prevent their sons from fighting for the Shah's army. He commended the employees of the Iranian National Oil Company for having joined the strike against the Pahlavi regime.[1]

To commemorate this proclamation issued from France by Khomeini to the Iranian people, Habib Sadeqi created a poster called "ʿAshura." It represents a traditional Muharram printed cloth with invocations in black calligraphy to Imam Hussein and his mother, Fatemeh. Such cloths are usually displayed on the walls of *husseiniyeh* during Muharram. The proclamation of Khomeini is attached to the cloth with masking-tape. The cloth is framed in green, with blood dripping from the bottom of the frame. The slogan in Arabic declaring "Every day is ʿAshura and the whole earth is Karbala" is written in white on the red blood. [Fig. 9.5]

9.6

9.7

145

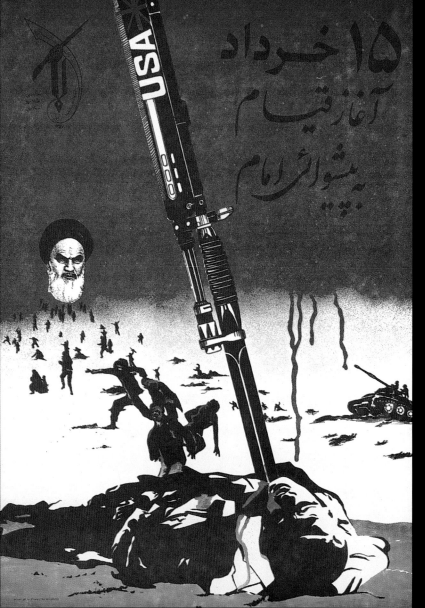

۱۵ خرداد
آغاز قیام
به پیشوائی امام

9.8

عاشورا،
پیروزی خون بر شمشیر

Indeed, the victory did come five weeks later, when the Shah left the country and the Ayatollah returned two weeks later to a tumultuous welcome in Iran. These events are best captured in the poster showing the Shah dressed up in his imperial uniform, crossing the Persian Gulf and heading west. He flees the land of Iran carrying two satchels (one marked with the Stars and Stripes and one with the Union Jack) full of billions of dollars and pounds sterling, leaving behind the refineries and oil rigs which had produced this wealth. He is accompanied by the Devil and a black dog—the dog is considered unclean in Islam because it is a potential carrier of rabies. The Shah has just barely escaped the hangman's noose. His nemesis, the Ayatollah Khomeini, has arrived from Paris (the Eiffel Tower and his Air France plane are seen in the distance). Holding aloft the Qur'an, with the banners of Islam and the Revolution behind him, he is banishing the Shah. This poster is painted in traditional coffeehouse, storytelling style, with a multitude of people and recent revolutionary events taking place against the backdrop of the map of Iran. However, this action-packed poster had a short life; and why? Some of the banners carried by the people declare the support of the people for Mahdi Bazargan, the first Prime Minister of the Islamic Republic, and for

Sadeq Qotbzadeh, the foreign minister; the former was removed from office and the latter executed by firing squad. [Fig. 9.10] A 5 rial postage stamp issued after the demise of Ayatollah Khomeini, juxtaposed with that poster, presents a notable contrast: the Shah was fleeing the power of religion and the anger of the people; the Ayatollah is pushed over the borders of Iran by rifles with bayonets attached, one marked "USA." This was issued to commemorate the Imam's exile after the uprising of 1963. [Fig. 9.11]

Another poster depicting the flight of the Shah is an outright caricature. Iran is a shiny red apple, its white pulp the map of the country. The revolutionary crowd in the map carries portraits of Khomeini and banners inscribed with religio-political slogans. A red tulip in full bloom rises from the valentine-shaped heart as if from the heart of a martyr, and an outsize swallow, the harbinger of spring, flies in pursuit of a Shah-headed worm whose skin pattern is the American flag. [Fig. 9.12] The poster put out by the United Islamic Associations of the Torkman-Sahra region connects the 5 June 1963 uprising with the irrevocable destruction of the monarchic regime by showing the crowned head of the Shah pounded by a clenched fist; the veins visible in its arm read, "There is no god but God." On the Shah's prominent

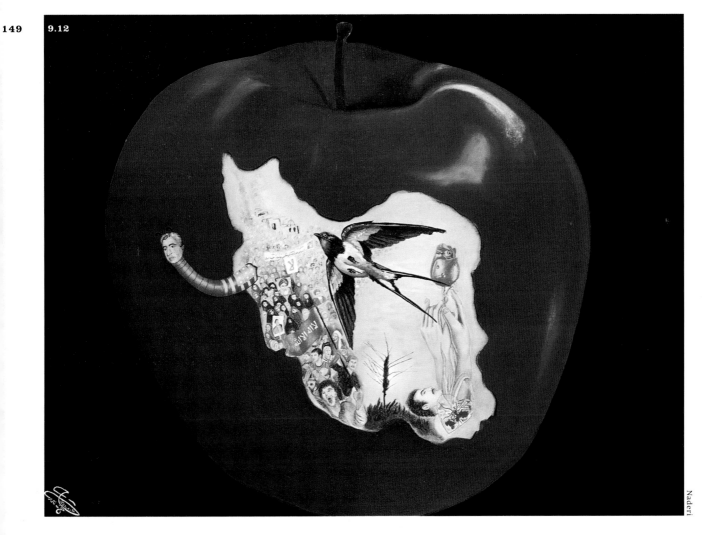

nose sits a pair of glasses with a heart in one lens and a dollar sign in the other, signifying here lust, greed, and corruption. [Fig. 9.13] When the Ayatollah Khomeini returned to Iran from his fourteen-year exile, he knew that the final victory of the Islamic Revolution had not yet been won. He still had to deal with the last government appointed by the Shah, the formidable imperial armed forces and an array of left-wing and nationalist groups who had jumped aboard the revolutionary bandwagon. To keep up the momentum of Islamic revolutionary preparedness, the Ayatollah did not waste a single minute on welcoming speeches at the airport, but drove straight through the packed streets of Tehran to the Behesht-e Zahra Cemetery, where the martyrs of the Revolution are buried. Amid the graves, he delivered one of his strongest orations, praising the dead and the living, who would fight on. To commemorate that event, a poster in a style reminiscent of Persian miniatures was put out, with echoes of Laertes' mourning speech from *Hamlet*. On the upper left-hand corner is a famous line from an early twentieth-century poet, ʿAref: "From the blood of the youth of the homeland tulips spring." This is translated into graphic terms by rows of tombstones, each with a red tulip growing from it. Juxtaposed to that, in the lower right-hand corner lies Shah Muhammad Reza Pahlavi, his insignia of power scattered about like Pharaoh's army; even the columns of the imperial palace at Persepolis are crumbling behind him. Khomeini plays the role of the agent of God, like Moses, and is about to lead the nation out of the Shah's/Pharaoh's slavery. Even the traditional dragon which often appears in Persian miniatures is spewing flames on the Shah. [Fig. 9.16] The same line of poetry quoted above was connected calligraphically into the shape of a tulip and made into a stencil which appeared on walls all over Iran. [Fig. 9.14] A child's vision of ʿAref's line appears in an illustration to a poem written by the 11-year-old Ali Haqiqi entitled "Martyr" and published in *Children of Revolution*. In this illustration, we see a revolutionary rally of children carrying a banner inscribed "Death to the Shah," their arms outstretched and fists clenched in proper revolutionary fashion. The rally takes place on green grass out of which the slightly altered words of ʿAref's line spring in red like tulips. (In this line the word "youth" is substituted by "martyrs.") [Fig. 9.15]

9.16

9.14

9.15

151

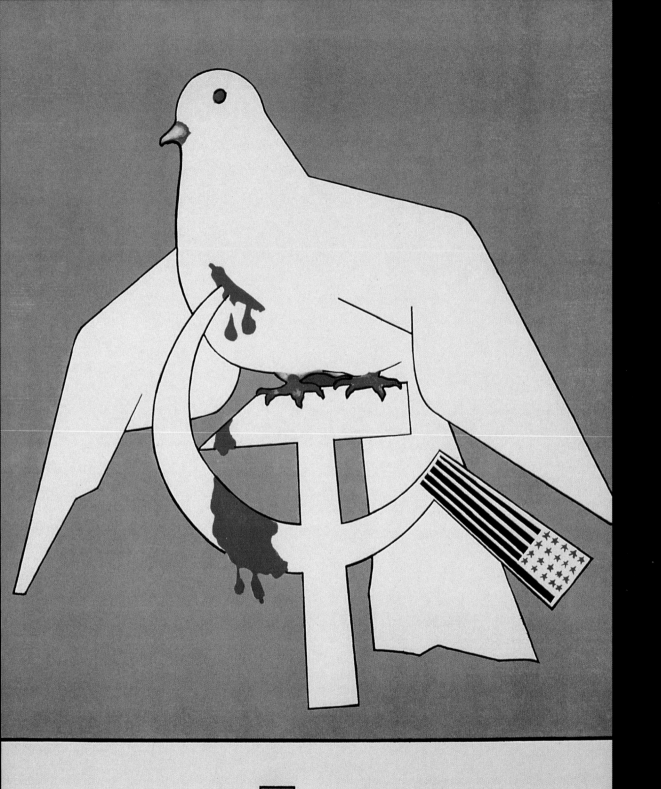

9.18

153

The victory of the Islamic Revolution, like any other revolution, did not bring immediate peace and stability to the nation. On the contrary, the country was in a state of flux. Many ethnic regions were threatening to break off as they were manipulated by internal and external forces. The Republic had once again to rely on the Karbala paradigm. Therefore, the Ministry of Islamic Guidance issued small posters based on the black-and-white photographs of the ᶜAshura speeches of Khomeini that inspired the uprising of 1963. In addition to the photographs, there were quotations from Khomeini equating the lot of the Iranian nation with that of Imam Hussein and his followers on the plain of Karbala. The establishment of the Islamic Republic was the great victory of the Islamic Revolution, but the struggle against internal and external enemies was by no means over. To represent the external enemies, a poster, marvelously effective in the simplicity of its imagery, was issued representing Iran in the form of a dove trying to perch on a hammer, only to be pierced by a sickle. This emblem of the Soviet Union, however, has a handle stamped with the American flag. Underneath the picture appears the word "Mirage," implying that Iran's reliance on one bloc or another would be a delusion. [Fig. 9.17] In another representation of the American flag, this time in a cartoon, the flag's stripes are hangmen's ropes complete with nooses. [Fig. 9.18]

Another poster, with a far more ghastly image of the external enemies, shows a cosmic hand (Iran) in outer space strangling a bug-eyed monster. One of the monster's eyes is an American flag, the other is the flag of the Soviet Union, while the monster's tongue is the flag of the People's Republic of China. The flags of the United Kingdom and Israel wave raggedly from this space alien's head. One wonders if Muhammadi, the designer of the poster, had seen classic American science fiction movies from the 1950s featuring bug-eyed invaders from Mars. [Fig. 9.19]

9.19

153

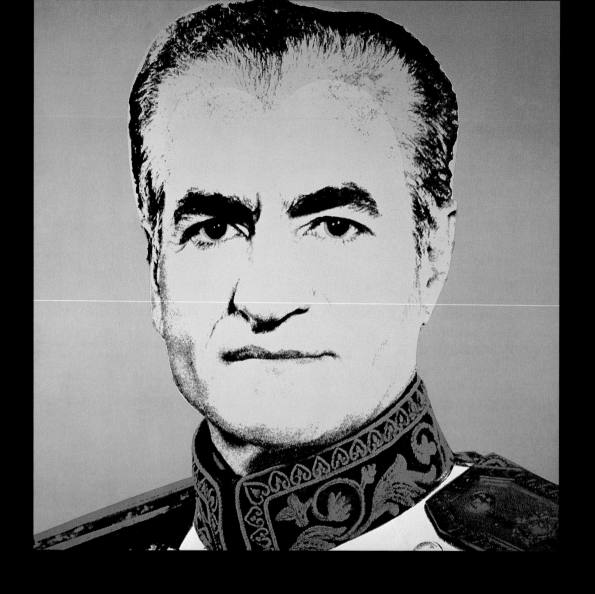

9.20

However, when it comes to the enhanced photo-image poster-portraits of the leaders of the Islamic Republic, there is no doubt about who inspired Ahmad Aqa Qolizadeh and Sedigheh Vosughi, the artists. It was none other than Andy Warhol, whose many portraits of the Empress and the Shah hung on the walls of the imperial palaces and in the Tehran Museum of Contemporary Art. Irony of ironies, in order to propagate the eternal verities espoused by the Islamic Republic, these poster artists used a style taken from the works of the Western media-hype artist famous for his statement that everybody gets fifteen minutes of fame, no more, no less! [Fig. 9.20]

Years before the 444-day-long hostage crisis, Khomeini had given voice to his anti-American sentiments in his sermons. This crisis which was felt all over the world as well as in Iran was also expressed in posters, graffiti, and postage stamps. This poster is based on photographs and additional images in watercolor or acrylic. It represents the takeover of the American Embassy in Tehran with men scaling the Embassy's main gate—favorite motif in the propaganda arising from this incident. From the compound of the American Embassy rises the Iranian Muslim fighter in full battle gear. On his chest we see the superimposed images of the Ayatollah Khomeini first being forcefully driven out of the country in 1964, and then returning home triumphantly in 1979. Both the image of the soldier and those of Khomeini are based on actual news photographs. The crowd

Alfred Yaqubzadeh

carries a poster portrait of the Ayatollah. On the Embassy walls appear the graffiti "Death to America" and "Long live Khomeini!" But the poster is entitled "The 15th of Khordad" (5 June 1963), thus depicting the takeover of the Embassy in 1979 as the successful implementation sixteen years later of the Ayatollah's anti-American sermons. [Fig. 9.21]

The gate of the American Embassy in Tehran figures in another poster which was originally the cover of a special publication by Sharif Polytechnic University. Here the Embassy complex, depicted as made up of bricks spelling out "USA," together with the walls and gate, is crushed by a huge fist made of cut-out photographs of Iranian crowds. Flattened beneath the walls and the gate in a pool of blood lies the Jimmy Carter-headed American eagle, its plumes the American flag. [Fig. 9.22] Until recently, the American flag, and sometimes the flags of the Soviet Union and Israel as well, were painted on the sidewalks leading to the entrance of the major hotels so that the hotel guests would inevitably tread on them.

Carrying effigies of enemies through the streets is an old Iranian tradition called ʿUmar Koshan (killing of ʿUmar). It could be compared to the burning of the guy accompanied by fireworks on Guy Fawkes Day in England. During the hostage crisis, ʿUmar

Masʿud Qandi

9.21

9.22

9.24

متر سال!!

9.23

Koshan became "Carter Koshan." This poster is a reflection of that political ritual. The head of President Carter is impaled on a spike above an American flag going up in smoke. The first part of the text underneath reads: "The heroic, wide-awake Iranian nation knows that setting fire to the American flag and Carter's ugly mug, the occupation of the CIA den of spies, and the hauling back of the Shah is the beginning of the battle against American imperialism." In a cartoon of the day, President Carter has been caught with the goods and faces a noose of "Oil." [Figs. 9.23 and 9.24] The Islamic Republic of Iran is out to fight "Corruption on earth" (*Mufsed fi-l Ard* in the Qur'anic phrase). In this poster, however, it seems that corruption comes primarily from the United States, going by the images of 100 dollar bills sticking out of the head of a *Schweinhund* and the copy of *Playboy* magazine in the breast-pocket of its suit. [Fig. 9.25]

The annual observance in Iran on the last Friday of Ramadan of the preparation for the liberation of Jerusalem is a political ploy aimed at the Islamic world as a whole. It provides an opportunity for many artists to compete in producing designs for book illustrations, posters, stamps, coins, and even banknotes. Characteristically, these

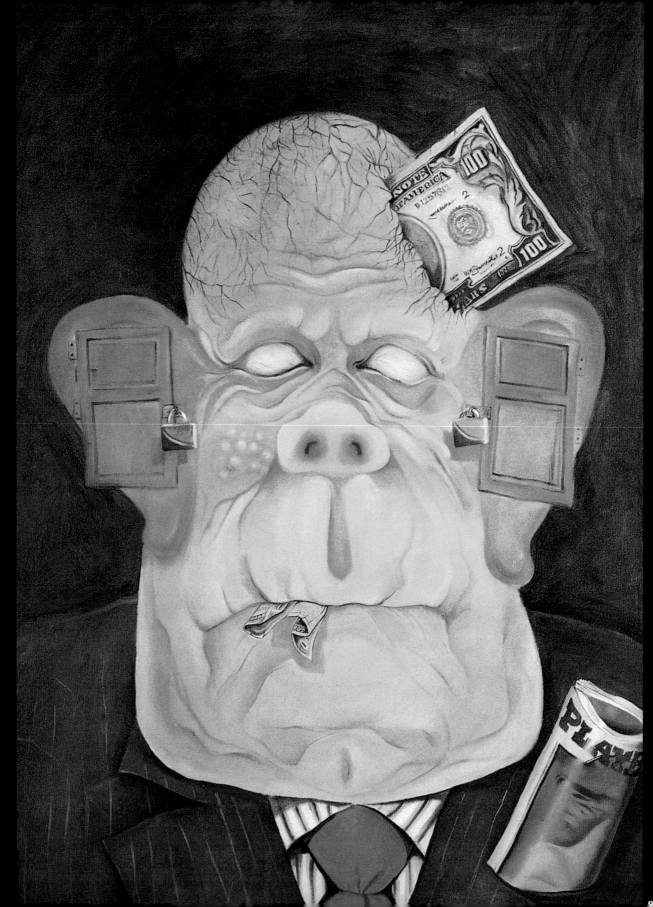

9.27

Hussein Khosrojerdi

9.26

159 designs feature the Mosque of the Dome in Jerusalem surrounded by barbed wire or smeared with blood. Another characteristic icon is the Star of David, always pictured in a menacing or oppressive manner. There is a poster and a stamp issued in 1991 for the World Day of the Child depicting a little child throwing a stone through a window with the Star of David on it. Although this is intended to honor the Intifada, it is bound to put the Westerner more in mind of Kristallnacht. [Figs. 9.26 and 9.27]

The protracted war with Iraq required endless sacrifice, determination, and almost superhuman heroism of the men, women, and children of Iran. The graphic artists did their part in mobilizing the country and in comforting the bereaved. Innumerable posters, murals, paintings, illustrations, and cartoons were dedicated to the war effort. An apocalyptic poster, rather in the style of the American painter Thomas Hart Benton, entitled "Guards of the Anemone Field" demonstrates the ethnic diversity of the Iranian Muslim fighters united in the struggle to defend the oilfields under the watchful and protective gaze of the Ayatollah Khomeini. [Fig. 9.28] The main burden of the war effort was on the shoulders of the fighting men. On this large twenty-four by nineteen meter mural on tile, we see them advancing fearlessly. The mural's image, based on a color photograph, was so popular that it was reproduced on posters and stamps, including one celebrating "Woman's Day" (*sic*), in which the soldiers are sent forth by Fatemeh Zahra, the mother of Hasan and Hussein. [Fig. 9.29]

Kazem Chalipa

9.28

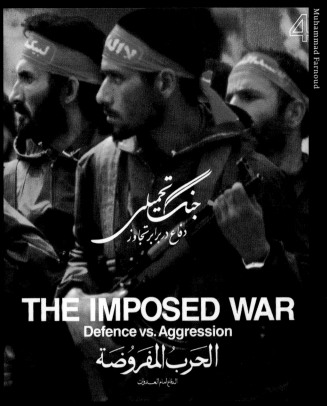

٤

جنگ تحمیلی
دفاع در برابر تجاوز

THE IMPOSED WAR
Defence vs. Aggression

الحرب المفروضة

الدفاع أمام العدوان

9.29

Many of those who died in battle are buried in the Behesht-e Zahra Cemetery south of Tehran represented in this poster. Above each tombstone is a metal stand housing a photograph of the soldier-martyr. The mood of the poster is seraphic rather than tragic; the cemetery is bathed in a golden and crimson glow, above which is a flight of souls into the deep blue. The brightly colored bandannas floating around their heads invoke Shiʿi heroes and heroines and the vengeance of God. [Fig. 9.30] In another Behesht-e Zahra poster, intended to comfort the bereaved women, a group of women veiled in *chador* sit around a flower-strewn tomb; they are joined by the radiant veiled apparition of either the sainted Zeynab or that of Fatemeh Zahra herself, come to commiserate with them. [Fig. 9.31]

The motif of self-sacrifice is represented in unflinching detail in a poster of the same name. The actual meaning of the title, "Ithar," is "Altruism, giving in abundance." Under a *mihrab* (prayer niche) stands a woman bearing the body of a fallen warrior in her arms. The entire lower half of her body is shaped like a red tulip. To her right is a long line of tulips turned mother's wombs holding the fetuses of male children, to her left another long line of fetuses

grown to manhood and bearing arms. She is surrounded by martyrs tied to stakes, and by row on row of headless martyrs (reminiscent of Karbala) in white shrouds ascending to paradise. Behind her is the white, headless figure of the Prince of Martyrs Hussein on his white steed. Finally, at the very top is a hand, its index finger pointing upwards to the Seventh Heaven and testifying to the oneness of God. The whole picture is framed by quotations from the Qurʾan—"Fight in the cause of Allah those who fight you" (2:190); "To him who fighteth in the cause of Allah whether he is slain or gets victory soon shall we give him a reward of great [value]" (4:74); and "Truly Allah loves those who fight in His cause in battle array, as if they were solid cemented structure" (61:4)—exalting those who die in the cause of God. This poster was reproduced on postage stamps and on murals. One mural close to the American Embassy in Tehran is three stories high. [Fig. 9.32] Another poster depicts martyrs in their white shrouds encircling an enemy tank like a swirling nebula. The poster is entitled "Blood Vanquishes the Sword." [Fig. 9.33]

The poster put out by the Art Department of the Islamic Propagation Organization shows a young boy ready to go to the front and taking leave of his sister who is clutching a Qurʾan in a

paroxysm of grief. The graffiti on the wall in the background focus on the teenagers who went to the front line, fought, and died there. Among the familiar slogans on the wall is an unusual statement by Ayatollah Khomeini; he hands over his title of *rahbar* (leader) to those teenagers and asks the nation rather to call him their servant. [Fig. 9.35]

Those boys who have not been drafted yet prepare themselves psychologically for the test of fire by participating in street demonstrations, carrying plastic rifles and plastic grenades, like those in the photograph. [Fig. 14.8 in the chapter: letters to Khomeini] When they are called to the front, the moment of departure is moving, as is shown in this poster honoring the "Day of the Student." It is ironic that images dealing with the death of children and adolescents departing for the front commemorate either the "Universal Day of the Child" or the "Day of the Student." This poster is based on an actual photograph taken by a photographer of the Kayhan group of newspapers. [Fig. 9.34] A boy in civilian clothes is saying farewell to his buddy or brother, dressed in military fatigues with a bandanna around his head. The bandannas are usually inscribed with such slogans as "God is Greatest," "Revenge

for the blood of Hussein", or "At your service, O Khomeini."

In rituals devoted to Karbala the tragedy is divided into many episodes focusing on many heroes. In the passion play, each hero asks Hussein for permission to fight the enemy. When permission is granted, the hero dons a white burial shroud, as he knows that he will die in battle. Then, a heart-breaking scene of departure takes place, followed by a battle in view of all the remaining members of the Hussein party, as well as the audience. The farewell scene captured by the black and white photograph in the poster is almost like a culmination of a rehearsal lasting several centuries. But this is not a photograph of a passion play—this is reality. The artist of this poster chose this photograph deliberately, because it fits so well into the paradigm of Hussein, and its many forms. Even comrades in arms, who form the background of the photograph, behave like participants in a Muharram ritual and seem to be in a state of catalepsy; they mechanically beat their chests like robots. The photographer, here, captures the essence of the anguish of parting reflected on the faces of the embracing boys and on the faces of those who witness it. Beneath this moving scene is written in bold letters, "Sing to my ear the hymn of how to live like a man…"

9.37

9.39

9.40

9.38

The demonization of perceived enemies started with the Shah, who was compared to Yazid, continued with President Carter, and culminated with Saddam Hussein, who was called Saddam Yazid. His effigies were carried through the streets and mutilated for the amusement of bystanders. In this photograph, on the necktie of the effigy is written "Death to Saddam and Israel!" The bad characters are usually associated with Israel, and in the caricature poster issued by the Revolutionary Guards on the occasion of the second anniversary of the "Imposed War," Saddam pops out in a tank from Menachem Begin's head. The caption underneath reads: "Saddam went crazy and became a thorn in the side of his own nation, our nation, and every other nation!" [Figs. 9.37]

Saddam is the Americans' wind-up toy; he was a war criminal —a Hitler—long before President Bush thought to call him one—and a mad mutt held by American and Soviet leashes alike; his dog license has the inevitable Star of David on it, and he is getting a richly deserved punch in the chops from the fist of the Islamic Republic of Iran. [Figs. 9.38, 9.39, and 9.40]

THE MOVEMENT OF IRAN IS NOT EXCLUSIVE TO IRAN ALONE: RATHER THE MOVEMENT IS OF THE DEPRIVED AGAINST THE ARROGANT AND TOWARDS THE PROTECTION OF ALL PEOPLE WHO RESPECT HUMANITY AND HUMAN RIGHTS. "Imam Khomeini"

9.41

The Iranian Revolution was the most important event of the Islamic resurgent movement. This movement, known also as militant Islam and political Islam, is to be found now in most Muslim countries. The resurfacing of Islam is a result of the dissatisfaction of the Muslim peoples with Soviet and Western models. Because the prime motives for the movement are not so much  religious as social and economic, they are of interest to non-Muslim Third World countries. The Revolution in the eyes of its makers was a movement of the dispossessed and downtrodden and should therefore appeal to all suffering people, both Muslim and non-Muslim. In this spirit, a poster was designed using two photographs:

9.42

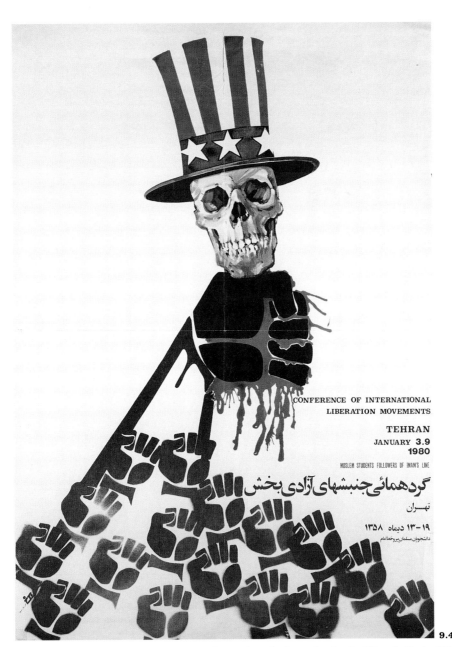

CONFERENCE OF INTERNATIONAL
LIBERATION MOVEMENTS

TEHRAN
JANUARY 3.9
1980

MOSLEM STUDENTS FOLLOWERS OF IMAM'S LINE

گردهمائی جنبشهای آزادی بخش

تهران

۱۹ - ۱۳ دیماه ۱۳۵۸

دانشجویان مسلمان پیرو خط امام

9.43

one, serving as the background, showing an enormous crowd of Iranians with raised arms and clenched fists, carrying banners, over which is superimposed a famous photograph by Werner Bischof

9.44

taken during a famine in Bihar, India in 1951, showing a bereft mother holding in one arm a hungry child, while begging God and passers-by with the other. The tragic expression on her face is self-explanatory as is the quotation in English beneath it, which is attributed to Khomeini. Since the caption is written in English only, this poster was obviously designed for a foreign audience. [Fig. 9.41]

The logo of Solidarity in Poland is now known all over the world. It is made up of silhouettes of people marching in demonstration, whose body contours spell out "Solidarnosć." The Ministry of National Guidance in Iran came up with a poster based on the same principle: a graphic depiction of a crowd of demonstrators with upraised fists which spell out an Islamic profession of faith, "There is no god but God." [Fig. 9.42] A conference in support of the "International Liberation Movements" was held in Tehran on 3-9 January 1980. Two posters designed for this event pretty much speak for themselves. [Figs. 9.43, 9.44 and 9.45]

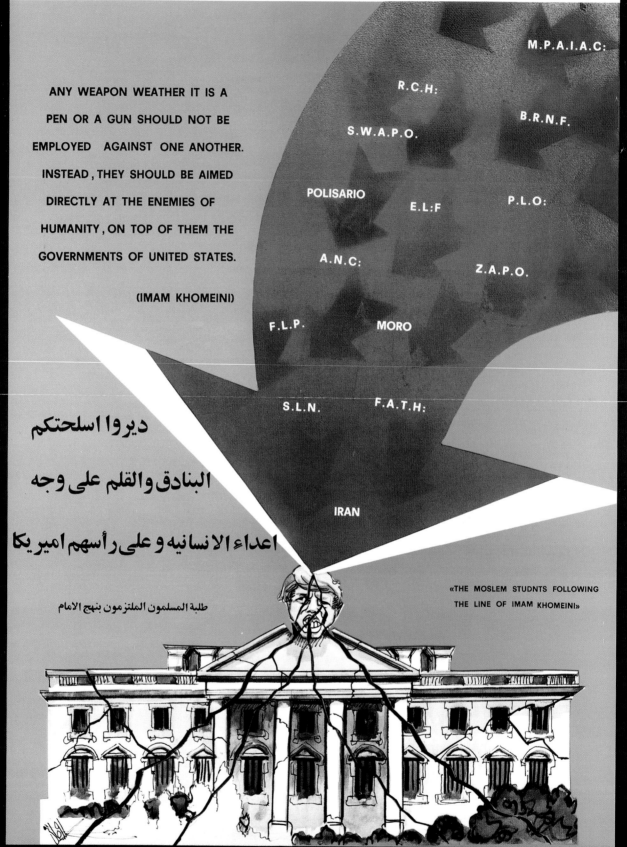

ANY WEAPON WEATHER IT IS A
PEN OR A GUN SHOULD NOT BE
EMPLOYED AGAINST ONE ANOTHER.
INSTEAD, THEY SHOULD BE AIMED
DIRECTLY AT THE ENEMIES OF
HUMANITY, ON TOP OF THEM THE
GOVERNMENTS OF UNITED STATES.

(IMAM KHOMEINI)

M.P.A.I.A.C:

R.C.H:

B.R.N.F.

S.W.A.P.O.

POLISARIO

E.L:F

P.L.O:

A.N.C:

Z.A.P.O.

F.L.P.   MORO

S.L.N.   F.A.T.H:

IRAN

ديروا اسلحتكم
البنادق والقلم على وجه
اعداء الانسانيه وعلى رأسهم اميريكا

طلبة المسلمون الملتزمون بنهج الامام

«THE MOSLEM STUDNTS FOLLOWING
THE LINE OF IMAM KHOMEINI»

9.45

9.46

Posters were designed primarily for internal consumption. Among those designed for external audiencies were some targeted at special groups, for example Shiʿites of the world, all Muslim countries regardless of sectarian persuasion, Third World countries, the superpowers, and the world at large. One intriguing poster seems to have been designed to appeal to the Christian world. Equally intriguing is a postage stamp issued to commemorate the birth of Christ. [Fig. 9.46]

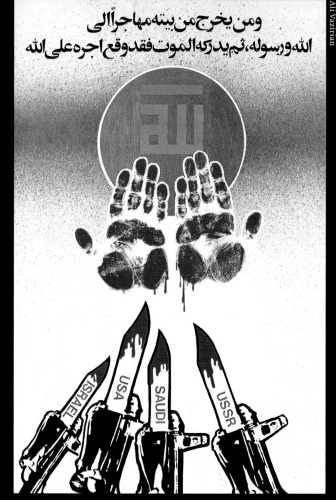

9.47

The Kaʿbah in Mecca is of special significance to Muslims the world over. Every Muslim prays in the direction of Mecca, and one of the Five Pillars of Islam is to perform the *hajj* (pilgrimage) to Mecca once in a lifetime. The Kaʿbah in Mecca is a symbol of Muslim unity. Therefore, many posters, stamps, and even banknotes featuring the Kaʿbah have been produced in Iran since the Revolution. In 1987, during Dhuʾl Hajj which is the month of pilgrimage, a shocking tragedy took place in that most holy precinct of Islam, which is forbidden to other than religious activities. The Saudi security forces responsible for keeping good order during the *hajj* tried to contain a political demonstration staged by the Iranian pilgrims. In the stampede which ensued, nearly 400 people, most of them women, were trampled to death. A flood of graphic art in various media commemorates this "Bloody Hajj." [Fig. 9.47] See also 6.4 a huge mural in Tehran devoted to the "Bloody Hajj."

The authorities in Iran stress the close and loving relationship between the Ayatollah Khomeini and his people. Like a votive image, a poster featuring the head of the Ayatollah serves as a medium for dialogue between the Iranians and their leader. The contours of Khomeini's face in the photograph are not sharp; a shy lingering smile complements the gentle look in his eyes. The face is translucent, giving it an air of serenity. Khomeini is a caring father who thinks about everyone who looks upon him. The fine calligraphy in two symbolic colors, green representing Islam, and red symbolizing blood and sacrifice, is superimposed on the photograph. Khomeini, like an actor playing the role of a god in a Greek tragedy, speaks in the first person, the nation plays the role of men, and the voice of a chorus is heard as well. [Fig. 9.48]

Khomeini: Many afflictions have beset me, but I can't divulge all of them. You are not alone O Imam!
Chorus: The whole Islamic community supports you.
The Nation: We are all your soldiers, O Khomeini!
We are all ears to listen to your commands, O Khomeini!

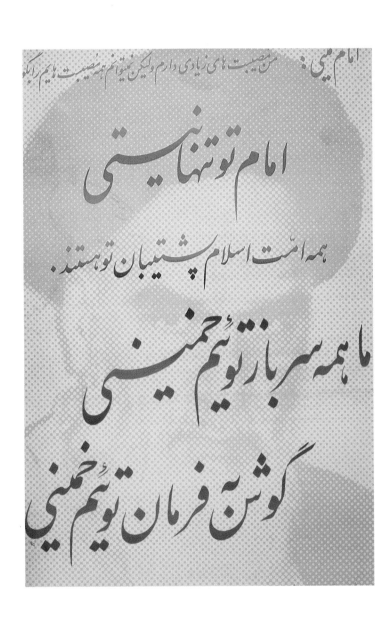

امام خمینی : من مصیبت های زیادی دارم ولیکن نمیتوانم همه مصیبت هایم را بگو

امام تو تنها نیستی

همه امت اسلام پشتیبان تو هستند.

ما همه سرباز توئیم خمینی

گوش به فرمان توئیم خمینی

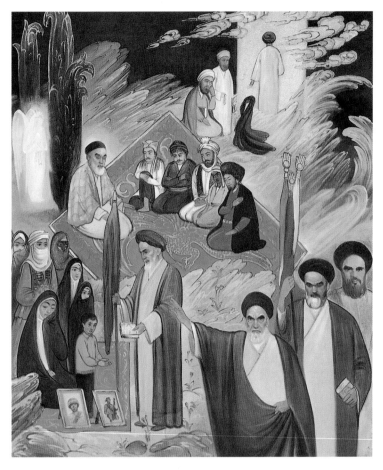

9.50 In the lower right-hand corner we can see Ayatollah Khomeini moving from young manhood to old age, a preacher and revolutionary, bearing the Qur'an in one hand and the standard of Shiᶜi Islam in the other. In the lower left-hand corner, he is consoling the women and young children who have given martyrs to the Islamic Revolution and the "Imposed War," extending the banner and the Qu'ran to them. In the center of the poster, the Ayatollah is represented as the patriarch unifying Iran's various ethnic groups. Finally, we see the Ayatollah departing this life, leaving his mantle behind. The mood of this poster is one of lively gravity in the tradition of Persian miniatures, and not without a certain respectful tenderness in notable contrast to depiction of most other totalitarian figures of the century.

Contrary to the multiplicity of outfits worn by the Shah — and by Saddam Hussein, for that matter — on government posters, and in official photography, state portraits, etc., the Ayatollah Khomeini always appeared in the traditional Shiᶜi clerical garb. Juxtaposed with the glittering opulence of the imperial court, the lifestyle of the Ayatollah exhibited a simplicity bordering on the ascetic. One graphic artist, however, was so carried away by this ideal image that in his enthusiasm he based a poster of the Ayatollah on the paintings by the seventeenth-century Spanish artist Murillo of the Blessed Virgin Mary surrounded by cherubim and crushing a serpent underfoot. [Fig. 9.49] All the stages of the Ayatollah Khomeini's life are depicted on the poster issued after his death by the Islamic Propagation Organization. [Fig. 9.50]

Until the middle of 1981, the left-wing and non-Islamic nationalist groups were producing posters as well. They were soon left out in the cold, and the stiffness of their works stands in startling contrast to the lively and passionate works produced by the Islamic graphic artists. Most of the posters created by the Left during the Revolution and in the early years of the Islamic Republic emphasize their support of the Ayatollah Khomeini, like the poster featuring the logo of the Mujahedin-e Khalq (People's Mujahedin) alongside a shoulder-length photograph of the Ayatollah. The others commemorate May Day and are full of slogans opposing American imperialism. "Workers of the world unite" could carry them only so far in this atmosphere. [Figs. 9.51 and 9.52]

9.51

9.52

But the atmosphere changed drastically in early 1981 when those who disagreed with the program of the Islamic Republic were branded as counter-revolutionaries and became the target of government propaganda. In Iran it is a time-honored perception that people turn villains under the influence of malign external forces, be they extraterrestrial (evil stars, or satanic influence—"If anyone withdraws himself from remembrance of [God] Most Gracious, we appoint for him an evil one, to be an intimate companion of him" (Qur'an 43:36)) or terrestrial (foreign powers). The villains are always depicted as puppets or marionettes manipulated by foreign hands. A poster turned into the cover of a book entitled *How I Became a Terrorist* is a very good example of this. The main thrust of that propaganda has been aimed at the Mujahedin-e Khalq. On this book cover the logo of the Mujahedin is stamped on the chest of the robot-like puppet. [Fig. 9.53]

Surely in the field of political posters, the graphic artists of the Islamic Republic of Iran have shown an almost unique artistic drive and flair.[3]

---

1 Ali Davani, Nehzat-e Ruhaniyun-e Iran (Tehran, n.d.), vol. 9: 4-18. **2** Ibid., pp. 21-5. **3** The pioneering study of Iranian posters was made by William L. Hanaway, Jr., "The Symbolism of Persian Revolutionary Posters," in Barry M. Rosen (ed.), Iran since the Revolution (Boulder, Colo., 1985). The best graphic material for further study of the revolutionary posters is contained in two luxuriously published volumes: Abolfazl Aliy and Davoud Sadegh Sa' (comp.), A Decade with the Graphists of the Islamic Revolution (1979-1989) (Tehran, 1989), and Mustafa Goodarzi and Davoud Sadegh Sa' (comp.), A Decade with Painters of the Islamic Revolution (1979-1989) (Tehran, 1989). Another important source is a volume compiled by Abolfazl Aliy, The Graphic Art of the Islamic Revolution (Tehran, 1985)

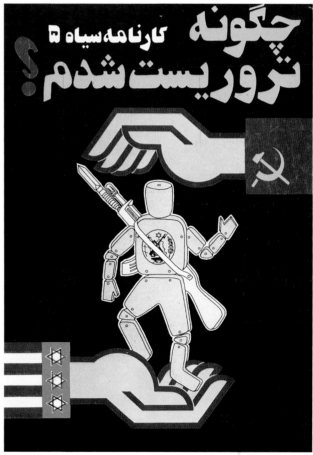

9.53

Ten

BETWEEN CONTENT
AND CAPTION:

READING THE
COLORFUL CODES
OF A REVOLUTION

THE REVOLUTIONARY GRAPHIC ART WHICH CAME TO FRUITION IN THIS PERIOD PLACES THE PROPAGANDA SIGNIFICANCE OF POLITICAL POSTERS AT THE CENTER OF MEASURING THE DIMENSIONS OF THE ART OF PERSUASION IN ANY REVOLUTION. IN THIS CHAPTER, WE SHALL CONSIDER SOME OF THE ICONIC MODES OF OPERATION THAT PUT THE SEMIOTIC REPERTOIRE OF THESE IMAGES IN THE SERVICE OF THE REVOLUTION. IN EVERY IMAGE, WHETHER OR NOT CONTROLLED BY A CAPTION, THERE IS A "LITERAL MESSAGE," AS BARTHES CALLS IT, WHICH IS REGISTERED AT THE MOST IMMEDIATE LEVEL OF ENCOUNTERING IT. "A PLENITUDE OF VIRTUALITIES" AND "AN ABSENCE OF MEANING FULL OF ALL THE MEANINGS" ARE THE TERMS WITH WHICH BARTHES IDENTIFIES THE IMAGE AT THIS DENOTED LEVEL.[1] FOR THE IMAGE TO BEGIN TO ESTABLISH THE PARAMETERS OF ITS IMMEDIATE AND DISTANT MEANINGS, IT WILL HAVE TO COMMENCE WITH THE MOST RECOGNIZABLE PICTORIAL REGISTRATIONS COMMUNAL TO ITS AUDIENCE.

10.1 Muhammad Ali Keshavarz's depiction of a political prisoner; his body is captured but his mind flourishes outside his body.

These pictorial representations are inevitably drawn from the common repertoire of the cultural heritage that makes all symbolic understandings possible. They may include colors, such as green and red (that in the Shi‘i *Farbenlehre* carry profound loads of signification), or shapes, such as a circle or a rectangle (which have equally enduring patterns of "meanings"). But at this denoted level there is an uncontrollable weight of mute inarticulation about the image that can lead just about anywhere. That is why Barthes insists that "the characteristics of the literal message cannot be substantial but only relational."[2] This relational function, though, carries the observer from a disturbing variety of contextual distractions to the immediate doorstep of the textual substance of the image, namely the possibilities of meaningful encounter with it. In the course of a revolutionary procession, and as the crowd gathers around the leading banners, the demonstrators enter their communal gathering with a variety of distractions, expectations, projections, etc. The immediate recognition of a poster with a picture on it, the shapes and shades of a turban and a beard, the certain lines of a clerical robe, all are pictorial invitations that collect the scattered attentions of the participants to the focal point of a relational significance. The function of this denoted image, before any possibility of meaningful connotation is realized, is to gather all the participants from their scattered points of reference around a common symbolic of collective reference and keep them alert and ready for the self-same image to perform its next function, which is to invite the expecting audience one step further into the vast domain of connoted meaning and signification that it inevitably entails.

Barthes further distinguishes between a photograph and a painting in terms of their possibility of mere denotation. Calling the image at this denoted level a "message without a code," he argues that a drawing "even when denoted, is a coded message."[3] The distinction, which is quite a crucial one, has to do with intentionality and manipulation. The mechanical registration of image, as in a photograph, involves a human mind less than a drawing. To be sure, even in a photograph such elements as framing, lighting, and angle are among the particular manipulations that are at the disposal of the photographer to exercise a certain degree of intentionality. But the object of photography has certain inherent qualities of matter-of-factness that limit the range of such manipulations. These limitations, however, are not inhibitive to a painter or a graphic artist, who has every dimension

10.2 Commemorating the death of the revolutionary leader, this poster, produced by the Art Bureau of the Organization for Islamic Propaganda, invokes powerful images from Persian iconography.

and minutiae of the production wide open to his or her creative imagination. Beyond the particulars of framing, lighting, and angle, the process of encoding a photograph usually starts after its mechanical operation is over and when it is being reframed for a specific purpose. But in a drawing the act of coding for future connotations begins instantly as the artist draws the first lines. The range of possibilities available to the artist, as he or she begins to denote and thus encode the image, is much wider and more complex than what Barthes suggests in saying that "there is no drawing without style"[4] or in drawing our attention, along with Saussure, to the factor of "apprenticeship." He also underestimates the range of encoding and denoting already available to the photographer. We need not, for our purpose here, explore such range of possibilities any further. Suffice it to say that although Barthes is right in realizing that photography and drawing have two separate "ethics"[5] of denotation, there are still innate possibilities of formal manipulation at both photographic and pictorial levels, textual and contextual, that can be put at the service of the subsequent uses of both connotation and signification.

Central to the revolutionary message is, of course, the connoted image, the iconographic image as it is intended to be received. Nowhere more than in the connoted image is the centrality of culture—and the common repertoire of meaning and signification it engenders—evident. Without the cultural context and energy to give it zest and interpretability, the connoted image will fall flat on its surface value, its mere denotability. At this level, the connoted image is, as Barthes has put it, "a normal system whose signs are drawn from a cultural code."[6] Codification is at the disposal of the graphic artist, the iconographer, the symbolizer. But the artistic codification is quintessentially limited to the shared pictorial sensibilities of the culture that the artist and his or her audience share. A focal point of remembrance, a shared memory of things past, brings together the codifier and his or her audience. The iconic field is where the two meet.

There is nothing predestinate or monolithic about this interpretative *rendezvous* on the iconic site. Multiplicity of meaning

and exegesis abounds on the rich pregnancy of the iconic field. Individual members of the shared symbolics enter the iconic field from a diverse set of directions and orientations. But, as Barthes has reminded us,[7] there is nothing anarchical about this multiplicity of readings. Both the multiplicity and the inherent limitations of the connoted image are culturally set. What accounts for the possibility of multiple readings ought to be seen in the particular corres-pondence between the universe of meaning engendered in the connoted image and the observing individual. "Such sign corresponds," Barthes has noted, to a body of "attitudes ... certain of which may obviously be lacking in this or that individual."[8] Thus every feasibility of reading is the dialectical outcome of a correspondence between a particular "attitude" in a given individual aroused by the specifics of certain constitutional forces in the iconic image.

This leads us towards a more dynamic view of the revolutionary process as mitigated through its iconic messages. There is no validity in believing that all revolutionary participants, full-fledged Muslims if we consider them all, entered the mobilized force with identical expectations, emerging from identical responses to the iconic banners calling for ideological loyalty. "The language of the image," Barthes has successfully demonstrated, "is not merely the totality of utterances emitted... it is also the totality of utterances received."[9] It is in this dynamic dialectic that we can get closer to the varied nature of correspondence between the aesthetic agencies of revolutionary mobilization and the psychological disposition of individual responses to them. Barthes's assertion that "the languages must include the surprises' of meaning"[10] carries us a considerable distance in accounting for certain disillusions on the part of the secular intellectuals who "misread" the verbal and iconographic messages of the Islamic origin. "But we thought this was our revolution" is the common denominator of much disillusion about the nature and outcome of the (Islamic) Revolution. The disillusion stems precisely from that "misreading" of the verbal, visual, and aural messages. To be sure, there is a certain element of ambiguity in all

10.4 A reinterpretation of the revolutionary woman.

such messages. The ambiguity cannot altogether be attributed to a Machiavellian deceit on the part of the cultural codifiers at the helm of the revolutionary movement. The possibility of "misinterpretation," which is nothing but a politically failed interpretation, leads us to the more conducive field of operation for the connoted image, namely its vibrant ideological charges. In these terms, Barthes defined "ideology" as the "common domain of the signified connotations."[11] The common domain can be either received or engendered, or is more probably a combination of both. In revolutionary ideology, and the rhetoric of its expectations, the power of reinterpreting the received history in engendering new terms of loyalty should never be underestimated.

Here is Khomeini giving authoritative voice to a rising conception of "Islam" as political mandate, a mandate which is engendered and defined via a revolutionary counter-interpretation that puts a sacred memory squarely at the service of the political: "If rulers are Muslims they ought to obey the jurists. They have to ask the jurists about the [Islamic] laws and regulations, and then act accordingly. Thus the true rulers are the jurists themselves, and the government ought to be officially given to them, not to those who because of their ignorance of the [divine] law have to obey the jurists."[12]

10.3 Identifying Saddam Hussein with death and destruction, this poster invokes fearful memories.

1 ROLAND BARTHES, "RHETORIC OF THE IMAGE," IN ROBERT E. INNIS (ED.), SEMIOTICS: AN INTRODUCTORY ANTHOLOGY (BLOOMINGTON, IND., 1985), P. 199. 2 IBID. 3 IBID. 4 IBID., P. 200. 5 IBID. 6 IBID., P. 201., 7 IBID. 8 IBID., P. 202. 9 IBID. 10 IBID. 11 IBID., P. 203. 12 AYATOLLAH KHOMEINI, VELAYAT-E FAQIH (TEHRAN, 1978), P. 60

picture that

THEPROPAGANDAUSESOF

mouth

AREVOLUTIONARYCINEMA

Eleven

IN A SURPRISE ATTACK IN THE SOUTHERN REGIONS OF THE COUNTRY, IN THE COURSE OF THE IMPOSED WAR OF IRAQ AGAINST IRAN, A GROUP OF OUR DEFENSELESS FELLOW-COUNTRYMEN ARE CAPTURED. UNDER THE PRESSURES AND TORTURES OF THE BA^{c}ATHIST MERCENARIES, THESE CAPTIVES RESIST HEROICALLY AND ARE STRENGTHENED BY THEIR ORDEAL... A FEW OF THE CAPTIVES DECIDE TO ESCAPE, AND THEY ARE SUCCESSFUL. AS SOON AS THEY REACH IRAN, THEY GO TO THE FRONT AND JOIN THE BATTLE AGAINST THE IRAQI BA^{c}ATHISTS.[1]

This is the synopsis of one of many hundreds of feature films which began to be produced immediately after the initial successes of the Islamic Revolution in Iran. Cinema has been by far the most popular form of entertainment in modern Iranian history. No other form of public entertainment comes even close to cinema in the range of its appeal in the popular culture. Traditional forms of public entertainment, such as *naqqali*, gradually gave way to the fascination of the Iranian public with these moving pictures that talked and enchanted their way into the modern Iranian consciousness. In this chapter we shall consider some of the salient features of Iranian cinema that made it an effective political instrument.

The origin of Iranian cinema goes back to the first decades of the twentieth century when the magic of the moving pictures began to cast its spell on the fascinated Iranian audience.[2] Since then there has been a steady growth of interest in both foreign and domestic films. The enchanting magic of American, European, Japanese, Arabic, and Indian movies were dubbed into Persian colloquialism and achieved a permanent niche in the modern Iranian aesthetic consciousness. Very soon Iranian film-makers began to translate local scenes and incidents to the enduring magic of the motion picture. From its populist and entertaining origins in the 1920s through the 1950s, the young Iranian cinema gradually gave rise to a much more aesthetically and intellectually ambitious film culture in the 1960s, through the revolutionary years, and into the 1990s.[3] Today, Iranian films are shown, and celebrated by prizes, in a number of international film festivals.

The Iranian cinema has been instrumental in the making and representation of the Islamic Revolution in a number of significant ways.[4] Although relatively recent in its introduction into the contemporary Iranian creative imagination, cinema very quickly found its significant place in the popular culture. As soon as the initial generations of imported films led to local production of Iranian feature films, the popular culture began to be reflected in, as indeed influenced by, a variety of cinematic genres. Once centrally located in the midst of the Iranian popular culture,

11.1 Very early in the revolution, the Islamic ideologues recognized the significance of cinema. This poster was targeted at foreign reporters, cameramen in particular, reporting the events of the revolution; Iranian filmmakers were soon mobilized to make both documentary and feature films extolling the virtues of the Islamic revolution.

cinema began to have a crucial role in the repoliticization of the Iranian collective consciousness.

Perhaps the most significant impact of cinema on modern Iranian politics is its opening up the limited access of the general public to the outside world. Exposure to and conceptions of the outside world were the province only of high-ranking officials of the governments or of wealthy merchants who for diplomatic or commercial purposes travelled abroad and saw and experienced things beyond what was possible or conceivable inside Iran. When movies began to come to Iran—from India, Europe, the Arab world, the United States, and Japan—vast and utterly unprecedented horizons were opened up for Iranians. In the worlds of active imagination they let loose, the magic and enchantment of the moving pictures were incomparable to the occasional and much more limited accounts of travelers which appeared, in a very small circulation, in books or periodicals. Those accounts of the outside world were considerably limited in the range and intensity of their popular reach. In a society where the overwhelming majority could not read or write these written accounts could not have reached beyond their immediate literate audience. But cinema was

«MILAD»
The First National Film Festival of Islamic Republic of IRAN
June 18–27, 1981

different. Movies that came from the outside world were censored, re-edited, expurgated, dubbed, and consequently made into semi-local productions. As a result, the "foreignness" of movies from Japan or America was considerably reduced. John Wayne and Raj Kapour became household names, their worlds and their adventures penetrating deep into the collective and individual consciousness of their Iranian audience.[5] These repeated experiences transported the Iranian audiences to worlds and universes never before dreamt of. From Los Angeles to Tokyo, from Paris to Bombay, the four corners of the world became visible, imaginable, almost touchable for Iranians. The inhibiting borders of illiteracy, ignorance, unawareness were broken up and Iranians began to see, hear, and directly feel the fears, hopes, anxieties, trials, and tribulations of people who were called John, Raj, Katsoyu, or Siegfried and yet were remarkably similar to themselves. The experience forever changed the mental landscape of Iranians.

As the global village began to emerge, as the world began to notice Iranians, they began to notice the world. From the streets of San Francisco to the mountain slopes of India, from the skyscrapers of New York to the back alleys of Rome, from the Parliament of England to the Russian Revolution, from Chinese peasantry to French bureaucracy, the vertiginous vision of multiplied worlds began to be imbricated in the Iranian mind. The avalanche of these visions began to evoke an unprecedented range of sensibilities, perceptions, attitudes. Such evocative mental conceptions could easily be provoked for any number of purposes—didactic or political. Through the enchanting magic of the moving pictures, the collective Iranian consciousness expanded far beyond anything achieved before. New heroes and demons, myths and magic, came to haunt and animate the living imagination of the people. In a growing cinematic culture there began to emerge a wide ranging assembly of emotions, perceptions, assumptions, and vague expectations of something disquieting, something irresistibly, though disturbingly, attractive. A culture of cinema emerged, elitist to populist in the range of its aesthetic appeal, in which new and unprecedented webs of affiliation became possible: an Iranian peasant could now identify with an Indian in love, an American in revolt, an Arab in turmoil, with a British comedian, a French cab-driver, an Italian farmer. Cinema became a universalizing medium, a catalyst of unmitigated identification, of unification, internationalization, mental and emotional expansion of the Iranian collective psyche. The introduction of cinema expanded the horizons of the

11.2 A national film festival regularly celebrates the ideals of the Islamic revolution. There is a continuous transference of revolutionary images, such as a red tulip, from popular culture into the active elements of a revolutionary cinema.

modern Iranian collective consciousness beyond anything achieved in its long and antiquated history.

Immediately related to this expansion and universalization of the Iranian collective memory is the qualitative transformation of its imaginative prowess. By watching movies, Iranians' passive and active imagination began to expand. They began to dream things they could not dream before, imagine things not in the range of their imagination before, and a vivid memory of things as they ought to be began to transplant things as they now were. The emergent imagination was more active, immediate, mnemonic to an unprecedented degree in the power of its visualization. Thanks to the vivid and unforgettable visualization of movies, Iranians began not just to imagine more things, things nowhere near their active consciousness, but to imagine them more vividly, compellingly. That intensified not just the range but the power, the quality, the nature of imagination. That activated imagination did not remain confined to matters exclusively cinematic. The audience carried its recharged imagination home, to school, to the market, even mosques, religious gatherings. This new, enlarged, rejuvenated, and even agitated imagination knew no boundary, respected no limit to its protuberant intrusion into every corner of the Iranian psyche.

A crucial by-product, perhaps an unanticipated consequence, of the Iranian assimilation into this new cinematic culture, was the creation of an unprecedented collective consciousness through participation in which Iranians were brought closer together. The same movies, such as an Indian drama or an American Western, were shown to Iranians as far apart as Tabriz and Ahwaz. Through such movies, not only did Iranians come to know about the outside world, but they were brought closer together. The movie culture created a third level of identification, beyond the local and the national, in which the younger Iranians began to participate. Left to their local cultural identities, there were considerable vistas and valleys of linguistic and cultural differences that kept Iranians separate. Although the Persian literary tradition, in the long history of which almost all Iranian regions and localities participated, did provide a common level of cultural identification, still this remained a highly exclusive and literary phenomenon, effectively inaccessible to the masses of the illiterate people. The story of cinema was drastically different.

Central to this emerging cinematic self-consciousness was the formation of a political awareness unprecedented in Iranian history. This political awareness was not limited to exposure to movies with an identifiable ideological message. Watching the cultural, social, political, and economic dimensions of foreign lands, even (or especially) if only in the background of the story-line unfolded in the movie, gave rise to occasions of reflection, of self-assessment, comparison, to questions of why, how, and what if. A cab-drivers' strike in Rome, a newspaper editorial board in London, a scene of acute poverty in Bombay, a decadent nightclub in Beirut, a corrupt politician in Washington, a dispossessed farmer in

11.3 Very soon after the revolution, the Fajr (The Dawn) Film Festival was institutionalized as the official forum for Iranians' interested in international cinema. It replaced the prerevolutionary Tehran Film Festival in which many foreign film makers participated.

11.4 and 11.5 The construction of a cinematically charged political consciousness in the pre-revolutionary period was crucial after the success of the revolution. In 1982, a week-long film festival commemorated "the Imposed war" with Iraq; in 1983, doves were depicted as symbols of a potential peace.

California appeared in any number of movies. Accumulated and juxtaposed, reviewed and remembered, these scattered and unrelated scenes would gradually merge into a collective political memory that heightened the level of ideological receptivity. Through visual imageries, the Iranians' political vocabulary expanded. Ideas of democracy, society, government, military, economy, production, workers, capitalists, international relations, superpowers, and a range of similar and interrelated questions emerged in the lexicon of the Iranian intellectual armament, giving expression and reality to otherwise mute and non-existent concerns, conceptions, anxieties.

Underlying this heightened political awareness was the overwhelming sense of relative deprivation that began to register itself on a mass, totally unprecedented, scale. Pictures of fantastic opulence and wealth in Europe and the United States were viewed by an audience in the slums of south Tehran. The power of this imagery lay in implication rather than in what it explicitly said or intended. The backgrounds of overstuffed shopping malls, super-markets, opulent neighborhoods, conspicuous consumptions, cars,

uninhibited sex (however censored for the Iranian audience) cumulatively gave rise to a recognition that life could be and was different in other parts of the world. Without these vivid pictures, the masses of Iranians rarely saw such uninhibited exhibition of wealth and luxury. Since the wealth and luxury of affluent Iranians were hidden from public view, they could scarcely excite the public imagination. But these pictures of affluence from faraway lands excited the fantasies and accentuated the relative or absolute poverty of the Iranian audience. With the later advent of television, these pictures of affluence were brought right into Iranian homes. There, in the very center of modesty and deprivation, the affluence of life in faraway lands became more pronounced, more disturbing, more conducive to a revolutionary disposition.

When the time was right and ripe, the political conscious-ness thus created and the sense of relative deprivation that accompanied it led to the active formation of Iranian political cinema. Films such as Daryush Mehrju'i's *Cow* (1969), Amir Naderi's screen adaptation of Sadeq Chubak's *Tanqsir* (1973), Ebrahim Golestan's *Asrar Ganj-e Darrah Jenni* (1974), Parviz Kimiavi's *Moghul-ha*

11.6 Amir Naderi's *Tangsir* (1973) was one of the most successful screen adaptations of a major Persian novel by the distinguished Iranian novelist Sadeq Chubak. Naderi expanded the political implications of the novel and turned the film into a major political event. Its leading character takes brutal revenge from the religious, political, and commercial authorities who had conspired to rob him of his lifetime savings.

(1973), and Parviz Kimi'ai's *Gavaznha* (1975) began to give cinematic expression to the rising awareness of a political consciousness. The Iranian political cinema was rich, diversified, and comfortably distanced from any stifling ideological muzzle or party program. Sohrab Shahid Sales' *Still Life* (1975) portrayed the unbearable solitude of a railway watchman without sentimentality or political advocacy. Parviz Kimi'ai's *Gavaznha* contrasted the lives of a drug addict and a political activist with remarkable poise and balanced sensitivity. The Iranian political cinema, as its cinematic culture in general, played a crucial role in preparing the Iranian masses for a revolutionary disposition. No less an authority than Ayatollah Khomeini himself is reported to have seen and passed a positive judgment on Mehrju'i's *Cow*. In a series of movies directed with stunning sensibility, Parviz Kimi'ai is to be particularly noted for such compelling films as *Qeisar* (1969), *Reza-Motori* (1970), *Khak* (1973), *Dash-Akol* (1971), and *Gavaznha*. These movies, and those of equal sensibility by Dariush Mehrjui'i, Bahram Beiza'i, Ebrahim Golestan, Bahman Farmanara, and Amir Naderi, were produced and directed, much to their credit, with no set political agenda. But through them a whole new political dictionary of cinematic

11.7 In Iraj Qaderi's film *Barzakhi-ha* (1981) a group of prisoners freed during the revolution try to escape the country illegally and instead end up in the front-line of fire in the Iran-Iraq war, the experience turning them into staunch nationalists. Familiar faces such as Muhammad Ali Fardin, Naser Malik-Moti'i, Iraj Qaderi, and Muhammad Ali Keshavarz were depicted in the film's poster for impact.

imagery was made public, in the compelling universe of which an alternative political culture began to be perceived, shaped, and understood. The emerging political culture of this cinema was not pointing to any particular ideological utopia; and yet it engendered an air of heightened political urgency, of revolutionary expectation one might say. To what immediate historical use this sense of urgency and expectation might be put was of no particular concern or significance to them. But when the right moment came, there was an active political imagination which was deeply rooted in Iranian cinema.

At the birth of the Islamic Revolution, cinema came to play a crucial role in the course and consequences of the cataclysmic event. One of the earliest targets of the reconstructed Islamic anger was the movie-house as a symbol of something beyond itself. A number of movie-houses were set on fire or blown up by Muslim activists. This is to be understood in the increasingly Islamic language that the revolutionary momentum adopted. The targets were not cinema and movie-houses in themselves but in their symbolizing of what the reactivated Islamic consciousness considered to be a corrupt and alien culture. By then, cinema had already served its historical function and given Iranians the necessary vocabulary of dissent and rebellion. On the verge of the revolutionary outburst, the Muslim revolutionaries bombed and set on fire focal points of their anger and anxieties. Undoubtedly, there was a strong, however latent, sense of ressentiment involved in this

destruction of the media that gave the Iranian masses the most vivid expression of what they desired most and achieved least: the figment of their own imagination they called "the West." Destroying the very means of access to the outside world, to the world of imagination, fantasy, and visions of things even beyond the realm of dreams, was perhaps the harshest and most difficult phase in the history of Iranian fascination with moving pictures. As movie-houses in Tehran and other major Iranian cities were blown up or set on fire, the youthful revolutionary watched the destruction of its own father. This was not the only, or even the most important, act of patricide in the course of the Revolution. Many similar acts, ranging from patricide to infanticide, found spectacular expressions. But cinema as an active and diligent father of political consciousness was among the first victims of its own children — murdered but soon to be resurrected by the same children for their post-revolutionary purposes. But the greatest and the most tragic act in the saga of the cinema and revolutionary Iran was to come in the summer of 1978, in the industrial town of Abadan in southern Iran. Some 400 people — women and children — were burned alive inside a movie-house while watching Parviz Kimia'i's *Gavaznha*. The event shook the already fragile Iranian body politic to its bones.

Cinema was almost immediately resuscitated, the revolutionary father resurrected, upon the success of the Islamic Revolution.[6] It was emphatically clear to the revolutionary functionaries of the nascent Islamic Republic that cinema was too powerful a medium of propaganda and persuasion not to be effectively utilized for immediate and more distant ideological and political purposes. The popularity of film in post-revolutionary Iran made it a particularly compelling ideological instrument. There are seventy-seven movie theatres in Tehran alone. In every major Iranian city there are a few theatres, always filled to capacity at every show. After the Revolution, the names of cinemas were changed from such fanciful American names as "Silver City" to more revolutionary names such as "Africa" or "Freedom."[7]

Feature films began to have revolutionary plots and, after the commencement of war with Iraq, anti-Ba^cath propaganda. Revolutionary valor and sacrifice were highly praised and celebrated in these films. In this period Mohsen Makhmalbaf emerged as one of the most successful directors with a solid command over his narrative strategies, all put squarely in the service of the Revolution. Savak, the hated secret police of the Pahlavi regime,

11.8 Parviz Kimia'i, as one of Iran's most celebrated film-makers, adopted his experience and talent to the purposes of the Islamic Revolution. In *Red Line* (1983), Kimia'i wove the domestic affairs surrounding a wedding into the wider social unrest which had accompanied the 1979 revolution.

11.9 In *Qarantineh* (1982), Mas⁥ud Asadollahi tested the loyalties of a son who finds out that his father was a high-ranking member of the SAVAK, the dreaded secret police under the Pahlavis.

became the subject of many movies during this period. Through such feature films as Mirlohi (*Ghosts*, 1983), Iranians began to exorcise their deep-rooted fear of the secret police. Quite a number of documentary films were made, all geared towards an active celebration of the Islamic Revolution in Iran. The Farabi Foundation was ultimately established as a state-sponsored agency supervising the production and distribution of feature films in the service of the Revolution.

1 Anon. (ed.), Sinema-ye Iran: 1358/1979-1363/1984 (Tehran, 1984), p. 78. 2 For a short history of Iranian cinema, see Jamsheed Akrami, "The Blighted Spring: Iranian Political Cinema in the 1970s," in J. D. H. Downing (ed.), Film and Politics in the Third World (New York, 1987), pp. 131-44. A more comprehensive account is to be found in Mas⁥ud Mehrabi, Tarikh-e Cinema-ye Iran (Tehran, 1984). 3 For a full discussion of this period, see Jamsheed Akrami's article, "Cinema II. Feature Films," in Encyclopaedia Iranica, vol. 5, fasc. 6, pp. 572-86. 4 For an excellent account of the political uses of cinema in Iran, see Hamid Naficy's "Cinema as a Political Instrument," in Michael E. Bonine and Nikki Keddie (eds.), Continuity and Change in Modern Iran (Albany, NY, 1987), pp. 265-83. For a brilliant theoretical statement on the political dimensions of film as such, see Mas⁥ud Zavarzadeh, Seeing Films Politically (Albany, NY, 1991). 5 For an account of the culture of movie-going in Iran, see the excellent piece by Hamid Naficy, "Autobiography, Film Spectatorship, and Cultural Negotiation," Emergence 1 (Fall 1989), pp. 29-54. 6 For a critical assessment of post-revolutionary cinema in Iran, see Reza⁥Allamah-Zadeh, Sarab-e Sinema-ye Islami-ye Iran (Saarbrücken, Germany, 1991). A full description of the subversive forces operative in cinematic culture in general and in Iranian films in particular has yet to be written. For a brilliant extension of the Bakhtinian theory of carnivalesque to film and subversive forces, see Robert Stam, Subversive Pleasures: Bakhtin, Cultural Criticism, and Film (Baltimore and London, 1989). 7 These statistics are collected in Sinema-ye Iran, pp. 37-48.

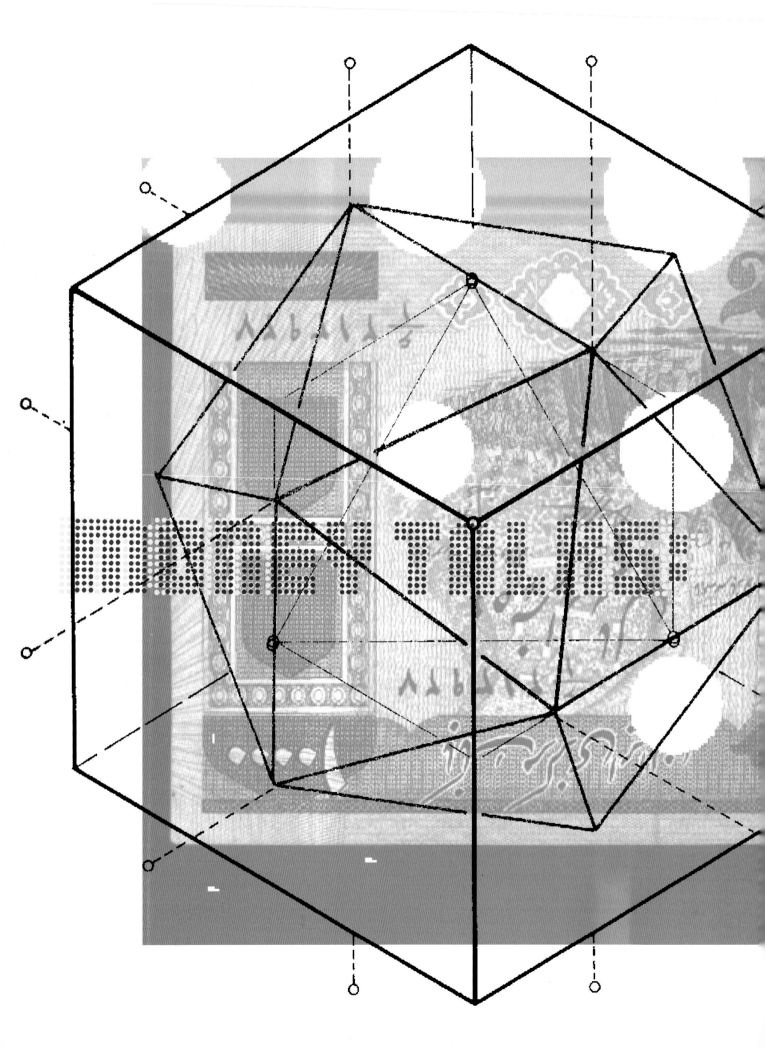

BANKNOTES AS INSTRUMENTS OF
propaganda

Twelve

POSTAGE STAMPS AND BANKNOTES ARE TWO OF THE MOST IMPORTANT MEANS BY WHICH A GOVERNMENT CAN LEGITIMIZE ITSELF[1] IT HAS BEEN STATED THAT "BOTH ARE A MONOPOLY— I.E., A SOVEREIGN ATTRIBUTE OF THE STATE AS WELL AS AN EFFICIENT ICONOGRAPHIC PROPAGANDA VEHICLE THEREOF. THEY CAN TELL US SOMETHING ABOUT THE OFFICIAL DISCOURSE OF THE STATE, THE ONE FOR WHICH IT ATTEMPTS TO ENSURE IDEOLOGICAL HEGEMONY."[2] MAINTAINING THE IDEOLOGICAL HEGEMONY OF THE STATE IS A CONTINUOUS EFFORT, REQUIRING A CONSTANT RE-AFFIRMATION OF MORAL AND POLITICAL LEGITIMACY. BECAUSE OF THEIR UBIQUITOUS PRESENCE IN THE DAILY LIFE OF THE NATION, STAMPS AND BANKNOTES ARE USED TO ADDRESS THE STATE'S DEEPEST IDEOLOGICAL ANXIE-TIES. IN THIS CHAPTER WE SHALL EXAMINE THE EFFECTIVE MODE OF PROPAGANDA AS CARRIED OUT VIA THE IRANIAN CURRENCY.

12.1

From 1864 to 1926, the Iranian banking system was managed by foreign banks. In 1926, the Bank-e Melli (National Bank) was established as the state bank of Iran. The 1960 Monetary and Banking Act established the Bank-e Markazi (Central Bank) as a repository for government accounts, to transact the business of the government, to represent Iran in all international monetary organizations, to maintain a balance of foreign payments, to issue banknotes, to control gold and foreign exchange transactions, and to sell government bonds. During the Pahlavi reign, stamps and banknotes were used to glorify twenty-five centuries of Iranian achievements and contributions to world civilization. They emphasize pre-Islamic architecture and art, modern industrial complexes, gigantic dams, and the latest means of transportation. The portrait of a monarch is also a prominent feature of Pahlavi stamps and banknotes—an essential symbol for the self-legitimation of a monarchy. The banknotes issued during the rule of the Pahlavi dynasty bear a portrait of the monarch, usually in full dress uniform. The portrait is found either in the center of the note or on the right-hand side. Next to the portrait are the national emblems of the lion and the sun, shown under the Pahlavi crown. The symbolic animals which were used to decorate Achaemenid (550-330 BCE) palaces and Sasanid (224-651 CE) silverware are another common motif. Sometimes, in an image borrowed from the friezes at Persepolis, a royal hero is shown killing a ferocious dragon, a traditional symbol of the triumph of good over evil. Other banknotes have the Furuhar, the winged image of Ahura Mazda, dramatically spread across the surface of the note. The reverse side of the notes is predominantly decorated with architectural motifs.[3] Images from the ancient period include the ruins of the palaces of Darius and Xerxes, the columns of the Apadana hall at Persepolis, the tomb of Cyrus the Great, and the friezes of tribute-bearers, fighting animals, and Darius on the throne from Persepolis. Architecture from the Sasanid and Islamic period is also used to decorate the reverse of some of the banknotes; included among them are the palace of Shah Abbas in Isfahan and two bridges, one Sasanid and the other Safavid (1501-1732 CE). Lastly, the magnificent snow-covered peak of Mount Demavand, which figures in many national legends, graces the backs of still other bills.

During the reign of Reza Shah, modern buildings and public works projects such as the Trans-Iranian railway, the port of Bandar-e Pahlavi, and the National Bank building were also used to decorate banknotes. During the reign of his son, Muhammad Reza, the use of modern motifs increased. The most striking designs used in this era feature the huge Karaj Dam, Tehran's Mehrabad Airport, the oil refinery at Abadan, and the triumphal Shahyad Gate. This gate at the approach to Tehran was built as part of the celebrations for the 2,500th anniversary of the founding of the Persian Empire by Cyrus the Great.

The decorative filigree used on Pahlavi banknotes draws its inspiration from Iran's pre-Islamic arts. The graceful fluted columns, animal-shaped capitals, rows of ancient Persia's "Immortal Guards" standing at attention, and rosette ornaments

12.2

12.3

CENTRAL BANK OF
THE ISLAMIC REPUBLIC OF IRAN **100**

100   ONE HUNDRED RIALS

12.4

دانشجویان عزیز

شما بازو و نیروی عظیم اسلام هستید، بکوشید علی‌رغم همهٔ مشکلات موجود ندای آزادی بخش اسلام را بگوش محرومین جهان برسانید .

(آیت ا... منتظری)

ایها الطلبه الاعزاء انتم قوة الاسلام و زراعه حاولوا ـ رغم کل الصعاب ـ علی ایصال نداء الاسلام المحرری الی کافة الشعوب المستضعفة فی العالم.

آیت ا... منتظری

Beloved Students,
You are the strong
arm and the great
power of Islam.
Struggle inspite of the existing problems. Take the liberation cry of Islam to the ears
of the deprived people of the world. (Ayatollah Montazeri)

12.6

from the friezes of Persepolis are all used to provide a decorative border. For the series first issued in 1971, and used until the Revolution, the filigree is based on masterpieces of the Iranian arabesque decorative tradition. This series also features an enlarged portrait of Muhammad Reza with a relaxed, though assertive and confident, look. This last series of Muhammad Reza Pahlavi bank-notes is very refined and artistically appealing.[4] [Fig. 12.1]

After the Revolution, the currency of the Pahlavi regime had to remain in use until it could be replaced with new coins and notes.

Obliterating the portrait of the Shah on postage stamps and using up the old stocks was not a very difficult operation.[5] But far more work was required to remove the image of the Shah from banknotes. Not only did his regime's currency bear his portrait, it also carried a watermark of his profile. The old notes were modified in three stages. The first stage resulted in the obliteration of the portrait of the Shah, the second in the obliteration of both the portrait and the watermark, and in the third stage the Shah's portrait was replaced with a picture of the mausoleum of Imam Reza in Mashhad and the watermark was covered on both sides with a dark colored seal. The seal bears the words "The Islamic Republic of Iran" in fine calligraphy.

As soon as the Central Bank of the Islamic Republic of Iran was ready to issue new banknotes, the authorities joined forces with graphic artists to make certain that the notes would carry the message of the new order. This passionate intensity directed toward reconstruction of monetary identity, a cornerstone of ideological identity, is almost unique in modern history. The only comparable change of a nation's currency was during the de-Nazification of Germany by the victorious Allies after the Second World War. "Nowhere in the Arab world," it has been observed, "have the last six decades produced a phenomenon like that which occurred in revolutionary Iran, where the whole pre-Islamic past, so vaunted under the Shah, suddenly disappeared from postal and monetary iconography."[6] Each banknote of the Islamic Republic utilizes the symbols of the new political mythology to carry messages on two interrelated levels. By utilizing depictions of events, persons, and places which are part of the official story of the Revolution, the banknotes serve to provide a narration of revolutionary history. These same images are also powerful reminders of the religious nature of the regime.

In order to see the new regime's movement away from the shahs' glorification of the pre-Islamic past and pro-Western ideology and towards an emphasis upon traditional Islamic attitudes and sensibilities, let us compare a 100 rial banknote issued by the monarchy with a note of the same denomination issued by the Islamic Republic. The last banknote of the Pahlavi regime was issued in 1976 on the occasion of the Golden Jubilee of the dynasty. The 100 rial note was as common in Iran during the late 1970s as the $1 bill in the contemporary United States. Portraits of

both Pahlavi rulers, father and son, appear on this banknote. Reza Shah, the founder of the dynasty, appears in three-quarters profile behind the portrait of his son, Muhammad Reza. The modern building of the Bank-e Melli, the National Bank of Iran, is in the middle foreground, to the left of the portraits. The cornerstone of this bank was laid by Reza Shah himself in 1934. The style of its architecture is neo-Achaemenid, with a massive stairway leading to a gateway supported by columns and flanked by pylons. The stairs

are flanked by lions while the pylons are guarded by "Immortal Guards" copied from the friezes of Persepolis. The columns are modeled like those of the Apadana Hall of Persepolis, with lotus-shaped bases and capitals in the shape of heraldic animals. Above the gate hovers the Furuhar. The window frames and the roof parapet are modeled like those found

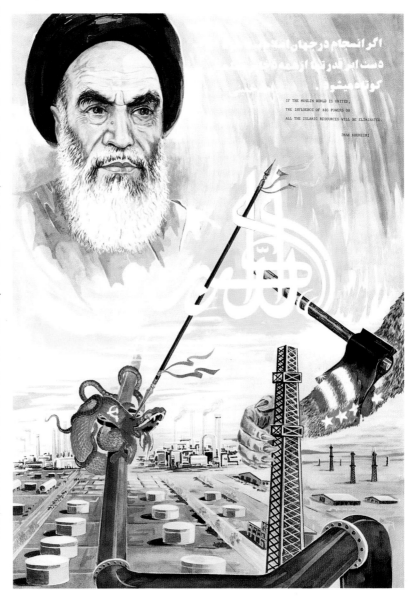

12.5 A poster illustrating the slogan "Neither East (the communist block) nor West (the capitalist western block)

جمهوری اسلامی ایران

٦٩/٢١ ٤١٧٧٢٩

٥٠٠ پانصد ریال

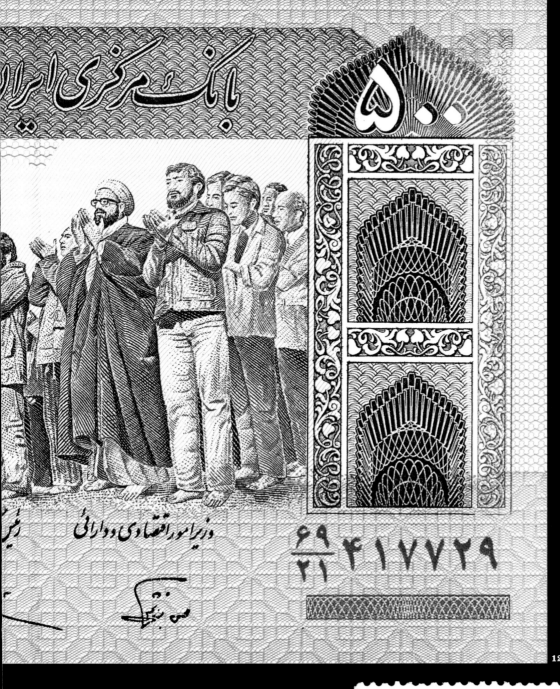

بانک مرکزی ایران

۵۰۰

وزیر امور اقتصادی و دارائی

رئیس

۶۹
۲۱

۴۱۷۷۲۹

12.7

3R. R.I.IRAN ۳ریال

12.8

12.10

at Persepolis. Muhammad Reza Shah's profile is visible in the watermark. The collective effect of the three figures, two kings and the monumental surrogate of the archetypal King Cyrus, is to demonstrate the continuity of the royal line in Iran. These images convey the message that there is a direct and recognizable line of descent from Cyrus the Great to Reza Shah the Great to Muhammad Reza Shah, "Sun of the Aryan Race." The modernity of the bank building, despite its archaic architectural quotations, suggests that, as a line in the monarchical national anthem states, "With the Pahlavis, the Iranian land became a hundred times better than it was in ancient times." [Fig.12.2]

On the reverse of the 100 rial note is the Pahlavi crown centered against a background of royal blue. The crown is

The 100 rial note issued by the Central Bank of the Islamic Republic of Iran can serve as a symbolic monument to the political changes brought about by the Revolution. This note was printed in the same lavender color and is almost the same size as the Pahlavi note it replaced. The portraits of the two clean-shaven Pahlavi monarchs are replaced by a bust of the formidably bearded Ayatollah Modarres.[8] He is shown in traditional Shi'i dress and wearing a turban. Beneath his bust are inscribed his name and his famous statement, "Our religion is our politics; our politics is our religion." This motto is the ideological foundation of the Islamic Republic. As Modarres stated and Khomeini demonstrated, there is no separation of religion and politics. The appearance of that statement on the banknote is the semiotic celebration of the

12.11

surrounded by two circles of twenty-five dots each.[7] The total of fifty dots is representative of the fifty years of Pahlavi rule. The bold inscription "The Fiftieth Year of the Pahlavi Reign" and the date of 2535 link the rule of the Pahlavis to that of Cyrus the Great, founder of the Iranian Empire. Shi'i clerics objected to this innovation in dating, since they reckon the year by counting from the date of the Prophet's migration (Hijra) from Mecca to Medina in 622 CE. The Muslim calendar computes time for religious purposes by the movement of the moon around the earth. For secular purposes, time may be computed on a solar basis as long as the year one corresponds to 622 CE. Any other means of reckoning time would be considered deviant by the Shi'i clerics. It is important to note that the dating of Iranian banknotes has been very erratic, with most lacking a date altogether. Only coins are usually dated.

victory of one brand of Islamic ideology over all other ideologies, especially that of the clerics who sought to establish a separation of religion and politics. [Fig. 12.3]

The victorious ideology is typified by the career of Ayatollah Sayyid Hasan Modarres. In matters of foreign policy, he was an advocate of the "neutral balance" between the Soviet Union and Great Britain.[9] This same policy is endorsed by the Islamic Republic in the slogan, "Neither East nor West, but the Islamic Government." [Fig. 12.5] On the reverse of the note is a picture of what was formerly the building used by the Iranian Senate, which is now the seat of the Islamic Consultative Assembly. The symbolic implications of the iconography are clear. Modarres has removed the Pahlavi shahs, one of whom was responsible for removing him from Parliament, which has itself been transformed into an Islamic Assembly.

While the symbols of the Islamic Republic's 100 rial banknote are almost completely Islamicized, one image remains from the vocabulary of the Pahlavi regime. At the front of the building are two columns in the form of chains. These chains represent the legendary chain strung from the throne room to the bazaar by the Shah Anushiravan, a Sasanid, for the purpose of allowing any subject with a grievance to alert the king by simply pulling on the chain. This "Chain of Justice" is central to the iconography of the Persian monarchy. Its symbolic presence in the design of the Senate building emphasizes that the Senate acts as a link between the monarch and his people, thus ensuring just rule. The point made by the transformation of the monarchist Senate into the Islamic Consultative Assembly is unaffected by the presence of this architectural quotation, so the particular reference to the monarchical past is ignored. [Fig. 12.4]

The watermark appearing on the new 100 rial note is a calligraphic arrangement of the words *la ilaha illa Allah* (There is no god but God) in the shape of a tulip, an Iranian symbol for love and sacrifice. The calligraphic tulip is an official emblem of the Islamic Republic of Iran, and all banknotes in the first series issued by the Islamic Republic have this symbol as their watermark.[10] The watermark on the 100 rial note is framed by the contours of a *mihrab*, which is the part of a mosque used to show the direction of Mecca.

In the medieval Islamic state, there were two major indicators of where power lay. A coin was struck in the name of the ruler so that all might see it. More significant was the inclusion of the ruler's name in the *khutbeh* during the Friday congregational prayer. From the early history of Islam, rulers or their representatives have often acted as *khatib*, spokesmen/preachers at the Friday prayers and on other major religious occasions. By means of the *khatib's* address at congregational prayers, important announcements are made, orders given, and official views on politics and issues of general interest disseminated. Bitter and violent criticism, sometimes even cursing, of enemies can be a part of the *khutbeh*. The Pahlavi monarchs did not make effective use of this tradition, relying instead on modern media to communicate with the general population. Ayatollah Khomeini, unlike the Pahlavis, used the *khutbeh* with great skill. This practice has been continued by the government of the Islamic Republic. Khomeini knew and appreciated the importance of orality in Iranian rhetorical culture. A network of mosques used *khutbeh* as a powerful supplement to the modern media during the Revolution. Khomeini was equally skillful in his use of modern media. It may almost be said that the final phases of the Revolution were directed by means of international telephone links and prerecorded cassettes of sermons that were played during the Friday prayers. In the Islamic Republic of Iran, traditional and modern means of communication are complementary.

Soon after his return to Iran, Ayatollah Khomeini called for the reinstitution of the *khutbeh* at Friday prayers and urged the faithful to attend. Though radio, television, and newspapers are mouthpieces for the Islamic government, important political announcements and condemnations are made at Friday congregational prayers throughout the country. This practice makes regional prayer-leaders more powerful than regional governors. The huge grounds of Tehran University have become the primary location for the government-sponsored Friday prayers. It was there on the first Friday of Ramadan in 1979 that the gifted orator Ayatollah Taleqani told the congregation that it was the Prophet Muhammad's intention that the Friday congregational prayers should be devoted to both worship and politics. Every Friday free buses bring thousands to the grounds of Tehran University.[11] Together they can pray, hear important speeches, and be mobilized. [Fig. 12.6]

The importance and excitement of the Friday prayers are effectively translated into imagery on banknotes. The 500 rial note portrays the leader of the congregation standing in front of rows of people of all ages and classes, as indicated by their apparel. One very revealing detail is a man of Turkoman appearance, whose hands are folded in the manner typical of Sunni, rather than Shi'i, prayer. This appearance of this man emphasizes that the universality of Friday prayer extends across sectarian lines.[12] Tribesmen are depicted standing among villagers, city-dwellers, military personnel, and clerics. Below the prayer rug of the leader is a caption in Persian: "Friday Prayer." On the lower left corner of the note is a picture of the famous theological seminary at Qom, where Khomeini once taught. Above it, contained by the outline of an arch, is the watermark. Depicted on the reverse is the main gate of Tehran University, which has been witness to many bloody encounters during the Revolution and now sees thousands pass through it every Friday on their way to the congregational prayers. [Fig. 12.7]

Ever since the French Revolution of 1789, a common image of "revolution" in the Western mind has been of a makeshift barricade behind which insufficiently armed citizens hide from the well-equipped forces of oppression. Similarly, the visual image of the Iranian Revolution of 1978-9 is of a massive column of people moving through a town. Thousands of marchers in formation hold their clenched fists above their heads, shout, and carry banners with religious and political slogans. This image, a reflection of the Muharram processions, dates back to at least the sixteenth century in Iran. by that time Shi'i Islam had become the state religion. The many symbolic props associated with the Muharram processions remind the people of suffering, injustice, sacrifice, and a determination to fight to the end. As Elias Canetti has noted, the Shi'i mourning procession "manifests itself with unforgettable power" and "the pain which the participants inflict on themselves is the pain of Hussein, which by being exhibited, becomes the pain of the whole community."[13]

In addition to self-mortification, the demonstrators move around town in columns, singing the praises of Imam Hussein and his companions and cursing the enemies of Hussein and his father

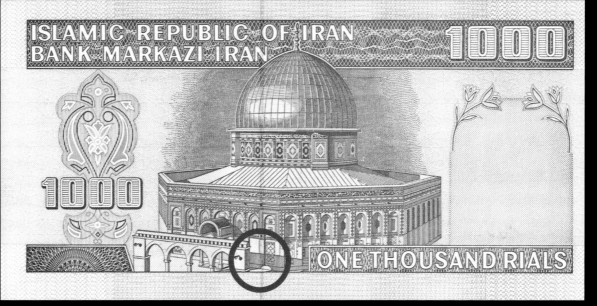

ISLAMIC REPUBLIC OF IRAN
BANK MARKAZI IRAN
1000

1000

ONE THOUSAND RIALS

12.12

...AMIC REPUBLIC OF IRAN
...NK MARKAZI IRAN
100

000

مسجد الاقصى ONE THOUSAND RIA...

and well-disciplined crowds shout religious and political slogans to prepare themselves for a sacrifice—even for death. A pictorial representation of such a procession appears on the 5,000 rial note. It depicts the revolutionary version of the traditional Muharram procession. The revolutionaries, with raised hands clenched into fists, stretch back towards the horizon. The front of the column is marching into the warm rays of a symbolic sun. The overall form of the column, curving back and forth as it narrows towards the horizon, is reminiscent of a standard depiction of a tree in traditional Iranian arts. This standard tree form is a symbolic reference to paradise in both the Iranian graphic tradition and the Chinese tradition, from which it is borrowed. People in all walks of life, both men and veiled women, are led by clerics holding portraits of Khomeini. They also hold up banners which read "Independence, Freedom, Islamic Republic" and "We are all your soldiers, O Khomeini." Such banners were in fact carried by demonstrators during the Islamic Revolution who pledged themselves body and soul to Khomeini. This graphic story on a banknote acknowledges the leadership of Khomeini, who inspired Iranian crowds during the Revolution and who then led them in the bloody war against Iraq. Equally prominent in the front row are clerics, who are represented as the leaders of the revolutionary procession. This is an appropri-

Ali. They may also curse those who oppose the "just" rule of the community's contemporary leadership. They also praise their leaders and extol their virtues. The Muharram processions served as a prototype for the massive revolutionary marches in Tehran and other Iranian towns during the Islamic Revolution. The logistics and passion of the Muharram processions were transformed into well-organized revolutionary marching columns.[14] The network of mosques, *husseiniyyeh*, and *tekiyeh* (places for stationary Hussein rituals) were converted from traditional assembly places into grounds for political rallies. After being religiously and politically stimulated, highly motivated crowds stream out from their places of assembly to join the groups moving out from other sites around the town to form a tightly knit river of humanity flowing through the main artery of the town. Emotionally charged, extremely vocal,

ation of revolutionary leadership by the clerical class, denying any other (secular) group a share of the glory. Most men in the procession are without neckties and the women are all wearing the *chador* (veil). This represents the Islamic nature of the revolutionaries. The poster with Khomeini's image and the revolutionary slogans are level with the signatures of the Minister of Finance and the Director of the Central Bank, each of these elements making the new revolutionary currency real and legitimate. [Fig. 12.8]

The signature of the "Minister of Economic and Financial Affairs," as the full title indicates, is yet another symbol of the monarchical period which has found its way into the Islamic state unnoticed. The word for "minister" in Persian, *vazir*, has a profound and irrevocable monarchical connotation. A *vazir* is a high-ranking official in the service of the shah. In effect, there is no *vazir* without

204

a shah. With the abolition of the monarchy, what could "Vazir of Economic and Financial Affairs" possibly mean? However, it can be argued that the term is so ingrained in Iranian political culture that no revolution can strip it of its meaning. Unlike the banknotes of the pre-revolutionary period, a portrait of the current ruler never

12.15

appears directly on the notes of the Islamic Republic.[15] This is a clever manipulation of symbolism, suggesting that Ayatollah Khomeini is not being imposed as a ruler but is the "chosen" representative of the people, who, out of love and devotion, are carrying his portrait. The way in which Khomeini's portrait is introduced into the currency by means of an illustration within an illustration shifts the ideological basis for his legitimacy away from one imposed by the state to one emerging from the devotion of the masses.

On the reverse of the 5,000 rial note, there is a picture of the shrine/mosque of Qom. The shrine is the tomb of the sister of the eighth Shiʿi Imam, Ali Reza. Qom is the most important center of religious learning in Iran. The main Shiʿi pilgrimage site in Iran, the shrine of Imam Ali Reza, is depicted on the reverse of the 10,000 rial note (and the 100 rial coin). On the front of the 10,000 rial note is a depiction of the revolutionary marchers almost identical to that on the 5,000 rial note. The only difference between the fronts of the two notes is color. The 5,000 rial note is cranberry red and the 10,000 rial note is grey-blue. It is rather unusual to have the same graphic design on banknotes of different

denominations. The mass marches depicted on the banknotes were weekly events in the Islamic Republic of Iran until the end of the Iraq–Iran war. They were intended to rally the people behind Khomeini and his successors in the struggle against internal and external enemies. The banknotes are the graphic representation of Khomeini's *Weltanschauung*. [Fig. 12.9]

The portrait of Ayatollah Khomeini also appears within the illustration on the 2,000 rial note. This bill commemorates the liberation of the Persian Gulf port city of Khorramshahr by Iranian troops. The figures in the illustration represent the three main branches of the Iranian armed forces: the Pasdaran-e Enqelab (Revolutionary Guards), Basij (Volunteers of the Mobilization Forces), and the Regulars. A portrait of Khomeini is held in front of the fighters, who are recognizable from their uniforms. One young man in the scene, a member of the Basij, is wearing a headband with the motto, written in red, "O Hussein," thus invoking the name of the "Prince of Martyrs." From those portions of the texts which appear on partially obscured banners, it can be deduced that the banners are in Arabic and therefore likely to be of a religious nature. [Fig. 12.10] In the background of the illustration is the battered Mosque of Khorramshahr. The flag of the Islamic Republic of Iran is flying from the left minaret. From the mosque's roof parapet hangs a banner on which are written the words: "At the dawn of victory we regret the absence of the martyrs." At the time, the crushing defeat of Iraqi forces in the battle of Khorramshahr (21-4 May 1982) looked like the dawn of a total victory in the then twenty-month-old war. Today, we know that was not to be the case. The recapture of Khorramshahr, however, erased from the Iranian forces the stigma of the loss of that important city to the Iraqis. The liberation of the city marked the transition of the Iranian forces from a defensive to an offensive posture. The victory was celebrated with festivities all over Iran. A special postage stamp was issued to honor the occasion. The illustration of this victory on the 2,000 rial note makes clear to the observer that the war is a holy war. The holiness of the war, officially called the "Sacred Defense," is further emphasized by the drawing on the back of the banknote, which depicts the Kaʿbah in Mecca, the holiest site in Islam and the focus of the *hajj*. [12.11] The Kaʿbah is the subject of many graphic designs

12.14

on both stamps and posters issued for the celebration of the annual "Week of Islamic Unity,"[16] the celebration of which is concurrent with the birthday of the Prophet Muhammad. The indirect message of these designs is that the Islamic Republic of Iran is a unifying force for all Muslims, regardless of sectarian differences.

The third most important site in Islam, after Mecca and Medina, is Jerusalem. According to a famous traditionalist, al-Zuhri, the Prophet Muhammad regarded all three as sites of equal importance for pilgrimage. Until the middle of the second year of the Hijra, the Prophet and his companions prayed towards Jerusalem. It was only then that the Prophet changed the direction of prayer towards the Kaʿbah in Mecca. Jerusalem has remained a sacred city for Muslims and is associated with the Prophet's miraculous night journey, the Isra, and his ascent to heaven, the

Day." After the 1967 Arab-Israel War, the Dome of the Rock became a symbol of the unified effort by the Muslims to liberate Jerusalem. Since 1979, stamps and posters have been printed for the occasion of Jerusalem Day on an annual basis. Most of these feature the Dome of the Rock as a centerpiece. Even a banknote featuring the Dome of the Rock has been issued. However, the first series with the image of the Dome had to be recalled, since the engraver mistakenly labeled it the "Mosque of al-Aqsa." The 1,000 rial notes now in circulation have had the erroneous label removed, but the label has not been replaced with a new, corrected caption. [Figs. 12.12] The Dome of the Rock also appears on a special minting of the 1 rial coin. This coin was struck in a yellow metal so as to resemble gold, and was issued one year after Khomeini proclaimed the observance of Jerusalem Day. Around the Dome is written the slogan, "On the

12.17

Miʿraj. "Glory to Him who caused his servant to journey by night from the sacred places of worship [Masjid al-Haram in Mecca] to the further place of place [Masjid al-Aqsa in Jerusalem], which We have encircled with blessings, in order that We might show him some of Our signs."[17] In Jerusalem there are two famous Muslim edifices: the shrine of the Dome of the Rock, built by the Caliph Abd al-Malik in the year 72 of the Islamic calendar (691 CE), and, next to it, the al-Aqsa Mosque, built by the Caliph Walid I in 96 AH (715 CE). It would be difficult to say which of the two is the more important. However, the Dome of the Rock is considered the oldest example of Muslim architecture. Its octagonal shape makes it an easily recognizable structure. When during the month of Ramadan in 1979 Khomeini asked the preachers at the Friday prayers to emphasize unity among Muslims, the last Friday in Ramadan was declared to be "Jerusalem

12.16 One of the many posters dedicated to the "Liberation of Palestine."

occasion of World Jerusalem Day, Blessed Ramadan 1400 AH." On the other side of the coin, under the number 1, are the Arabic words Yaum al-Quds (Jerusalem Day). The rare use of Arabic on a contemporary Iranian coin underlines the Islamic nature of the symbolism. To emphasize the necessity of devotion and sacrifice for the sake of Jerusalem, the edge of the coin is milled with symbolic tulips. [Figs. 12.14 and 12.15]

On the back of the 1,000 rial note is a picture of the Madrasseh Fayziyyeh in Qom. This famous madrasseh (seminary), the pride of Qom, the center of religious learning, is located in one of the four courtyards of the shrine of Fatemeh, sister of the Imam Ali Reza. (It is the tomb of Fatemeh which appears on the back of the 5,000 rial note.) For the past five decades the Madrasseh Fayziyyeh has been linked to the name of the Ayatollah Khomeini. It was there that Khomeini delivered a series of anti-Shah and anti-American sermons which precipitated the 15th of Khordad (5 June) uprising in 1963. That uprising is regarded by the leadership of the Islamic

Republic as the beginning of the revolutionary movement. Graphic representations of the uprising are usually centered on the Fayziyyeh building. Sometimes the sun, in the shape of the emblem of the Islamic Republic, is shown rising behind the building. In other drawings, the courtyard of the Madrasseh is shown as a river of blood, [12.17] or, as on the banknote, the image of the building alone is enough to convey the symbolic reference. The 1,000 rial note is remarkable as it is the only banknote with edifices on both sides. Usually one side, the front, depicts a human story while the back is given over to the picture of a building. [Fig. 12.18] The uncommon design of the 1,000 rial note has been brought into line with the general principles of design of the Islamic Republic's currency. The second series issued after the death of Ayatollah Khomeini bears his portrait on the front, replacing the picture of the Fayziyyeh Madrasseh.[18] The new design of the 1,000 rial note is ingenious. Replacing the Fayziyyeh Madrasseh with a portrait of Khomeini suggests, in the language of symbols, that the Ayatollah has come out of his college and into full view on the surface of the note. The majestic portrait of the Ayatollah inspires awe in its simple grandeur. The proportions of his turbaned and bearded head are perfect. His sparkling eyes are situated equidistant from the top of his turban to the bottom of his beard. They are also in the center of a sun-like disk, which consists of glowing rays emanating from his head. The border design on the front and the picture of the Dome of the Rock remain as on previous issues. In this fashion, the link between Khomeini and the liberation of Jerusalem is made even more explicit. [Figs. 12.19]

In addition to the 1,000 rial note, the banknotes that have

been redesigned in the years following the death of Ayatollah Khomeini include the 5,000 and 10,000 rial notes. The 10,000 rial note is completely changed. It is a cheerful, modernist arrangement; there is a portrait of Khomeini to the right of center; a traditional decorative design of flowers, foliage, and geometric patterns in predominantly blue and green tones balances the front of the bill. No doubt the designer had in mind the symbolic meaning of green in Islamic culture: it is both the color of paradise and of the Prophet Muhammad's family. The portrait of Ayatollah Khomeini is identical to the one appearing on the new 1,000 rial bill. The color of the portrait is different, and instead of being shown against a sun-like disk, his head is partially surrounded by radiating semicircles, alternately blue and pale gold, forming a halo. It seems as if the poster of Khomeini carried by the marchers on previous issues has been brought to the foreground and the image of the Ayatollah alone is enough to deliver the message of the revolutionary struggle. Like the Shah's portrait on the 1971 series of banknotes, the portrait of Khomeini conveys a sense of confidence, strength, hope, and tranquility. The watermark is a replica of the portrait. On the back of the new 10,000 rial bill is a picture of Mount Demavand. Its even, conical slopes and snow-covered heights graced many Iranian banknotes of the pre-revolutionary era. Demavand is connected to many Iranian myths and legends. It has been celebrated by poets, miniature painters, and carpet-weavers; it even plays a part in the national epic, the *Shahnameh*. By associating the portrait of Khomeini with the image of Demavand, the designers of the banknotes have placed him in the succession of national heroes who have preserved Iran in times of need. [Fig. 12.20 and 12.21]

The redesigned 5,000 rial notes have almost the same design on the front as the new 10,000 rial notes, differing only in color and the details of the filigree. This is in keeping with the identical images appearing on the front of the earlier 5,000 and 10,000 rial notes. On the back of the new 5,000 rial bill is the soothing image of a pair of birds nestled amongst flowers and foliage. Both birds are gazing upon a radiant sun-like design which forms a halo on the other side. The tranquility of this image implies that the Islamic Republic is bringing about a similar contentment in Iranian society, a new national sentiment and a looking forward to renewed prosperity resulting from the effort to

12.18

12.19

12.20

rebuild after the devastating war with Iraq. The less strident tone of the new issues portrays the Revolution as a *fait accompli* and signifies the increased confidence of the political regime in its own permanence.

The 200 rial note is another example of how there are no fixed rules in the design of Iranian currency, as long as the banknotes convey an effective message. On the 200 rial note the building appears on the front and the human story on the back. The front of the bill has a picture of the Friday Mosque in Yazd. The back of the bill illustrates the Jihad-e Sazendegi (Jihad for Construction). This Jihad recruited volunteers from all walks of life to improve the well-being of the residents of small towns and villages throughout Iran. It was initiated by Khomeini on 19 June 1979. Now the Jihad is a government ministry and its activities have expanded beyond its original goals. During the war with Iraq, the Jihad was responsible for building defensive fortifications, even on the front itself. Many of those who took part in the Jihad building trenches and bunkers died under enemy fire. The organization does not differ greatly from the many volunteer corps established by the Shah. It is the Islamic ideology of the Jihad that sets it apart from the programs instituted by the Shah, whose White Revolution Corps were also honored on a banknote. The 100 rial note issued in 1971 shows members of the Literacy, Rural Development, and Public Health Corps. On the 50 rial note issued in the same year, the Shah himself is shown handing out land deeds to farmers as part of his land reforms.

On the current 200 rial note, above the sign "Jihad-e Sazendegi," we see men with shovels building a gravel road across barren terrain. A tractor with a driver is standing next to the workers, while in the background there is a village at the foot of some gently rolling hills. The Mosque of Yazd is on the reverse of the note. Yazd is situated on the edge of the Great Desert, and is surrounded by villages whose inhabitants are remarkable for their survival in the harshest of natural environments. The image of this mosque emphasizes the Islamic dimension of the Jihad-e Sazendegi and its concern with the population in remote areas of the country. This is the same population that provided the majority of the forces

used as cannon fodder during the war with Iraq.

In addition to their function as currency, the banknotes of the Islamic Republic of Iran are a means of demonstrating that Islam dominates the economy just as it dominates the political life of the nation. The imagery of the banknotes is a daily reminder to the general public of the pre-eminent role played by Islam in all walks of life. Ayatollah Modarres' famous statement, "Our religion is our politics; our politics is our religion," is quoted only once on the banknotes, but it is implicit in all the currency issued by the Islamic Republic of Iran. Banknotes are used daily for commercial transactions. They travel thousands of miles into the remotest parts of the country. As instruments of ideological persuasion, they are the cheapest and most effective mechanism for convincing the general public as to who is in charge. The ideological opponents of the Islamic Republic may say whatever they want about the (il)legitimacy of the government, but as soon as they reach into their pockets to pay for a piece of bread, at the moment the bread is in one hand and their change is in the other, they have accepted the legitimacy of the *status quo*.[19]

---

1 An earlier version of this chapter first appeared as "Khomeini's Iran as Seen through Bank Notes," in David Menashri (ed.), The Iranian Revolution and the Muslim World (Boulder, Colo., 1990), pp. 85-101. 2 Emmanuel Sivan, "The Arab Nation-State: In Search of a Usable Past," Middle East Review, Spring 1987, p. 21. 3 As a general rule, the obverse of a banknote is inscribed in Persian and the reverse in a Latin transliteration. There are exceptions to this rule. Banknotes issued during the reign of Reza Shah in 1933 and 1936 were inscribed in Persian only, as were those issued by Muhammad Reza in 1945 and 1947. Furthermore, the 1938 series is inscribed in French on the reverse. The Islamic Republic, despite its explicit hostility towards the West, uses English on the reverse, that is to say, "Five Hundred Rials" or "Ten Thousand Rials" is spelled out in English. On some banknotes Bank-e Markazi, instead of being transliterated, is translated to "Central Bank of the

210

CENTRAL BANK OF
THE ISLAMIC REPUBLIC OF IRAN
TEN THOUSAND RIALS

10000

10000

12.21

ISLAMIC REPUBLIC OF IRAN." **4** SEE MAJMU'E-YE ESKENASHA-YE MONTASHER SHODEH DAR DOWRAN-E PANJAH SALE-YE SHAHANSHAHI-YE DUDEMAN-E PAHLAVI (TEHRAN: BANK-E MELLI PRESS, 1976). **5** SEE PETER CHELKOWSKI, "STAMPS OF BLOOD," AMERICAN PHILATELIST 101, NO. 6 (JUNE 1987), P. 556. **6** SIVAN, "THE ARAB NATION-STATE," P. 23. **7** THIS DESIGN SERVED AS THE OFFICIAL INSIGNIA OF THE GOLDEN JUBILEE AND WAS WORN ON LAPELS, PRINTED ON BOOKS AND POSTERS, DISPLAYED ON BUILDING FACADES, AND EVEN MADE INTO A GIANT NEON SIGN. **8** BORN NEAR ISFAHAN IN 1871, MODARRES BECAME FAMOUS AS AN ISLAMIC SCHOLAR, TEACHER, PREACHER, AND POLITICIAN. REGULARLY RE-ELECTED TO PARLIAMENT (MAJLES), HE WAS A CHARISMATIC LEADER OF THE OPPOSITION TO REZA SHAH. IN 1927 REZA SHAH BLOCKED MODARRES' RE-ELECTION TO PARLIAMENT AND SENT HIM INTO INTERNAL EXILE IN THE EASTERN PROVINCE OF KHORASSAN, WHERE MODARRES DIED NINE YEARS LATER UNDER SUSPICIOUS CIRCUMSTANCES. **9** THROUGHOUT THE NINETEENTH AND EARLY TWENTIETH CENTURIES, IRAN WAS SANDWICHED BETWEEN TWO COLONIAL SUPERPOWERS: RUSSIA (LATER THE SOVIET UNION) AND GREAT BRITAIN. THIS HISTORY PROVIDES A RICH SOURCE FOR SYMBOLIC COMPARISON TO THE REVOLUTIONARY GOVERNMENT'S PERCEPTION OF ITS OWN POSITION BETWEEN THE EQUALLY HOSTILE UNITED STATES AND SOVIET UNION. **10** ON LATER SERIES THE WATERMARK WAS CHANGED. MONEY IS OFTEN CARRIED IN PEOPLE'S POCKETS, WHICH COULD LEAD TO ACCIDENTAL ACTS OF IRREVERENCE, SO THE TULIP EMBLEM WAS REPLACED WITH A PORTRAIT OF HUSSEIN FAHMIDEH, THE 12-YEAR-OLD BOY WHO DIED WHILE DESTROYING AN IRAQI TANK. HE IS ALSO HONORED ON A DOUBLE POSTAGE STAMP. THE INAPPROPRIATE NATURE OF CURRENCY AS A PLACE TO DISPLAY THE NAME OF GOD IS FURTHER EMPHASIZED BY THE USE OF THREE DOTS TO COMPLETE THE TITLE "AYATO(LLAH)" IN THE CAPTION BELOW THE IMAGE OF MODARRES ON THE 100 RIAL NOTE. **11** TEHRAN UNIVERSITY WAS ESTABLISHED IN 1934. THE CAMPUS IS LAID OUT IN A U SHAPE, WITH BUILDINGS AROUND THE PERIMETER AND A LARGE OPEN CENTRAL SPACE. THIS CENTRAL AREA HAS BEEN USED FOR A VARIETY OF PURPOSES, FROM TENNIS AND SOCCER MATCHES TO POLITICAL RALLIES AND, AFTER THE REVOLUTION, FRIDAY PRAYERS. **12** AYATOLLAH KHOMEINI WAS VERY MUCH CONCERNED WITH THE IMAGE OF THE ISLAMIC REPUBLIC OF IRAN. HE WANTED IT TO BE AN EXAMPLE TO ALL MUSLIM COMMUNITIES, REGARDLESS OF SECTARIAN AFFILIATION. **13** ELIAS CANETTI, CROWDS AND POWER (NEW YORK, 1978), P. 150. **14** SEE PETER CHELKOWSKI, "IRAN: MOURNING BECOMES REVOLUTION," ASIA, MAY/JUNE 1980, PP. 30-45. **15** THE PORTRAIT OF KHOMEINI APPEARS ON POSTERS DEPICTED ON THE 5,000 AND 10,000 RIAL NOTES. SUCH POSTERS ARE SOMETIMES OF GIGANTIC SIZE AND ARE CARRIED IN MARCHES AND DISPLAYED ON THE WALLS OF TOWNS AND VILLAGES. SOMETIMES THESE PORTRAITS ARE PAINTED DIRECTLY ON WALLS, SUPPOSEDLY IN ACTS OF SPONTANEOUS DEVOTION BY THE PEOPLE. **16** AMONG THE SPECIAL ITEMS ISSUED FOR THE CELEBRATION OF ISLAMIC UNITY WEEK IS A REMARKABLE 10 RIAL COIN. UNLIKE OTHER IRANIAN COINS, WHICH ARE IN PERSIAN ONLY, THIS COIN HAS THE MOTTO "O MUSLIMS, UNITE! UNITE!" IN BOTH ENGLISH AND ARABIC. IT ENTERED INTO CIRCULATION SHORTLY BEFORE THE ANNUAL HAJJ, PROBABLY IN THE HOPE THAT IT WOULD BE CARRIED ABROAD BY IRANIAN PILGRIMS. **17** QUR'AN 17:1. **18** IN ORDER TO PROTECT THE IMAGE OF KHOMEINI FROM DESECRATION, THE NOTES WITH HIS IMAGE ARE DEEMED BY THE GOVERNMENT TO HAVE LOST THEIR VALUE, AND ARE LESS LIKELY TO BE ACCEPTED FOR FINANCIAL TRANSACTIONS, IF THEY ARE DAMAGED OR DEFACED IN ANY WAY. **19** IT IS INTERESTING THAT DESPITE THE EFFORTS OF THE NEW REGIME TO EFFACE ALL VESTIGES OF THE MONARCHY, THE VERY NAME OF THE CURRENCY, "RIAL," HAS ITS ROOT IN THE MONARCHICAL TRADITION. THE TERM "RIAL" IS LINKED TO THE ENGLISH WORD "ROYAL," AND IS DERIVED FROM THE NAME OF A SPANISH COIN OF THE FIFTEENTH CENTURY, THE REAL. THIS COIN WAS, FOR A TIME, THE PREFERRED MEANS OF PAYMENT IN NORTH AFRICA AND THE MIDDLE EAST AND GAVE ITS NAME TO THE CURRENCIES OF SEVERAL NATIONS.

SWIFT
COMPLETION
OF
APPOINTED
ROUNDS:

stamps with a revolutionary purpose

Thirteen

Neither snow nor rain nor heat nor gloom of night shall stay these couriers from the swift completion of their appointed rounds." These words, recorded by Herodotus, and carved in stone on the facade of the main post office in New York City, describe the world's first postal system, created by Iranian kings some twenty-five centuries ago. Today, the postage stamps of the Islamic Republic of Iran are attempting to project the concept that no vicissitudes shall stay the completion of the appointed rounds of the Islamic Revolution. This chapter is devoted to an examination of these revolutionary stamps.

13.1

Every political order has its own line to draw. In the Shah's day, stamps, like banknotes, exalted both the ancient pre-Islamic Iranian civilization and the latest modern achievements under the aegis of the Pahlavis. Like the banknotes, the graphics of the stamps concentrated on the breathtaking art and architecture of the Achaemenid and Sasanid dynasties. A profile or portrait of the monarch was almost always shown on the stamps, appropriating for the Shah all the glorified memory of a reconstructed past. After the Revolution, a number of these postage stamps remained in use, but the image of the Shah was crossed out and the words "Islamic Revolution" stamped across its entire surface. Similar techniques have been employed in other countries following a drastic change of regime. This allows the new government to use up old stocks while awaiting new issues and demonstrating a complete departure from the past. This departure is effectively represented by the superimposed signs of the new order, which triumphantly conceal and effectively deface aspects of the old order. The Pahlavis did the same thing when they overthrew their predecessors, the Qajars. Leftover Qajar stamps were used, but the portrait of the last Qajar monarch, Ahmad Shah, was crudely defaced. [Figs. 13.1 and 13.2]

The break with the *ancien régime* is perhaps better illustrated by a series of stamps devoted to the "forerunners" of the Islamic revolutionary movement. The depiction of these turbaned men illustrates the change of orientation from the Western apparel and ideology of the Shah's era to the traditionalist Islamic attitude of the Khomeini regime.[1] On the left side of each of these stamps is a picture of a minbar, demonstrating the Islamic orientation of the individual pictured.[2] [Fig. 13.3]

The more than 400 stamps issued by Iran since the Revolution are designed to convince her people that the Islamic Republic is here to stay and that the masses must be consolidated against internal and external enemies. To the rest of the world, these stamps bear the message that the Islamic Republic of Iran is the leader of a worldwide and resurgent Islam, unafraid of any threat, even from the superpowers. These stamps, the silent but evocative heralds of revolt, proclaim to the world the triumph of a revolution founded on faith and based on an unfailing and emphatic conviction regarding all moral and ideological commitments that matter to a resurrected political culture. By means of their illustrative and textual elements, these stamps express clear and symbolic themes. Most of them commemorate events such as the creation of the Islamic Republic of Iran; the uprising of 5 June 1963; Islamic Unity

214

13.2

day as "the victory of blood over the sword."[4] An allegorical representation of that pronouncement in the form of a sword being broken by a trickle of blood appears on a stamp issued in 1980 to celebrate the first anniversary of the Revolution. [Fig. 13.5] The stamp issued in 1981 for the Revolution's second anniversary shows a large red tulip surrounded by drops of blood. In the background is the date, "The 17th of Shahrivar." The blood on this stamp probably refers not only to the Revolution, but also to the bloody war with Iraq, in which Iran had already been engaged for almost a year. [Fig. 13.6]

Another commemorative stamp, issued in 1985, with Ayatollah Khomeini's pronouncement in Persian and English, shows red tulips growing out of a pool of blood on a green foreground. [13.7] The motif of red tulips is used frequently on the stamps of Iran. The tulip is indigenous to Iran and is often eulogized in Persian poetry, as a symbol of love and sacrifice. On a 1979 stamp the Islamic Republic is represented by a tulip emerging from a crowd of people. The leaves of the flower are green, the color of Islam, and are formed by a calligraphic pattern that spells out "The Islamic Republic"; the petals form the word "Allah." This directly links the political success of the Islamic Revolution to sacred certitude in the Muslim consciousness. [Fig. 13.8]

In the foreground of the "Seventh Anniversary of the Victory of the Revolution" stamp, a crowd pulls down the statue of a monarch on horseback. Above the crowd, the stems of seven red tulips spell out, in Arabic, "Verily we have granted thee a manifest victory,"

Week; the anniversary of the Prophet Muhammad's appointment to prophethood; the birthday of the Mahdi (Hidden Imam), which is called "The Universal Day of the Oppressed"; "Liberation of Jerusalem Day," also called the "Universal Day of Qods"; the annual week of mobilization for the war effort against Iraq; and the legacy of Ayatollah Khomeini.

The 8th of September (17th of Shahrivar) is central among the events and dates commemorated in the early days of the Islamic Republic. That day in 1978 represents what is considered to be the blood-birth of the Revolution. On that day, scores of demonstrators were killed by the Shah's troops in one of Tehran's main squares, an event which may be regarded as the point of no return for the revolutionary movement in Iran.[3] Among the first stamps issued by the Islamic Republic is one dedicated to the "martyrs" of 8 September 1978. It depicts a revolutionary crowd carrying a dead man aloft and holding a banner printed with the words "Independence, Freedom, Islamic Republic." The graphic style of the stamp is that of Socialist Realism, a clear Soviet influence. [Fig. 13.4] Ayatollah Khomeini described the events of that

13.3

13.6   13.7   13.8   13.9

This is a verse from the Qur'an (48:1). [Fig. 13.9] Arabic, the sacred tongue of Islam both spoken and in its calligraphy, had the sanctity and the power of holy writ for the revolutionary crowds, though the majority, like most Iranians, did not understand the language. By frequent use of Qur'anic quotations in Arabic, Khomeini's regime tried to depict itself as the vanguard of the Islamic world. With the passage of time, more and more Arabic inscriptions appeared on Iranian stamps, as well as on the banners carried by demonstrators in Iranian towns. This is of religio-political significance: while Iran was at war with an Arab country, it wanted to show the Arab world that the fight was not against Arabs per se, but against the "corrupt, irreligious" regime of the Iraqi Baʿath Party.

Ever since Hussein's tragic martyrdom at Karbala, the desire to avenge him and to spill blood for his holy cause has been omnipresent in the Shiʿi community. Every believing Shiʿite wants to identify with his suffering, passion, and martyrdom. This paradigm represents not only a personal commitment, but a communal one. It is as if the fighting men become Hussein and the youth become Ali Akbar and Qassem, Hussein's son and nephew respectively, who, according to tradition, fought gallantly and died at Karbala. It is believed that Hussein, the "Prince of Martyrs," will act

as an intercessor on the Day of Judgment and usher into paradise those who shed their blood and tears for him. In this ideological remembrance of the past is the central theme of the Revolution. Khomeini succeeded largely because he was able to convert popular beliefs and Karbala rituals into mass mobilization. During the eight years of bloody war with Iraq, these ideas were used to encourage men and boys to go to the front and to soothe the families of the maimed or killed. This mechanism was effective in maintaining the momentum of the war as "holy sacrifice and martyrdom." The repeated Iranian offensives were called Karbala I, Karbala II, and so on, reminding the warriors what they were fighting for.

According to tradition, the tragedy at Karbala involved not only Hussein, but his relatives, children, and companions—seventy-two persons in all. Hussein's womenfolk were also present during the slaughter, and many contemporary Iranian women identify with Zeynab, Hussein's sister. During the war they were all Zeynabs, bereaved and heartbroken. During this period, the birthday of Zeynab was commemorated as "Nurse's Day" (*sic*) and stamps were issued to honor those who cared for the wounded soldiers. [Fig. 13.10] Women appear on very few Iranian stamps, but the annual issue in honor of "Woman's Day" (*sic*) is an exception to the

13.13

پُست جمهوری اسلامی ایران

حجاب

20 R. R.I.IRAN ریال ۲۰

13.12

13.14

one in the crowd, the men and women of Iran alike, could liberate themselves from the burdens of war, curse the enemy, and share their personal griefs. Further through identification with the women of Karbala, the women in the marches became an "orchestra of grief" in public, leading to catharsis, which in turn eased their individual sorrows.[5]

A good illustration of this is a poster which was inspired by rule. Celebrated on the birthday of Fatemeh Zahra, daughter of the Prophet Muhammad, wife of Ali, and mother of Hussein, "Woman's Day" honors the chastity and endurance of women. [Fig. 13.11]

During the war against Iraqi aggression, the participation of women in street rallies and marches, while organized, was genuinely spontaneous. Although the women did not mingle with the men, the discharge of the crowd was so intense that they fell into step with them. According to Canetti, during a discharge, all distinction of class, upbringing, and gender are removed, and every-

a photograph of women taking part in a revolutionary march. It contains all the characteristics of the photograph of the crowd: density, energy, equality, and direction. The direction is indicated by the image of a militant woman dressed in blood-red, hovering above the marching crowd of women in their black *chador*. Her hand held high in exhortation, she seems to urge them onward. The palm of her hand almost touches another palm atop the flagstaff. That hand symbolically represents the severed hand of ʿAbbas, Imam Hussein's half-brother and standard-bearer. The outstretched fingers of the hand also stand for the five holy personalities among the Shiʿites. The unfurled flags in symbolic colors flying over the women add a dynamic forward thrust to the procession. On one of the green flags is written "O Zahra!" To emphasize the revolutionary spirit, a rifle barrel rises from the background, behind the shoulder of the hovering image. A portrait of Ayatollah Khomeini, based on a photograph, is carried by one of the *chador*-clad women. Khomeini appears with his hand raised high as well. Another woman carries a quotation from Khomeini, written in black on the white background: "A man ascends to heaven from his mother's lap." [Fig. 13.14]

These crowds of women dressed in *chador*, who have proved especially appealing to Western reporters, were also incorporated into a postage stamp. It kept the same design as the poster, but due to the scale of the stamp the rifle and the quotation from Khomeini were removed. The invocation on the flag, however, was expanded to read, "O Fatemeh Al-Zahra!" Another "Woman's Day" stamp depicts a woman holding a little boy already designated as a future martyr: he wears a red headband and is wrapped in a white shroud. [Fig. 13.12] A stamp entitled *Hejab*, which means "veil" in Persian, shows a veiled woman with a rifle over her shoulder. This stamp shows that the veil does not hamper a woman's activities, it only emphasizes her chastity. [Fig. 13.13]

13.15

The official cause of the Iraq–Iran war, started by Iraq on 22 September 1980, was a border dispute. This dispute was similar to the German claim on Gdansk (Danzig), which was the basis of Hitler's excuse to invade Poland in 1939. The actual origins of the war lay in the Ba'athist's fear that the Iranian Revolution would spread to Iraq. Iraq has a Shi'i majority, and important Shi'i holy

Islamic imprint. One of the three categories of Iranian armed forces, the Volunteers, are represented on a 1983 stamp entitled "The Preparation Day." [Fig. 13.16] The volunteer forces, known as the "Mobilization of the Oppressed," were comprised mainly of teenagers and old men. They were the Shi'i equivalent of the Second World War kamikaze. They wore head-bands inscribed with slogans such as "God is Greatest" and "Revenge for the Blood of Hussein" and served as an advance guard, clearing minefields with their own bodies in anticipation of an immediate ascent to paradise. The Revolutionary Guards, the Pasdaran, would move in after the Volunteers. This corps was originally established as a "people's revolutionary militia." On the battlefield, in the initial phase of the war, they prepared the terrain for the regular armed forces. A brown stamp based on the Pasdaran logo shows a crowd overshadowed by a large assault rifle in the grasp of a giant hand. Above the rifle is a quotation from the Qur'an (8:60) in Arabic: "Against them make ready your strength to the utmost." [Fig. 13.17] A third stamp depicting the regular armed forces shows planes, warships, tanks, and artillery in the background. [Fig. 13.18] The regular forces represent the remnants of the once powerful imperial forces, the best trained and equipped in the region until the Khomeini regime executed or purged officers whose loyalty to the Islamic Republic was suspect. As the war progressed, the Pasdaran achieved the upper hand over the volunteers and the

218

regular army, which was left with few spare parts and little ammunition. A 1982 stamp "In Honor of the Sacrifices of Islamic Warriors against the Imposed War of Bath's [*sic*] Party" shows all three branches of the armed forces together. A hand in the foreground carries the green flag of Islam on which is

13.16   **13.18**

places such as Karbala and Najaf are located within its borders. Towards the end of 1970, the Iraqi Shi'ites were very active and vocal under the leadership of Ayatollah Muhammad Baqer Sadr. Friction between the Ba'athist government and Iraqi Shi'ites increased after the Ayatollah declared the Ba'athist regime to be "un-Islamic." Before Iraq invaded Iran, Muhammad Baqer Sadr, an old friend of Ayatollah Khomeini

13.20

13.17   **13.19**

and a noted Shi'i authority, was executed by the Iraqi regime together with his close companions. A stamp to honor his martyr-dom was issued by Iran in 1982. The *minbar* in the left foreground of the stamp is stained with blood. The implication is that those who committed that crime acted against Islam. [Fig. 13.15]

Stamps devoted to the Iranian fighting machine also carry an

IN HONOR OF THE SACRIFICES OF ISLAMIC WARRIORS AGAINST THE IMPOSED WAR OF BATH'S PARTY.

inscribed, "Help from God and Speedy Victory." [Fig. 13.19] This quotation, taken from the Qur'an (61:13), means: "However great the odds against us, we are sure of victory with God's help." This emphasizes the Islamic, rather than Iranian, nature of the war.[6]

A stamp issued in 1981, devoted to the martyrs of the war, portrays the dead minister of defense, Mustafa Ali Chamran, surrounded by a cloud of fire. In the background, men carry the bodies of martyrs wrapped in white shrouds. [Fig. 13.20] A double stamp issued in 1986 for the "Universal Day of the Child" portrays, on the right-hand stamp, a young boy and a pronouncement by Khomeini: "Our guide is that boy of 12 years of age. The value of his little heart is greater than could be described by hundreds of tongues and hundreds of pens. He threw himself with a grenade under an enemy tank and destroyed it. [In doing so] he drank the sweet elixir of martyrdom." On the left-hand stamp is a graphic illustration of this event, drawn by a child. It depicts the martyred boy lying prone, prior to throwing himself under the tank. A flag of the Islamic Republic is beside him, and the oncoming tank bears Iraqi insignia. At first glance, the mood presented by the double stamp seems almost placid. The full horror emerges only after realizing how the portrait of the youth, the adjacent text, and the child's painting are related, and how the Day of the Child is celebrated in today's Iran, paradise or no paradise. [see Fig. 8.7]

Two stamps honoring the fifth anniversary of the "Sacred Defence" — that is, against Iraq — are the graphic apotheoses of martyrdom. One shows a cupola of the tomb of the Imam Hussein at

13.24

shows a four-petaled red flower, the stem of which is inserted into (or grows from) the barrel of a rifle. [Fig. 13.24] The stamen on each petal is a large bullet. Beneath the flower are the words "Islam is Victorious." A Qur'anic quotation (2:193) is used on a stamp commemorating the 2,000th day of the war: "And fight them until there is no more oppression." It is written on a flat scroll overlaying a tulip from which a clenched fist emerges. This design, in green and white, is superimposed on a map of Iran. The words

13.21

13.22

13.23

Karbala with the red flag symbolizing blood and sacrifice. On that stamp, inscribed in Arabic, are the words: "Every day is ᶜAshura; the whole earth is Karbala; each month is Muharram." [Fig. 13.21] On the second stamp is the picture of a martyr with a beatific expression on his face being carried to paradise. His headband is inscribed *Labbaik ya Khomeini!* (Here am I awaiting your commands, O Khomeini!) The expression *Labbaik* is traditionally reserved for God and is uttered by Muslim pilgrims on their way to and upon their arrival at the holy Kaᶜbah in Mecca. [Fig. 13.22]

In 1982 Iran began to designate one week each year as "War Week." The purpose of the week was to further mobilize the morale of the nation; and stamps were among the means used to accomplish this goal. One stamp, issued for the 1984 observance,

"2000th Day of Sacred Defence" appear in Arabic on the right, in English on the left, and in Persian near the base. [Fig. 13.23] Qur'anic quotations are considered the word of God and are not taken lightly in the Islamic world. The verses which follow the Qur'anic citation used on this stamp are: "And all worship is devoted to God alone; but if they desist [from fighting] then all hostility shall cease, save against those who [willfully] do wrong." This quotation, often printed in Iranian magazines and newspapers, was meant to indicate that peace with Iraq was possible only if Saddam Hussein's forces were to quit. Khomeini's animosity towards the Iraqi regime stemmed from the time he lived in exile in the holy city of Najaf in Iraq, from which he was expelled to Paris in 1978. Khomeini has always identified himself with Hussein, the grandson of the Prophet. When Hussein

13.25

was surrounded by enemy forces at Karbala, he had two choices: he could pay allegiance to Yazid, the ruler at the time, and go free; or face death for himself and his male companions. Hussein, like Khomeini, was incapable of compromise. He chose death and the maintenance of the Shi⁽i faith. Khomeini has publicly stated: "I am like Hussein. I am not like Hasan." Imam Hasan, older brother of Imam Hussein, compromised politically with the Ummayad caliph in Damascus. This uncompromising stand is illustrated by a stamp and a poster representing young, middle-aged, and old men with semi-automatic rifles at the ready, their determination to fight to the death visible on their composed faces. A *chador*-clad woman stands behind them like the women of Hussein's encampment at Karbala. The inscription, which is visible only on the poster, reads: "Standing tall on the lofty edifice of martyrdom and shouting: 'War, war till victory.'" [Fig. 13.28] Saddam Hussein, the President of Iraq, is always referred to as Saddam Yazid in Iran. A 1983 Iranian stamp bears the title "Saddam's Crimes Conference" in English, Persian, and Arabic. It depicts the wings of a large dove of peace flanking a map of Iraq and a fist grasping a gun, apparently to liberate the country from its oppressor. [Fig. 13.25] Thousands were slaughtered or wounded during this battle between political personalities. In order to show the world the Iraqi atrocities against humanity, a stamp was issued honoring the Iraqi Kurds who died in Halabja at the hands of their own government by chemical warfare. [Fig. 13.26]

At every opportunity, the Khomeini regime equates the past with the present, utilizing the religious fervor inspired by the Karbala paradigm to stir up the masses. For example, when the Iranian opposition bombed a high-level meeting of the Islamic Republican Party in June 1981, about 100 people died in the explosion, including the party leader, Ayatollah Beheshti. But only seventy-two deaths were reported, so that the tragedy would conform to the paradigm. These martyrs are mourned annually. A 1986 stamp which memorializes this event is imprinted "Fifth Martyrdom Anniversary of 72 Companions of the Islamic Revolution." This is an obvious allusion to the seventy-two martyrs

of Karbala. In the foreground of the stamp is a picture of Beheshti next to an exploding bomb. Above him, a flight of doves soars towards heaven, symbolizing the souls of the martyrs. [Fig. 13.29] Ali, the father of Hussein, is known as the "Martyr of the Altar" because he was assassinated while on his way to a mosque to pray. In the years since the Revolution, quite a few Shi⁽i clerics have been killed in similar circumstances. Many of them have been memorialized on stamps. A stamp issued on 21 April 1982 honors Ayatollah Dastgheib and Ayatollah Madani. Both these holy men were killed in 1981, the former while on his way to Friday prayers in Shiraz, the latter in Tabriz. On the stamp, both are pictured in religious garb in front of a *mihrab*. [Fig. 13.30]

The assassin of President Anwar Sadat of Egypt, the Egyptian soldier who shot a group of Israeli civilians, and a leading ideologue of Egypt's Muslim Brothers are honored with stamps in Iran. The message in such official and public expressions of solidarity is one of support for militant Islam. Iran aligns herself with Shi⁽ites all over the world, but also supports resurgent Islam regardless of sectarian considerations. During Sadat's presidency, the codification of Islamic law was under discussion in the Egyptian Parliament. At the same time, mosques were being built throughout the country and veiled women and bearded men were becoming more and more visible. Even on

13.26

13.28

13.29

American television, President Sadat was often seen at prayer. Yet, when Khalid al-Islambuli assassinated Sadat, the Khomeini regime responded by memorializing al-Islambuli with a stamp and putting his name on one of Tehran's main avenues. It must be remembered that Khomeini hated Sadat for criticizing his brand of Islam as well as for having provided the deposed Shah of Iran with a safe haven. Al-Islambuli's ideology was very close to Khomeini's own: both men believed that the enemy at home must be subdued before the external enemy could be attacked. The statement "I am Khalid al-Islambuli; I have killed Pharaoh and do not fear death" shows the similar thinking of the two men. To the "fundamentalists," Pharaoh and Shah represent oppressive dictatorial regimes that must be overthrown in order to establish Islamic societies. The al-Islambuli stamp is based on an Egyptian press photograph of the assassin at his trial, after which he was executed. On the lower left of the stamp is a bloodstain. [Fig. 13.31]

Another "fundamentalist" honored by an Iranian stamp is Sayyid Qutb, the leading ideologue of the Muslim Brothers, who, after many years in Nasser's prisons, was executed in 1966. [Fig. 13.32] Qutb, like Khomeini, advocated the propagation of Islam by the book and by the sword. He also shared an aversion to non-Muslim cultures. A third Egyptian portrayed on an Iranian stamp is Sulayman Khatir, a soldier who shot seven Israeli civilians in 1985 near the disputed area of the Sinai, the last area to be settled by the Camp David accords between Egypt and Israel. Subsequently, Khatir

was found dead in an Egyptian prison. As depicted on the stamp, the blood coming from his heart is an indication that the authorities in Iran do not accept the official Egyptian explanation of Khatir's death as suicide by hanging. The Mosque of al-Aqsa in the background of the stamp indicates that he is among those who have fought for the liberation of Jerusalem. The Khatir affair generated a wave of anti-Israeli and anti-American sentiment in Egypt. Many in Egypt interpreted Khatir's actions as an expression of opposition to the peace treaty between Egypt and Israel. For a long time after Khatir's death, posters with his picture were omnipresent in Egypt, and his portrait travels the world on an Iranian stamp. [Fig. 13.33]

IN MEMORY OF THE MARTYRS OF ALTAR

Sheikh Ragheb Harb, who died under strange circumstances in 1983, was a symbol of resistance to the Israeli occupation of southern Lebanon. Two years after his death, he was declared a significant martyr by Lebanese Shiʿites. But before that, in 1984, he had already been honored with an Iranian stamp. [Fig. 13.34] In the light of the stamp honoring Harb, the absence of a stamp honoring Musa Sadr, the leader of the Lebanese Shiʿites, is conspicuous. The leader of the movement of the "Disinherited and Oppressed" and the founder of Amal, the Shiʿi militia in Lebanon, Musa Sadr vanished while visiting Qaddafi in Libya in 1978. Because his death has not been proven, no stamp has been issued in his honor. Similarly, while Khomeini was alive, not a single stamp was issued with his likeness, although huge posters of him plastered the walls of most Iranian towns and shops and were carried in processions. On the other hand, there is a stamp for Khomeini's son, Mustafa, who was found dead in Najaf in 1977 at the age of 45. Because autopsies are prohibited by Islamic law, the cause of his death has never been established, but he was promptly elevated to the rank of martyr. [Fig. 13.35]

After the death of Ayatollah Khomeini, the government of the Islamic Republic of Iran could issue commemorative postage stamps and banknotes with his portrait. In the Islamic Republic, as in the United States, pictures of living persons may not grace official government-issued stamps and banknotes. With Khomeini's death, the official graphic endeavors of the government could vie with semi-governmental and non-governmental enterprises in glorifying the leader of the Revolution and founder of the Islamic Republic. The first stamp issued after Khomeini's death features a partial bust of the Ayatollah wearing a skullcap and is based on a photograph taken shortly before he died. The expression on his face is one of profound meditation. The emphasis of the stamp's design

is on simplicity and sincerity. [Fig. 13.37] Another stamp depicts an enormous funeral procession. The crowd of mourners strike their heads as a sign of impassioned grief. The banner carried by the throng reads: "Khomeini! Khomeini! Until the appearance of the Mahdi [Savior], your way is being followed." Hovering over the procession against the blue sky is the turbaned head of the Ayatollah, surrounded by the wings of doves in flight to symbolize the ascent of the soul to heaven. [Fig. 13.38] A third, more formal, stamp features the bust of Khomeini in clerical garb. This is the same portrait that appears on the new series of 1,000, 5,000, and 10,000 rial banknotes. [see Figs. 12.19 and 12.20]

The stamp commemorating the establishment of the Islamic Republic on the 22nd of Bahman issued two years after the Ayatollah's death is unusually large, ten centimeters high and four and a half centimeters wide. A crowd of revolutionaries seen dimly in the background is being showered with colorful flowers as the Ayatollah raises his hand in blessing. By describing the day as "divine" on the stamp, those who issued the stamp — that is, the government — present themselves as sacred, or at the very least sanctioned by God. [Fig. 13.36] A series of fourteen stamps devoted to the life of the Ayatollah Khomeini is the most telling of the issues. The stamps, in denominations from 1 to 1,000 rials, highlight the events of, or associated with, the Ayatollah's life, from his birth to his death. The right-hand side of each stamp features Khomeini in two-thirds profile. Each stamp's story is presented in a drawing which emanates from the contours of his face. The most salient events of his life are

13.31

13.32

13.33

represented on the 3, 5, 10, and 20 rial stamps, that is from his speech denouncing the Shah at Qom on 5 June 1963, through his return to Tehran after fourteen years of exile. The 3, 10, and 20 rial stamps are based on photographs of the events in question. But from the graphic point of view, the 5 rial stamp is the best of the series. It shows two rifles, one marked "USA," pushing the Ayatollah Khomeini, resplendent in his Shiʿi clerical garb, out of a map of Iran. [Fig. 13.39] [see Fig. 9.11]

Islamic unity is the subject of stamps issued annually on the birthday of the Prophet Muhammad. Most of these stamps feature the holy Kaʿbah surrounded by the faithful of all races. Such stamps attempt to depict Iran as a force for the unification of all Muslims. Another series of Iranian commemorative stamps, which have a similar purpose, celebrates "The Universal Day of Ghods," which is the last Friday of Ramadan. The 1980 commemorative stamp bears the inscription "Let Us Liberate Jerusalem" in English, Arabic, and Persian. On this stamp, the Mosque of the Dome of the Rock is encircled by barbed wire in the form of the Star of David. The barbed wire is being pulled down by two, presumably Muslim, hands. There is similar symbolism on other stamps in the series, all of which show either the Mosque of the Dome of the Rock, the al-Aqsa Mosque, or a map of Israel. [Figs. 13.42 and 13.43]

Other international issues are subjects for Iranian stamps. The stamp issued in 1983 for United Nations Day shows a

13.36

claw-like hand, representing the five permanent Security Council members, bursting through one side of the United Nations building. "Veto" is written on the wrist, which is being severed by the sword of Islam. The hilt of the sword is formed from the emblem of the Islamic Republic. This stamp is a reference to Khomeini's statement, painted in English and Persian on the walls of the old American Embassy compound, that the veto power of the permanent members of the Security Council represents a form of oppression. Another anti-UN Security Council stamp criticizes Resolution 598, which called for an end to the Iraq–Iran war. The major paragraphs of the resolution can be read on Security Council stationery resting on a table in the middle of the stamp. A hand holding a pencil marked with the Iraqi national emblem and colors has drawn a big question mark on the paper. This suggests that the United Nations is siding with Iraq, allowing Iraq to dictate to the Security Council. In diagonally opposite corners of the stamp are two small maps which elaborate Iranian views of the conflict. In the lower left corner the map shows the border between Iran and Iraq and the position of the military front. In the upper right corner there is a map of Iraq and a silhouette of a prisoner of war with his raised hands being bound with barbed wire. A small white dove flying out of the prison indicates that prisoners have died in captivity. [Fig. 13.44]

A stamp issued in 1985 is entitled "Anniversary of Afghanistan Occupation and Muslim Afghans Resistance." On this stamp, a map

13.34

13.35

13.37

13.38

Flagellants at Khomeni's funeral, like those who mourn Imam Hussein in the Muharram.

13.39

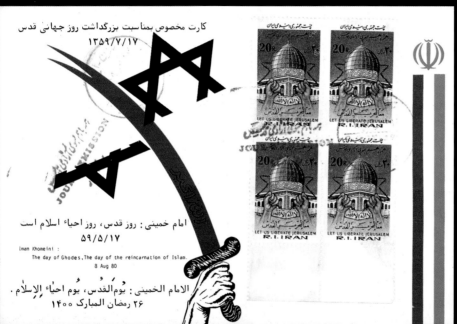

کارت مخصوص بمناسبت بزرگداشت روز جهانی قدس
۱۳۵۹/۷/۱۷

امام خمینی : روز قدس، روز احیاء اسلام است
۵۹/۵/۱۷

Imam Khomeini :
The day of Ghodes, The day of the reincarnation of Islam.
8 Aug 80

الإمام الخمینی : یومُ القدس، یوم احیاء الإسلام .
۲۶ رمضان المبارک ۱۴۰۰

13.42

of Afghanistan filled with clenched fists is attacked by multiple bayonets which shower down from the north. Thus, although the Soviet Union is not explicitly named, the source of the aggression is clearly implied. The use of a map of Afghanistan filled with *mujahedin*, became standard in the stamps issued annually to commemorate the Soviet invasion of Afghanistan and the Muslim Afghan resistance. [Fig. 13.45]

    Several anti-American stamps were issued representing the hostage crisis that occurred during the Carter administration.

The first, issued in 1983, shows the enlarged torso of a blindfolded hostage in front of a burning American flag. Below, a group of Iranians scale the main gates of the American Embassy in Tehran. The stamp is titled "The Takeover of the U.S. Spy Den." [Fig.13.50] Another stamp with the same title was issued eight years after the hostage-taking. It shows the same gate to the Embassy and a clenched fist shattering the American eagle. [Fig. 13.47] On a 1985 stamp, the broken seal of the Embassy with "CIA" stamped across it is surrounded by documents reassembled by the hostage-takers

THE 9th ANNIVERSARY OF THE SACRED DEFENCE

place. The timing of their issue probably reflects the needs of contemporary political expediency. The stamps of the Islamic Republic of Iran, like the stamps of other totalitarian regimes, serve a propaganda function. Both the sender and the receiver of the letters to which they are affixed receive a powerful message. Within Iran, one of the most powerful is that martyrs go to heaven and are honored on postage stamps.[8]

13.49   **13.48**

13.44

from the shredded papers of the Embassy chancellory. [Fig. 13.46] A stamp issued in 1986 is imprinted with the words "Failure of U.S. Military Aggression against Iran" in English, Arabic, and Persian.

228

It depicts the charred body of an American pilot in the foreground and, in the distance, a demolished American plane and helicopter. The image on the stamp is based on a photograph taken after the abortive attempt to rescue the hostages in April 1980. (This

photograph has also been made into a poster.) The Arabic inscription on this stamp is taken from the Qur'an (105:1): "Have you not seen how your Lord dealt with the people of the elephant? Did He not make their treacherous plan go astray?" This verse occurs at the beginning of a chapter in the Qur'an that describes the manner in which God repulsed an attempt by Abraha the Abyssinian to take over Mecca. The

13.45

huge invading force included elephants. The custodians of the Kaʿbah could not defend it against such a strong force, so, according to the Qur'an, the Almighty sent a flock of birds which showered the invaders with stones and annihilated them. The symbolic links between this event and the failure of the American rescue — mission in the dust storm are plentiful.[7] [Fig. 13.48]

What is interesting about all these stamps is that they were issued years after the events they depict took

13.46   **13.47**

62.08.15

13.50

1 In September 1928 Reza Shah ordered all male citizens to dress in the European style. The prohibition of traditional headgear like turbans and fur hats, and the imposition of the "Pahlavi cap" (a cylindrical hat with a bill) and later, in 1935, a European type of brimmed hat, met with strong opposition. This led to the spilling of blood when an anti-hat demonstration in Mashhad was crushed by the security forces. The abolition of the veil in 1936 also met with resistance from women and men. See "Clothing in the Pahlavi and Post Pahlavi Periods," Encyclopaedia Iranica, vol. 5: 808-11. **2** Some of the figures on the stamps, like Kuchik Khan (1881-1921), would be difficult for Western scholars to describe as "forerunners" of the Islamic movement. In the case of Kuchik Khan, his Jangali revolutionary movement's anti-dictatorship stance is enough for the new regime to co-opt him into its historical roots. **3** The authorities of the Islamic Republic claim that thousands were killed, but according to reliable sources 164 was the number of dead accounted for. Ahmad Ashraf conducted research on this topic at Tehran University in 1978-9. His findings were never published. This information is based on personal conversation with Dr Ashraf. **4** That honor was also attributed to other important dates of the Revolution such ʿAshura, December 1978. **5** Elias Canetti, Crowds and Power (New York, 1978), p. 148. **6** According to tradition, the banner used by Hussein at Karbala bore the same inscription. The same banner is used in the taʿziyeh performances of the martyrdom at Karbala. However, in the last four years of the war Islam was not enough and Iranian patriotism had to be stressed as well. **7** The commentary to the Qur'an by A. Yousuf Ali: no. 6275, p. 1792: "The lesson to be drawn is twofold... God will protect His own... For men in all ages it is: a man intoxicated with power can prepare armies and material resources against God's holy plan; but such a man's plan will be his own undoing..." **8** For more details, see Peter Chelkowski, "Stamps of Blood," American Philatelist 101, no. 6 (June 1987), pp. 556-66, and "Postage-Size Propaganda," New York Times Magazine, 15 February 1987, pp. 38-41. See also "L'Iran Poste La Mort au Grand Satan," Penthouse, Edition Française, 22 (November 1986), pp. 80-8. In 1984 the Iranian Consulate General in Milan, Italy issued an interesting catalogue of stamps printed in Iran after the Revolution, by an anonymous author, 5 Anniversario della Vittoriosa Rivoluzione Islamica dell'Iran.

Fourteen

the power of proximity
in children's literature

THE RECEPTIVITY OF THE YOUTHFUL IMAGINATION MUST REPRESENT SOMETHING PRIMEVAL IN THE HUMAN CAPACITY TO BELIEVE AND BE ENCHANTED. ALL THE DISGUISES OF RATIONALIZATION ARE ABSENT IN THAT STATE OF MIND WHERE THE BEDEVILING FORCES OF FASCINATION HAVE A FREER HAND AT THEIR MAGIC. CHILDHOOD IS THE KINGDOM OF MAGIC AND ENCHANTMENT. WHEN THE ROUTINE LIFE DOES TURN REVOLUTIONARY, THE PRIMAL FORCES OF FASCINATION HAVE A RICH AND READY FIELD FOR RELENTLESS CULTIVATION. THE MAGNETIC PRESENCE OF THE CHARISMATIC FIGURE, THE FATHER-FORCE THAT UNLEASHES AND TAPS THE REVOLUTIONARY MOMENTUM, DEEPLY MOVES AND INSTANTLY ATTRACTS ALL THE IMPRESSIONABLE IMAGINATIONS TO ITS CENTER OF GRAVITY. THERE THUS ARISES AN IRRESISTIBLE URGE FOR PROXIMITY TO THAT CENTER, FOR BEING NOT WITH BUT IN IT. THERE LIES, IN THE BOSOM OF THE REVOLUTIONARY SAGE, SOMETHING PRIMAL, SOMETHING ENDURING, THAT MOVES, STIRS, AND CULTIVATES THE EXPANDING IMAGINATION OF THE YOUTH. THE YOUTHFUL IMAGINATION DOES NOT MERELY NEED, IT EFFECTIVELY LIVES ON DEMAND AND DOCTRINES OF FASCINATION. WHEREAS FOR THE ADULT THE MECHANISM IS ALWAYS SOMETHING OF A COLLECTIVE REFASCINATION, FOR THE YOUTH IT IS THE FIRST AND FOREMOST INSTANCE OF A VIVID HISTORICAL ENCHANTMENT. THE CHILDREN OF A REVOLUTION ARE ITS FIRST AND FUTURE CONVERTS, ITS EXTENSION INTO THE FUTURE. THE ACTIVE IMAGINATION OF THE YOUTH DOES NOT MERELY RECEIVE THE PUBLIC INGREDIENTS OF ITS PRIVATE CONCEPTIONS; IT CONSTRUCTS, AT ONE AND THE SAME TIME, THE MOST IRREDUCIBLE TERMS OF ITS CREDULITIES, LIMITATIONS, THE FANGS AND FURY OF ITS CONCEALED AND CRAFTED PREJUDICES. THERE IS A POWER IN THE PROXIMITY OF THE REVOLUTIONARY SAGE LIKE NO OTHER FORCE OF ATTRACTION. YET TO BE DEFASCINATED (ONLY TO BE LATER REFASCINATED) WITH THE WORLD, THE YOUTHFUL MIND NEEDS NO MITIGATING AGENCY OF ENCHANTMENT. IT IS DRAWN TO THE REVOLUTIONARY FORCE LIKE A MOTH TO A FIRE.

232

In this chapter we wish to consider some of the particular sensibilities that were activated as the ideologues of the Islamic Revolution sought to instill their doctrines in the minds and souls of their younger adherents. In early 1980's the Unit for Literary Creativity of the Institute for the Intellectual Development of Children and Young Adults in Iran organized a national competition entitled "A Letter to the Imam." For six months, from March to September, the referees received some 2,700 letters addressed to Khomeini. Twenty-nine letters were selected as the best by a panel of judges.

Occasionally moving the members of this panel to tears, these letters were written by children aged between 7 and 17. The prize-winning letters were sent to Khomeini's office. The organizers

14.1 Pacifier in mouth, machine-gun in hand and in full Islamic regalia, under the protective gaze of the revolutionary grandfather.

232

of this competition knew of no better prize than a private audience with the "Imam." On 23 Esfand 1362/14 March 1984, Ayatollah Khomeini received the organizers of this event and the twenty-nine finalists.

The children were waiting for the Imam's arrival impatiently. As soon as the Imam saw the children, a fatherly smile blossomed on his most gracious face. The children all broke into tears. We all cried. These were tears of joy. The Imam received the children with open arms. The children gave the Imam a book in memory of this occasion. They showered his hand with kisses. The Imam prayed for all the children, one by one. When we returned, the children were all silent in the mini-bus. Obviously, it was the impact of the Imam's visit. We felt we were washed by a bounteous rain of piety. The kind glances of the Imam had touched our souls. The children were in ecstasy. As if they had just smelled the fragrance of a beautiful flower.[1]

The letters have been sent from all over the country, reflecting an array of emotions and sensibilities. Hediyeh Hamidi Afshar, 7 years old, wrote from Tehran that she loved "the Imam," that she wished she could be with him: "I badly miss you. I want to see you but the Pasdar's won't let me... My mother wishes to see you too... I love you."[2] Khomeini is perceived as awe-inspiring but kind.

He is repeatedly referred to as "father" and "grandfather." Sedigheh Yazdani, 9 years old, wrote from Damghan that she never saw her own grandfather but now considered Khomeini "a kind and faithful grandfather."[3] She too wished to see Khomeini and regretted that she could not do so. Narges Rashidi, also 9, went so far as to invite Khomeini to her hometown: "I wish even for once you could come to Zarand so that the people of Zarand could see you closely. For God's sake, please come to the children and the people of Zarand."[4] Afshin Shakuri, 9 years old, wrote from Zanjan that he was Khomeini's "little soldier."[5] Children spoke openly of their distant wishes: "Dear Imam, I wish to invent something that would make poor people rich, blind people see, crippled people healthy, so that I would help good people. I wish the peasants would not get sick and dirty. I wish they could have schools, new clothes. Please pray for me so that I can do all these things. [And then he closes with an abrupt] Goodbye."[6] Children were happy to grow up under his protection and Islamic care. They wished they could sacrifice their lives for his revolution.[7] Zahra Dehbashian wrote from Mashhad. She was 10 years old, and her father was a laborer, making 150 tuman (at the current exchange rate, about 70 cents) a day. She received 1 tuman a day as allowance, and was saving all her money to buy things for the

234

14.2 Depictions of Iraqi bombarded schools became the supreme sign of children's sacrifice for the revolution. The reference to "human rights" was intended as a mockery of President Carter's presidential campaign promise.

14.3 In this poster entitled "Guards of the Realm of Light" by artist K. Chalipa, children are encouraged to take part in the revolution under the protective gaze of the revolutionary leader.

soldiers at the front: "So far I have contributed two boxes of crackers, a bottle of lemon juice, two kilograms of potato and onion, two cans of fruit preserves, some rice, some tea leaves, and a few sugar cubes."[8] Ten-year-old Amaneh wrote from Shiraz to express the wishes of her entire family that "God Almighty would, for the sake of Islam, take away from our lives and add it to yours." She assured the revolutionary leader that they were strictly following his orders and not celebrating the Persian New Year. She yet had something to confess: "During the New Year celebrations, our parents, just not to break our hearts, bought us some seeds. That's all."[9] Some were at a loss for the right words. "Among all the Persian words," wrote Shayan Neᶜmatian, 12 years old, from Tehran, "I cannot find a word that can best describe you."[10]

There is a vast and uninhibited expression of love for Khomeini. Maryam Mokhlesi, 12 years old, wrote from Damghan, "O, my leader! I love you. As much as butterflies love the flowers, with the depth of all the seas, as much as a mother loves her beloved child, even more than all these, I love you... As long as this world exists, and the earth moves around, and the sun shines, I will remember you, and I will love you like the dance of butterflies around the flower and the candle." She also wrote that "when you

came I was only 7 years old. I did not know where you were coming from. But I knew that you were the spring of our Revolution." She remembered her dolls: "When you had not come yet, we children used to play with our dolls, ignorant of the fact that at the time we ourselves were puppets to injustice and tyranny. When you came we had no desire to play with dolls any more. They became old and after a while they broke. Then we began to make wooden guns (although I was a girl, I learned it from my brother). Childish games had no meaning for us any more. We felt grown up, very proud of the wooden guns we carried on our shoulders." She concluded, "O, idol-smasher Khomeini! You are like a teacher who teaches us the lesson of faith, of sacrifice. You warn us all the time."[11]

Majid Alipour, 12 years old, from the village of Neqab, blamed "the criminal America" and "the treacherous Shah" for all the catastrophes in Iranian villages. "The treacherous Shah made cities prosperous and ruined the villages. That is why the villagers became destitute."[12] From another village, Behshahr in Mazandaran, 12-year-old Majid Valipour Kalti wrote to Khomeini about his eyeache which made him almost blind. He also told of his dream of Khomeini, after which his problems with his eyes were gone. "But you see, Imam, only my mother believed my dream. All others

14.4 The artist Ahad Yari transformed this farewell black and white photograph, which ended in the death of the young hero at the front, into a compelling icon of maternal love and youthful sacrifice, framed and separated from the human realm.

Abbas

laughed at me. But that's alright. God knew I was not lying." He also wrote of his younger brother: "Imam, I wish, when I grow up, to save enough money to build a school at the center of our village so that children don't have to cross the highway in order to go to school. If our village had a school, my younger brother would not have been crushed under the wheels of a mini-bus, and would not have made my mother sad for ever. But I also know that if he too were here, he would have written to you how much he loved you, and how much he would love to kiss you."[13]

Children wrote poems for Khomeini, quoted the Qur'an for him, reminded him of his own aphorisms, and begged his pardon for having talked too much.[14] They endeared themselves to him, called him grandfather, and prayed for his health and long life. Hamideh Moslehi, 13 years old, from Juybar, wrote that she once saw him in a dream, and that in the morning she could not rest until she had told her dream "to two or three revolutionaries."[15] They talked like him, imitated his catch-phrases, condemned "East and West," and begged for the victory of "the valiant fighter of Islam."[16] Ziba Taherian, 13 years old, from Isfahan, wrote that when she was 5 or 6 years old her brother, who was later killed for Islam, showed

14.5 Children's images of war with Iraq often blamed it on the United States government. In this picture, by the fourteen-year old Marzieh Rudbari, the bombing of Iranian villages is attributed to the United States Air Force.

14.6 and 14.7 [next page] Participation of children in Muharram processions, in which they metaphorically participated in Shi'i martyrs sufferings through ritual self flagellation, anticipated their mobilization during the war with Iraq. The transformation from real chains to plastic grenades to real grenade on the battlefields is sudden and spontaneous.

her Khomeini's picture: "Since then, your love sat in my heart, and I am convinced it will never leave my heart."[17] Khomeini's picture had central significance in the lives of these children.

O dear Imam! Perhaps what I am about to tell you may appear as sheer madness. But believe me it is the truth. You see, when I look at your handsome picture, your beautiful smiles deeply move me. Whenever I do something good, your picture smiles at me, and whenever I commit a sin, if I look at your picture, the smile is gone from your lips. I feel that this is not a picture. This is your most gracious being. O dear Imam, please consider me worthy of your presence so that I may see you, because meeting my leader enlightens my heart. Well, I am not going to take your precious time any longer. I hope you will answer my letter. I conclude my letter with my best wishes for your health and the Mahdi's Revolution (may God hasten his return!), for the victory of the soldiers, and for the health of the clergy.[18]

240

240

14.9 A poster sets the Iraqi bombing of civilian targets in Iran against President Carter's "Human Rights" campaign. The Islamic Republic linked the United States and Israel to Saddam Hussein in a trilateral campaign against the Islamic Revolution in Iran. Children were among the main casualties of war with Iraq. The poster by Agha Gholizadeh is based on the photos by Muhammad Farnoud and Bahman Jalali.

14.8 A collage, prepared by the Ministry of Education (Division of Art), commemorating and celebrating every major symbol and event surrounding the revolution led by Khomeini. Towering over the poster is the red tulip, symbolizing youthful sacrifice; the tulip stem separates the two pages of a calendar. On one page the Pahlavi era is crossed out and, on the next, the Islamic Revolution is successfully celebrated with blood stains. The poster is inundated with the revolution's major slogans. On the hand mark on the left side of the picture is written: "Greetings to Khomeini." Moving down the poster, the revolutionary narrative leads to the war with Iraq. The small graves at the bottom are inscribed with names of real children, aged 10 to 18, who were killed during the revolution and the war.

14.10 A picture, by thirteen-year old Sara Kashipaz depicts the wedding of a young couple, with the young groom having lost a leg in the war.

14.11 A young hero is being killed in a Ta⁽e⁾ziyeh passion play of *The Two Children of Muslim*, Husseiniyeh Mushir, Shiraz 1976.

Children felt guilty if they were sick or not strong enough to fight for Islam: "My body is so feeble, and it is so weak, that I cannot lift a kettle." This is Ma⁽c⁾sumah Musaviani, 15 years old, from Tehran. "I have two younger brothers and an older brother. They are students. My mother is sick too. There is no one to help me get better. As much as I can I send money to the front."[19] Others showered him with praise: the pious man, the faithful man, the capable leader, the leader of Iran, the sea, full of kindness, the just ruler, truthful, destroyer of falsehood, the steadfast, the mountain of faith, a sword that cuts the enemy down, beloved of the weak, heart of the lovers, guardian of the faith who knows the Qur'an by heart, the old soldier, the leader of men, from the family of the Prophet, the Abraham of the time, the son of (Imam) Hussein, the beloved of the martyrs.[20]

From a total of 2,700 letters, only twenty-nine were selected by the jury. Of these a disproportionate number, nineteen, were written by young girls, nine by young boys, and the identity of one is not known. The girls are much more open in expression of their love, the boys in their respect. Of the twenty-nine letters, eight were

14.12 One of the first sentences that a first year schoolchild learns how to write in Persian is "Baba ab dad" ("Dad gave water"). Sixteen months after the Iraqi invasion of Iran, the children were learning how to write "Baba Khun dad" ("Dad gave blood").

from Tehran, seventeen from various provincial towns, and four from small villages. One was 7 years old, three were 9, three were 10, four were 12, three were 13, three were 15, seven were 16, and five were 17. One 13-year-old girl quoted the Qur'an to Khomeini; one 15-year-old girl quoted him one of his own aphorisms. Eight children, all from 15 to 17 years old, wrote their letters in the form of a poem. Four were boys, four girls. With the exception of one, all the poems were in classical Persian prosody. The one "modern poem," by Sakineh Goljarian, 17 years old, from Gonabad, addressed Khomeini as "O Gardener!"[21]

Fifteen-year-old Mitra Azimi, who quoted Khomeini's statement about the virtues of peasants, wrote from Babol that she had painted the statement in the pages of her reading textbook.[22] She also gave a report of the situation of her village Gavankola, its residents, their problems and difficulties. But she assured Khomeini that they would tolerate all these for the sake of the Islamic Revolution. They studied and formed Islamic organizations in their village just as Khomeini had instructed. She assured him that the peasants would multiply their efforts so that Iran would be agriculturally self-sufficient, independent of the superpowers. She wished him a long life, as long as the coming of the Mahdi.[23] Until then, the 16-year-old Nahid Bari assured Khomeini from Bakhtaran in a beautifully composed *ghazal*, he was the hope of all children and young people.[24] From Shirvan, another 16-year-old, Zahra Eftekhari, wrote to Khomeini that "our birthday was the day you were born." She also wrote of the day she and her fellow Shirvanis saw Khomeini's triumphant face "on the magical screen of the television."[25] A combination of such sentiments and images led Babak Nik-Talab to compose a *ghazal* for the revolutionary leader in which he is elevated to the mythological archetype of all virtues and aspirations. Another 16-year-old girl, Raheleh Ahmadi from Gorgan, linked Khomeini's virtues to all the beauties and miracles of nature — moonlight and creek, young fish and fresh blossoms, flowers and pearls, gardens and diamonds.[26] Another 16-year-old, Mozhgan Talebi from Jiroft, compared Khomeini to Jesus Christ and Moses, called him the executor of Muhammad's law, and compared his spirit to the brilliant sun.[27] Similar sentiments are expressed in Mahdi Thaqafi's poem. This 16-year-old from Mashhad saw in Khomeini a Noah who piloted his countrymen's ship — with a pun on Khomeini's first name, he called him "the Spirit of God," his spirit a prism of God — and then proclaimed that "All our history is indebted to you."[28] From the village of Nur to the capital, Tehran, two other 17-year-old poets thought of similar hyperboles for their beloved leader.[29]

One sick child, who signed with only his first initials and whose gender cannot be determined (probably a boy) openly stipulated that the only way he could contribute to the Islamic Revolution was for Khomeini to pray for him to get well. He was 16 years old and wrote from Qaᶜin Shahr. There was something wrong with the child's leg and eye: "O magnanimous Imam! Please ask God Almighty to cure my sickness. O Imam! I want to do something for God. But with this illness in my leg and in my eye I cannot. O magnanimous Imam! I cannot fight against the enemies of Islam with this illness. Whenever my face, eye, and leg are well, then I will fight against the enemies with all my life."[30]

Sediqeh Dust-Mohammadi, a 17-year-old girl from Kerman, took upon herself to write on behalf of all other children. "I wish I could bring the message of all Iranian children to your attention. But I cannot." But she decided to write: "Let me tell you about myself, that is to say ourselves, about the children, teenagers, and the youth of our Iran. To tell you about ourselves, of our love for you, of our endeavor to safeguard the Revolution, of our mourning for the martyrs, of the loneliness of our hearts. When we wish to see your face a drop of tear sits on our cheeks, and in our hearts a strange sadness dwells."[31] "Like a truthful messenger," she wanted to report of their collective participation in the revolutionary demonstrations. They had lost their own fathers, but Khomeini was now their father. Children now had only three objectives: to work for God, to follow Khomeini, and to honor the blood of the martyrs. Sediqeh concluded that she wished she could see Khomeini in person even once. This, she assured him, was the wish of "thirty-six million Iranians."[32]

One of the children, 17-year-old Zahra Habibian from Tehran, had actually seen Khomeini:

That day they had brought us from school to your house. I had a peculiar feeling. I felt as if I was the only one who was coming to meet you. I did not even see that huge crowd. I was telling myself, "How would I face him?" I thought it impossible to see one of "the friends of God." But after an hour or two, when I entered the Husseiniyeh of Jamaran, I was just beside myself. I had a strange feeling. Every moment, anxious as I was to see you, was like a lifetime. But nothing seemed to happen. As soon as the door from which you used to enter the balcony moved or opened, the crowd fell into a strange silence. But when the door opened and one of the guards or someone else came to the balcony, people would be so disappointed. At times they would say to each other: "Well, maybe the Imam will not come!" Others would say, "O no, God forbid!" At any rate, time was going idly by when the door was opened and all of a sudden I saw you. Believe me, I could clearly hear my heart beating. I did not know what to do. Should I laugh or cry! You kept waving your kind hand to the crowd. I could not believe it was you. You see, on the television, I had seen you somewhat differently. But now, right in front of my eyes I was watching a person which was light incarnate. If I had any power at that time, I would have stopped the time, so that I could see you more. After about twenty minutes you moved toward the door. I could not believe that you wanted to leave... I kept on crying. Even now, after some two years since that day, whenever I am reminded of those moments, tears come to my eyes. I only have one wish in my life, actually, two wishes: one is to see you one more time, and the other is to be fortunate enough to be graced by martyrdom. I know I am not worthy of either of these wishes. But I beg you to pray for me to have my wishes fulfilled. You see, just like you, I am a Sayyid too. I think I am entitled to see my own cousin one more time, very humble and insignificant as I am. Zahra Habibian.[33]

There must be some power, some inexplicable attraction to the magical center of charismatic gravity. These children,

14.13 A picture by twelve-year old Marzieh Alizadeh depicts a funeral procession of a young victim of the war.

14.14 A picture of Behesht-e Zahra Cemetery by thirteen-year old Sara Kashipaz.

testimonies of something primeval enduring in all, have one single overriding wish: to be near Khomeini, to see him close to, to feel him, touch him. They are attracted to him with awe and admiration, fear and love. Their mute attraction either succumbs to nervous informality or struggles for affected formalism, it hides behind either poetic conventions or the leading revolutionary slogans. They are desperate to appease him, to show how revolutionary they are, to prove how much they are willing to sacrifice, including the final, supreme sacrifice of their young lives. In his presence, they seem to seek security, but find themselves in a state of awe. They seek reassurance for their debilitating anxieties by calling him either a strong father or a weak grandfather. In his fatherly power they seem to find help for their external fears, in his grandfatherly weakness, they quell their inner anxieties.

Children are not too distant pictures of adults. They begin with the most immediate anxieties. Children need no mitigating force of re-enchantment with the world, of archetypally coming to terms with their fears and fascinations. They are not removed from the central forces of their self-fascination by any experience of defascination. The theological language of "innocence" marks that primeval state of a fascination when the whole world is open to magic. Khomeini's concern about children was equally intense, and central to his desire to ensure continued success for his reinvention of "Islam." He was particularly attentive to publications which were directed towards young readers. Addressing a group of journalists, he once observed that the words and images that go into a journal must be carefully selected. "For fifty years," he believed, "whenever [people in] our society opened a journal, or listened to radio, or watched television, they were all misguided. These [journals] were all [designed] so that no righteous young person would be brought up...Whoever wants to write [sic] a journal, [he/she] must be prepared to educate the next generation. Do something for the next generation...We are all duty-bound to do something for the next generation. We have to educate [our] children at home, primary and secondary school. I wish you all success, so that your journal would be educational. Do not write much! Write well!"[34] If anything, the chief task of journalism in Khomeini's republic was to educate children, so that they grow up to become responsible Muslims.

Teachers were another group whom Khomeini addressed and reminded of their responsibility in educating children: "These youngsters are the hope for the future of the Islamic country."[35] Children were entrusted to teachers and instructors, and they must be raised to become dedicated Muslims. Should responsible teachers fail to educate the children properly, they would grow up to become prey to "the false propaganda" of the enemy. Khomeini admonished those children who were "misguided" by the Mujahedin, a radical Islamic group which first supported and then opposed Khomeini's Revolution. "You young boys and girls! What have you seen from your corrupt leaders other than [empty] claims and misguidedness?"[36] Addressing the young Mujahedin followers, Khomeini asked: "You young people! Why have you surrendered your mind to others? Why do you lack independence of judgment? Why do you not examine the situation of your leaders yourselves?...Why do you not think?"[37] These youngsters were the potential soldiers that Khomeini needed for his cause, for "Islam" as he had now re-envisioned it. "We do not wish that you young people, who can be a treasure for this nation, be wasted—first mentally and then physically."[38]

The primary function of children's education was to transform "the Western person" (*insan-e Gharbi*) to "the Islamic person" (*insan-e Islami*).[39] Thus education was central in the Islamic Republic. Educational problems were the source of all other problems. Compared to the cultural damage that the monarchical regime had perpetrated on Iran, economic problems were minimal. From primary schools to universities, all institutions of learning were devoted to the education of "the Western person." "We must begin," Khomeini decreed, "with children, and our only concern should be the transformation of the Western person to the Islamic person."[40] Should this "Islamic person" be created, no external enemy could pose a danger to the Islamic state. "We have to believe that we are somebody," Khomeini emphatically declared. And for that purpose children ought to be carefully educated by responsible and religiously upright individuals. Then "We can recreate the culture that made Avicenna."[41] Addressing a group of parents, he once encouraged them to be diligent in the Islamic upbringing of their children. "The objective of your enemies," he emphasized, "is to divert your children from Islam...Be careful and educate the children and the youth Islamically."[42] With that end in mind, he thought that the war with Iraq had had the positive effect of creating a remarkable energy in the youth, and he celebrated the creation of this positive energy.[43] The immediate consequence of this youthful energy, Khomeini reminded a group of military leaders,[44] was that tyrants and despots would think twice before trying to take advantage of a country that they thought had been weakened.

The children's letters to Khomeini, whether orchestrated or genuine, are indications of a degree of success in achieving a fundamental redefinition of character, from the youngest and most impressionable stage, conducive to "Islamic ideals." Khomeini was the chief architect, the singular voice of authority, in designating the specifics of this Islamic character. Children thus directly identified with his constructed ideal through the intermediary of a state propaganda machinery. Khomeini was fully aware of the necessity, power, and effectiveness of this machinery, and used it to the best of his ability. The older generation, he thought, had been corrupted by years of "Westernization." It was an Islamic miracle that the Revolution had happened the way it did. But now it was time to institute Islamic guidelines so that no future generation would emerge alien or hostile to its Islamic heritage and duties. A link, a magnetic field, was thus created and sustained between Khomeini and children. They were molded into loving him, he was there to set them on the right path, and the stage was prepared for the militant formation of "the Islamic person."

1 Anon. (ed.), Nameh'i beh Imam (Tehran, n.d.), p. 4. 2 Ibid., p. 5. 3 Ibid., p. 6. 4 Ibid., p. 7. 5 Ibid., p. 8. 6 Ibid. 7 Ibid., p. 9. 8 Ibid., p. 10. 9 Ibid., p. 11. 10 Ibid., p. 12. 11 Ibid., p. 13. 12 Ibid., p. 14. 13 Ibid., p. 15. 14 Ibid., p. 36. 15 Ibid., p. 16. 16 Ibid. 17 Ibid., p. 17. 18 Ibid., p. 18. 19 Ibid., p. 19. 20 Ibid., pp. 20-1. 21 Ibid., pp. 42-4. 22 Ibid., p. 22. 23 Ibid., p. 23. 24 Ibid., p. 24. 25 Ibid., p. 25. 26 Ibid., p. 27. 27 Ibid., p. 28. 28 Ibid., p. 30. 29 Ibid., pp. 33, 37-8. 30 Ibid., pp. 31-2. 31 Ibid., p. 34. 32 Ibid., p. 36. 33 Ibid., pp. 39-40. 34 Khomeini, Sahifah-ye Nur (Tehran, 1982), vol. 15: 38. 35 Ibid., p. 95. 36 Ibid., p. 184. 37 Ibid., pp. 184-5. 38 Ibid., p. 185. 39 Ibid., p. 192. 40 Ibid. 41 Ibid., p. 193. 42 Ibid., pp. 197-8. 43 Ibid., p. 240. 44 Ibid.

Fifteen
DAYS OF OUR HISTORY:

RECONFIGURING THE
[roman/islamic/christian]
CALENDAR

Perhaps no other recurrent symbolic of collective identity represents the deep cleavages within contemporary Iranian society than the daily calendar by which it regulates its routine presence in history. This calendar consists of three distinct dates, representing the three divergent – at times deeply hostile to each other – universes within which a Muslim Iranian lives in time. The three deeply opposing dates, representing the three calendars, are Iranian, Islamic, and Christian (or what is now rather polemically called "common"). A typical Monday, for example, 16 December, 1996, will be marked as such, and next to it would be two other dates, 26 Azar, 1375, and 5 Sha'ban, 1417 [Fig. 15.1]. In a typical, desk-top, calendar, the central date, the one marking the Iranian day, is depicted in a larger frame and with larger numbers. This is the visual celebration and numerical privileging of the Iranian calendar. We are Iranians and this is our time. The one immediately to its right is the Islamic and the one to its left is the "common" calendars. While both the Iranian and the Islamic dates are in Arabic script, the "common" date uses Latin letters. That is the first and most immediate sign of tension in the Iranian-Islamic identity and the necessity of keeping up with "the Christian world," as it were. The affinity between the Iranian and Islamic letters and numbers reminds everyone that as Iranians we are Muslims. We use the same letters and numbers. Usually the sanctity of the Islamic calendar, however, is marked by the authoritative Naskh script being used for the Arabic names of the month, while the flirtatious Nasta'liq being used for the Iranian.

15.1

15.2

The visual and emotional affinity between the Iranian and the Islamic calendar, however, is offset by the fact that while the Islamic calendar is lunar, the Iranian is solar, exactly as the Christian calendar. The result is that the Iranian and the Christian calendars are almost always identically concurrent, while the Islamic lunar calendar constantly changes from one year to another, always falling eleven days shorter than the solar Iranian and Christian calendars. *We may be Muslims, but we have something seriously common with Europeans.* These sometimes clear sometimes subtextual innuendoes in an Iranian's way of figuring out the time are the constant source of confusion of identity. Take the sacrosanct month of Muharram, for example. This month on the Islamic calendar is an extraordinarily important month for a Shi'i Iranian, because on the 10th of this month in the year 61 AH/680 CE the third Shi'i Imam, Hussein, was martyred. Its correspondence with the end of Shahrivar, for example, could indicate some modification in the decision as to when the schools ought to start after the summer holidays. A concurrence of Muharram with the Iranian national New Year, Nowruz, can really be a source of grave aggravation in the country, when the religiously minded Iranians will ignore the New Year, while the nationalistically oriented ones will opt to celebrate it regardless of that coincidence. *Are we Muslims or Iranians first?* The strong anti-Arab sentiments which was constitutional to the Iranian nationalist project in the nineteenth and twentieth century come into play in the deciphering of the multiple calendars with which Iranians figure out their time.

In this chapter we shall consider some of the effective ways in which the post-revolutionary Iranian calendar was reconstructed to generate and sustain an "Islamic" memory.

Another sacred month on the Islamic calendar with potential points of conflict with practical and symbolic reasons is Ramadan. This month-long period of fasting may coincide with summer when the days are long and enduring hunger and thirst quite difficult. This month may alternatively coincide with the Iranians celebrating their national New Year when eating, drinking and partying would not be possible if they are also to fast. The 21st of Ramadan, when in the year 40 AH/661 CE the first Shi'i Imam, Ali, was assassinated, is a particularly sacred and somber date in the Shi'i memory. Should this day coincide with the New Year celebrations, there is again cause for confusion and split loyalties among Iranians. Conversely, there can be many occasions in which the Iranian and the Islamic identities may perfectly match and reinforce each other in a happy and positive way, as in Prophet Mohammad's birthday, for example, on the 17 of Rabi' I, may coincide with Noruz, or the day he was chosen as the messenger of God on the 27th of Rajab, or the 'Id Ghadir Khumm, the day of the nomination of Ali as Prophet Mohammad's successor according to the Shi'ite belief, on the 18th of Dhi al-Hajjah, or the birthday of Ali on the 13th of Rajab, or the birthday of the Eighth Shi'i Imam al-Reza on the 11th of Dhi al-Qa'dah, or the birthday of the 12th, the Hidden Imam, on the 15 of Sha'ban, or the 'Id al-Fitr at the end of the fasting month of Ramadan.

While during the Shah's time much emphasis was being put on the Iranian calendar, after the revolution it was the Islamic calendar which was overwhelmingly noted. During the Shah's time, attention to the Iranian calendar was carried to its rhetorical conclusion when in 1971 the ideologues of the monarchical regime decided to change the base of the calendar from the migration of the Prophet Mohammad from Mecca to Medina to the coronation of Cyrus the Great. The year 1350 of the Iranian calendar, i.e. 1350 solar years after the migration of the Prophet from Mecca to Medina, suddenly became 2535, i.e., this number of years after the presumed coronation of Cyrus the Great. During the 2500th anniversary of the Persian monarchy, the event was fantastically celebrated throughout the country but particularly at the Persepolis where the foreign heads of states joined the Iranian royal family. The Shah of Iran gave his official address at the foot of Cyrus' grave, assuring the ancient monarch that "Cyrus! Sleep soundly, because We are awake!" The following days, there were reports of rebellious mullahs going to the pulpits in the poor neighborhoods of the capital and echoing the king's statement with a twist, "Cyrus! Sleep soundly, because the whole nation is in dire poverty!" Ayatollah Khomeini issued a statement from his exile in Najaf denouncing both the celebration of 2500 years of monarchy and the changing of the calendar. One of the first things that the Shah was forced to do as a concession to the revolutionary uprising of 1978-79 was to reverse himself on the imperial calendar and re-institute the original base of the Iranian calendar to the migration of Prophet Mohammad from Mecca to Medina.

After the revolution one of the principal objectives of its ideologues was actively and pervasively to Islamicize the Iranian calendar. Not only the most famous Islamic events but the most obscure occurrences were recorded on the daily calendars. Days of the week were all inundated with the birthdays and death anniversaries of distant figures in Shi'i martyrology. By far the most significant development in this respect was when events in early Islamic history were given renewed and appropriate

60 Rls.   ولادت حضرت مهدی (عج) ، روز جهانی مستضعفین   ۶۰ ریال
SAVIOUR MAHDI'S BIRTH DAY. THE UNIVRSAL DAY OF THE OPPRESSED
1993   ISLAMIC REP. OF IRAN   ۱۳۷۱
15.3

significance. One crucial case in point is when the birthday of the Prophet is celebrated as the first day of a week-long celebration of "The Week of Unity," in the course of which Muslims of the world were all invited to set aside their differences and unite. The stamps that were released to celebrate this day and this week [Fig.15.2] invited in Persian, Arabic and English, the three languages of the Iranian calendars, all Muslims to unite with each other on the day of their Prophet's birthday. The minaret and the copula of the Prophet's mosque in Medina, the house of Ka'bah, the text of the Qur'an, a rising sun, the multitude of Muslims, and two hands clasping each other in unity are among the signs and symbols used on these stamps. These stamps were used by millions of Iranians to send letters and packages throughout the world, thus placing the Islamic Republic at the center of a global revivalism of Islamic unity.

Equally significant is the designation of the birthday of the Twelfth, the Hidden, Imam as "The International Day of the Down-Trodden." In the stamps issued to commemorate this day [Fig 15.3] an emerging sun is reached for by a multitude of hands. Here, a significant aspect of Shi'i eschatology is globalized as a political event of universal appeal. According to a central dogma of Shi'ism, the Twelfth Imam disappeared from human sight in the year 874 CE. His return, or parousia (zuhur) in order to establish universal justice is the defining factor of Shi'i eschatology. In the reconstituted Islamic calendar of the Islamic Republic, the birthday of the Twelfth Imam is universalized far beyond its Shi'i confinements by being designated as a day in which all the poor people of the world ought to expect a savior. The color red in the background of the merging sun hints at a period of bloodshed which is to anticipate the coming of the Mahdi. The active globalization of specifically Shi'i occasions in fact has an equally important impact on the Islamic Revolution itself which thus sees itself as a vanguard movement anticipating more global changes in the world. Here not just the Muslim world but the entire globe, and thus the significance of English phrases on these stamps, is cast into a proto-Islamic shadow by having it anticipate a global revolution under the guidance and leadership of the Twelfth, Hidden Imam. Now, in Iran proper, Ayatollah Khomeini was never formally identified as the Twelfth Imam, a doctrinal abomination which he and most Iranian Shi'is would emphatically denounce. However, the Shi'i millenarian expectations of the return of the Twelfth Imam actively informs their historical embrace of revolutionary movements led by the Shi'i clergy.

Another crucial day which was re-assigned with a revolutionary significance is the birthday of Fatemeh, an extraordinarily significant character in early Islamic and Shi'i history. Fatemeh was the prophet's daughter and Ali's wife. She is thus connected to four major figures in early Islam: Her father Prophet Mohammad, her husband, the first Shi'i Imam Ali, and her two sons Hasan and Hussein, the second and third Shi'i Imams respectively. Along with these four figures, Fatemeh completes the five leading saintly characters of the early Shi'i memory, collectively known as "Panj Tan-e Ahl-e Aba" ('The Five Person of the Mantle' i.e. the Mantle of the Prophet), and represented by the five fingers and the palm of the right hand. The significance of Fatemeh in Shi'i sacred memory was given a new contemporary twist when her birthday was adopted

as "The Day of Woman." The stamp which was issued on this occasion [Fig. 15.4] reveals the kind of revolutionary woman now being celebrated in the Islamic Republic. The most immediately recognizable aspect of the Muslim revolutionary woman is her veil. In fact we scarcely see the face of the woman and her body is completely covered. Raised over her right shoulder is a banner calling on "O Zahra!" ('O The Most Pure One') which is an honorific title of Fatemeh, while from her left shoulder hangs the right hand of a young child carrying a machine gun. Religious piety, revolutionary chastity, and breeding soldiers for the revolution are the three instant messages with which this stamp identifies and celebrates the faceless and bodiless Iranian woman. The hidden argument of this stamp is of course against the image of the Iranian woman constructed and celebrated during the Pahlavi regime: Without the traditional veil and alienated from the Islamic symbols of her identity. While during the Pahlavi regime, it was the birthday of the female members of the royal family which was recognized as the "Mother's Day," or the day that Reza Shah forced Iranian woman out of their veil as the "Woman's Day," after the revolution it was the saintly memory of Shi'i characters that was politically remembered for revolutionary purposes. The figure of Fatemeh was a particularly poignant one because even before the revolution, Ali Shari'ati, one of its principal ideologues, had written a book on her, called "Fatemeh is Fatemeh," and represented her as a model revolutionary figure for contemporary Iranian woman.

As much as days important in early Islamic history could be renewed with contemporary significance, events of more immediate origin could equally be celebrated and universalized with larger significance. The day that Ayatollah Motahhari, one of the principal ideologues of the Islamic Revolution, was assassinated in 1979 from then on was celebrated as "The Teachers Day." The stamps which were annually released to commemorate that day [Fig 15.5] feature a picture of Ayatollah Motahhari with various symbols of books, red tulips, and candles accessorizing his memory. There were quite a number of reason why the name of Motahhari should be identified with "The Teachers Day." He was one of the principal ideologues of the revolution and as such he in effect "taught" Iranians the right way. He was also a professor of religious studies at Tehran University. But perhaps most significantly, he was a student of Ayatollah Khomeini when he was teaching at Qom Seminary. A host of religious and revolutionary sentiments were thus invested in the name of Motahhari and his associations with the Islamic Revolution. Identifying "The Teachers Day" with Ayatollah Motahhari had the added benefit of idealizing a revolutionary religious leader as the model teacher, thus carrying his authority into the educational establishment. This was a particularly significant gesture because the radical Islamicization of the educational system was paramount on the revolutionary agenda.

By far the most memorable date in the early revolutionary upheavals of 1978 was Friday the 17th of Shahrivar 1357 (8 September, 1978) when hundreds of demonstrators were fired at by the

پست جمهوری اسلامی ایران

ولادت حضرت فاطمه زهرا«س»
روز زن

۲۰
ریال

ISLAMIC REPUBLIC OF IRAN

یا زهرا

1988

20
R1s.

BIRTH ANNIVERSARY OF
HAZRAT FATIMA (A.S) -WOMAN'S DAY

15.4

پست جمهوری اسلامی ایران

20
ریال

ISLAMIC REPUBLIC OF IRAN

پست جمهوری اسلامی ایران

THE COMMEMORATION OF TEACHER'S DAY.

ISLAMIC REPUBLIC OF IRAN

بزرگداشت روز معلم

5 R1s.   ۱۳۶۶   1987   ۵ ریال

15.5

Shah's army. The Seventeenth of Shahrivar from then on became known as "Yaum Allah" ('The Divine Day') because it was from this day forward that downfall of the Pahlavi regime was almost inevitable. It was on this day, the celebration thus implied, that the Divine judgment was cast on the fall of the Shah and the victory of the Islamic Revolution. The stamp which was released to celebrate the anniversary of this date [Fig 15.6] featured a prominent page from a typical desk-top calendar in which the three coinciding dates on the Iranian, Islamic, and "Common" calendars were noted: The 17th of Shahrivar, the 5th of Shawwal, and the 8th of September. The wounded body of a demonstrator is being carried away by his comrades. These three revolutionaries and an entire crowd behind them defiantly raise their hands against the firing guns of the Shah's army. The spilled blood of the fallen friend is the price that Muslim revolutionaries have paid for their ideal. By calling, and thus celebrating, this day as the "Divine Day of 17 Shahrivar," the Muslim ideologues are in effect appropriating not just all of those demonstrators but the entire evolutionary movement as "Islamic."

"Islamicizing" the Iranian calendar, and with it the Iranian revolution of 1979, meant an active attention to symbolic references to competing ideologies. Celebration of May 1 as "The Labor Day"

has traditionally been identified with the secular left. The ideologues of the Islamic revolution could not altogether neglect this day. Whatever they could not neglect, they sought to assimilate into an "Islamic" mold. The Tudeh Party, The Fada'ian-e Khalq Organization, and the Mujahedin Organization were the chief political rivals of the Islamic Republic and for all of them "May 1" was a principal symbolic appropriation of Iranian workers. Instead of leaving the symbolic power of "May 1" to them or creating an alternative labor day, the ideologues of the Islamic Republic sought to redefine it in an "Islamic" manner. In posters that were distributed on the occasion of "May 1" [Fig 15.7], in four languages "Islam," as re-defined by Ayatollah Khomeini, is proclaimed as "the only supporter of the worker." Quoting from the Sixth Shiʿi Imam Jaʿfar al-Sadiq, workers endeavors are compared to "Fighting in the Path of God." Against a background of industrial hardware, a group of workers have taken time out for their collective prayers. The figures represent the cross-sections of Iranian ethnicities. Their stern and hardened faces, reminiscent of Soviet socialist realist graphics, exudes a nobility which the ideologues of the Islamic Revolution sought to invest in Iranian workers. The celebration of 1 May as "The International Labor Day" is a major attempt to appropriate a crucial symbolic force in the arsenal of the socialist movements. Here the ideologues of the Islamic Republic sought actively to defuse a major rhetorical momentum historically at the disposal of the Iranian left. By recognizing and celebrating it as such, they have assimilated 1 May into an "Islamic calendar," which by definition "Islamicizes" every day of remembrance recorded in its pages. The assimilation of 1 May into the Islamic calendar also gives an aura of global universality to the annals of the revolutionaries, as is also evident in its noting "The End of World War II" on 8 May and "The Beginning of World War I" on 1 August. But the recognition of 10 December 1948 as the day when the United Nations ratified "The Declaration of Human Rights" is perhaps the most effective of such universalizing strategies of the Islamic calendar. On many occasions Khomeini had denounced the United Nations and its Declaration of Human Rights, asking why it was never applied to Iranians suffering under the Pahlavis. But by 1987, some eight years into the Revolution, the day of its ratification was assimilated into the Islamic calendar.

The thorough Islamicization of the Iranian history meant not only appropriating the symbolic powers of the secular left but also the secular nationalists. Iranian nationalism, next to "Islam" perhaps the most passionate ideological movement in the colonial and post-colonial periods, had to be incorporated into the emerging consciousness

15.6

الكادُّ على عيالِهِ كالمجاهِدِ في سبيلِ اللهِ
«امام صادق»

الاسلام وحده يحامى الذين يعملون «الامام خمينى»

ES IST EINZIG UND ALLEINE DER ISLAM, DER DIE ARBEITENDEN MENSCHEN SCHÜTZT. (IMAM KHOMEINY)
C'EST UNIQUEMENT I'ISLAM QUI PROTÈGE LES HOMMES TRAVAILLEURS. (IMAM KHOMEINY)
ISLAM IS THE ONLY SUPPORTER OF THE WORKER. (IMAM KHOMEINI)

ISLAMIC REPUBLIC PARTY · INT. SECTION

of a politicized "Islam." The commemoration of 29 Esfand (19 or 20 March) as "The Nationalization of the Oil Industry" is meant to incorporate a major turning point in Iranian anti-colonial nationalism. What is crucial here is that both during the reign of Mohammad Reza Shah and that of the Islamic Republic, the name of the principal engineer of that extraordinarily important event, i.e., Mohammad Mosaddeq, is omitted from the national annals. Although the Muslim ideologues after the revolution sought to acknowledge the anti-colonial movement of 1950's, any reference to its principal charismatic leader is eliminated. This became an extremely effective way of both taking advantage of the anti-colonial memory of the nationalist movement, while denying its leaders any recognition. As part of the same strategy, religious leaders of minor historical significance are renarrated into a more prominent role in this revised history of modern Iran. The 30th of Tir (21 or 22 of July) was now celebrated as "The Resurrection of the Muslim people of Iran under the leadership of Ayatollah Kashani." Here, the position of Ayatollah Kashani, arguably a less significant figure than Mosaddeq in the nationalist movement of the early 1950's, which gradually led to Mohammad Reza Shah's departure from Iran, is privileged over that of Mosaddeq by literally eliminating any reference to his role. Along the same lines is the remembrance of 3 Shahrivar (25 or 26 August) as "The Occupation of Iran by the Allied Forces and the Escape of Reza Khan from Iran." The commemoration of this event of 25 August 1941 has a multiple function of discrediting the legitimacy of the Pahlavi regime, signaling the imperialist history of the Allied Forces, and the partial appropriation of that history into the new Islamic historiography. To add further religious fervor to this discrediting of Reza Shah, 17 Dey (7 or 8 January) is remembered as "The Unveiling of Women" by Reza Khan's Instructions." While under the Pahlavis the 17th of Dey was celebrated as a day when Iranian women were liberated from their traditional bondage, here the day is remembered with a negative connotation and a derogatory reference to Reza "Khan," which strips the deceased monarch of his claims to kingship. It is the same sort of delegitimizing strategy which is operative in the commemoration of 3 Esfand (22 or 23 February) as "The Coup d'Etat of Reza Khan." This is in fact the commencement of the Pahlavi regime in the 1920's when Reza Shah plotted his succession of power to the Qajars. To bring that monarchical history to a closure, the 22nd of Bahman (9 or 10 February) is now celebrated as "The Victory of the Islamic Revolution in 1357/1979, and the toppling of 2,500 year-old Monarchy" [Fig. 15.8].

The downfall of the Qajars, and with it the Constitutional Revolution of 1906-11, assured a renewed significance for the ideologues of the Islamic Revolution and a massive process of appropriation commenced on the major symbolic of the nineteenth century. The 18th of Dey (8 or 9 January) is devoted to a major delegitimation of the Qajar monarchy. On this day, in 1851, the renowned prime minister of the Qajar period, Amir Kabir, was murdered. In the annals of Iranian reformists, modernists, and

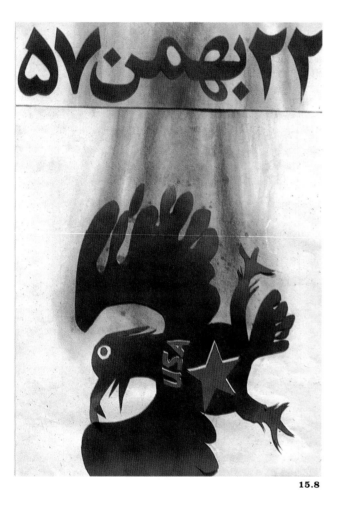

15.8

nationalists, Amir Kabir is remembered as a major nationalist of the nineteenth century who opposed the influence of foreign powers, initiated a series of major modernist reforms, chief among them the establishment of Dar al-Funun as the first secular college in Iran. His reforms, occasionally demanding radical changes in the medieval operations of the Qajar monarchy, were the culmination of more than half a century of development of a secular discourse of political self-awareness, dating back to the earlier part of the century. Amir Kabir's cultural, social, and political reforms were arguably a turning-point in a series of major institutional changes in the nineteenth century that gradually led to the Constitutional Revolution. The commemoration of his murder is noted by Muslim ideologues as "The Martyrdom of Mirza Amir Kabir by the Order of Naser al-Din Shah." The key operative word here of course is martyrdom (shahadat) which is meant to appropriate Amir Kabir as a "Muslim martyr," a highly unusual epithet for the nineteenth-century champion of secular reforms in Iranian social and political institutions. "By the Order of Naser al-Din Shah" is a further emphasis, intended to delegitimize not only Naser al-Din Shah and the Qajars, but the whole institution of monarchy. The same is true of the commemoration of 21 Mordad (11 or 12 August) as "The Martyrdom of Mirza Reza Kermani." Mirza Reza Kermani was the man who assassinated Naser al-Din Shah, on which charge he was hanged on 12 August 1896. Again the key term "martyrdom" is applied to Mirza Reza Kermani, without any reference to why he was killed. But perhaps the most controversial of all revisionist historical appropriations is the commemoration of 16 Sha'ban as "The Anniversary of the Martyrdom of Shaykh Fazlullah Nuri." Shaykh Fazlullah Nuri [See Fig. 15.9 for the celebration of his memory on a stamp] was a staunchly anti-Constitutionalist cleric who was hanged by the Constitutionalists. It is a curious fact of the Islamic Republic's revisionist historiography of the Constitutional period that while (in order to appropriate it) it celebrates its major figures and events, it equally canonizes its staunchest enemy, Shaykh Fazlullah Nuri. This can only be explained as yet another major act of "Islamicization" to which the Muslim ideologues of Iran have subjected their history. In this respect, the anniversary of the Constitutional Revolution on 14 Mordad 1366 (5 August 1987) of 1285/1908 was bracketed between "The Martyrdom of His Holiness Muslim [Ibn Aqil]" in 60AH/679 CE and "The Martyrdom of Dr. Sayyid Hasan Ayat" in 1360/1981. Here an early Muslim martyr and his most recent counterpart embraced and thus appropriated the Constitutional Revolution to define it as "Islamic."

The most celebrated days on the Islamic calendar of the year were reserved for those occasions that marked the event and the gradual success of the Islamic Revolution. The 12th of Farvardin (31 of March or 1 April, but totally unrelated to April Fool's Day, which does not mean anything in Iran, despite the fact that the following day, 13 Farvardin, is a national picnic day, when everyone spends the day in the countryside, wishing all the bad luck of the thirteenth day of the first month of the year away) was to be celebrated as "The

Day of the Islamic Republic" because on this day in 1979 Iranians participated in a national referendum and, according to official reports, overwhelmingly voted for an "Islamic Republic." The 20th of Farvardin (8 or 9 April) was reserved for the day of "The Complete Break in the Relation between Iran and the United States," marking the hostage crisis of 1979-81. Long suppressed under the Pahlavi regime, 15 Khordad (5 June) finally entered the annals of Iranian revolutionary history, marking "The Bloody Uprising of 15 Khordad 1342," also known as "The Uprising of the Muslim People," or the "Rebellion of Truth against Falsehood." The events of Khordad 1342/June 1963 were instrumental in shaking the Pahlavi regime to its foundations, a forewarning of the events of 1978-9 [Fig. 15.10].

Quite a number of days were given new significance on the basis of their place in the new Islamic reconfiguration of the Iranian Revolution. For example, 2 April 1987, where the birthday of Imam Hussein is celebrated is noted as "The Guardians of the Revolution Day." Here there is a very strong identification of perhaps the most vibrant and courageous image in Shi'i martyrology, that is the figure of Iman Hussein, with a recognition of the Pasdaran, the Muslim militia which emerged immediately after the Revolution as the military arm of the revolutionaries. The same is true of 14 April 1987, when the birthday of the twelfth Shi'i Imam, who is now considered to be in occultation and whose return is anticipated, is also celebrated as "The International Day of the Oppressed." There is a direct correspondence here between the promise of ultimate salvation, signaled by the birth of Savior Mahdi, and the day of remembering the oppressed. There is also an accidental

15.9

۱۵ خرداد ۱۳۴۲

15.10

gathering of two events that give added momentum to the rhetorical build-up in this calendar. Consider, for example, 28 March 1987, when the celebration of Prophet Mohammad's designation as a prophet on 27 Rajab, a highly festive occasion in the Islamic calendar, happened to coincide with 8 Farvardin, which is still in the two-week-long national New Year holiday celebrations. The birthday of Abu al-Fazl, a major Shi'i martyred saint (3 April 1987), also coincided in that year with "The International Day of Children's Books."

In a spirit of ecumenical, interreligious reconciliation, the birthday of Jesus is recognized and celebrated as a prophet (and expressly not as the son of God). This calendar reference does more than simply acknowledge the birth of Christ. While there is an active "Islamicization" of Christ, in the adding of the traditional benedictory phrase of "peace be upon him" after his name and thus signaling his Qur'anic significance, there is also an appeal to the Christian community inside Iran, particularly Armenian-Iranians, some of whom actively participated in the Revolution. This calendar recognition of Christ's birthday and the commencement of the Christian New Year, while alerting Iranians to two major holidays in the Christian world, also invites the Christian-Iranian community into the defining space of the Islamic Republic.

Beyond the Iranian boundaries, there is an active identification with revolutionary movements in the Third World. The 6th of October is remembered for "The Revolutionary Execution of [Anwar al-]Sadat, the Egyptian Dictator, by Muslim Forces in Egypt." The 30th of January is remembered for "The Assassination of Mahatma Gandhi," and 13 April is celebrated as "The Convening of the First Non-Aligned Nations" in 1956. This reaching out to identify with other Third World countries is obviously more pronounced when it comes to other Muslim nations. The 5 November is celebrated as "The Birthday of the Noble Prophet, Peace and Benedictions be upon Him and His Family, according to our Sunni Brothers' Sources." Like all other Muslims, the Shi'ites are very particular about the historical accuracy of their sources. In fact, the very veracity of Shi'ism is contingent upon the belief in the accuracy of these sources. Recognizing the birthday of the Prophet according to Sunni sources is thus a major step forward to reach the overwhelming majority of Muslims. The same spirit is present in commemorating the death of Allamah Iqbal Lahuri, the Pakistani poet and Muslim revivalist, on 21 April 1984.

Making new, revolutionary, and universalizing connections was as crucial in the reconfiguration of an Islamic calendar as breaking the old ones. Cento was a regional cooperative treaty between Iran, Turkey, and Pakistan, which Iran annulled in 1979 and marked on 25 March. Calling it "a colonial treaty," the ideologues of the Islamic Revolution in effect sought to declare their independence from any real or presumed power that the United States might exert over the region via such collateral treaties.

What we see in this active reconfiguration of the Islamic calendar in (and for) Iran is a specific contraction of a historical and fictional narrative to generate and sustain a revolutionary self-understanding. Hundreds of days of the calendar are devoted to the generation of such an historical/pictorial narrative, and then the narrative is given matter-of-fact reality by virtue of a day devoted to it, for example "The Day of Dentistry," 12 April. The structural identity of this reconfigured calendar is at the root of a new, emerging historiography which not only defines the 1978-9 Revolution as "Islamic" but recasts the whole history of Iran into this new mode. The historical and fictional narratives, as Paul Ricoeur has demonstrated, have a close affinity in their modes of operation in claiming truth. The temporality of all acts of historical/fictional narrative is constitutional to all its claims to truth. As Ricoeur puts it, "what is ultimately at stake in the case of the structural identity of the narrative functions as well as in that of the truth claims of every narrative work, is the temporal character of human experience. The world unfolded by every narrative work is always a temporal world. Or time becomes human time to the extent that it is organized after the manner of a narrative; narrative, in turn, is meaningful to the extent that it portrays the features of temporal experience." This connection between temporality and narrativity is blatantly evident in every page of the re-Islamicized Iranian calendar. When 10 Shahrivar (1 or 2 September) is designated "The Day of Interest-Free Banking," an ideological intervention is projected, on this very page of the calendar, between the temporal nature of all historical narratives and a particular ideological, reconfiguration of that narrative. There is no ideological (that is, historical/fictional) reconfiguration of a narrative without the necessary manipulation of its related temporality. The re-Islamicized calendar is the occasion of that manipulated temporality. The ideologues of the Islamic Republic did not, of course, limit themselves to manipulating the daily temporality of the revolutionary event. They were engaged in a thorough revision of Iranian history, giving full expression to their Islamic reading of major events. But on this elementary, routine, and mundane level, every day of the year was given an Islamic coordinate, 1 Sha'ban 1408 to match and balance the nationalist signifier, 30 Esfand 1366, and to neutralize and keep at bay the imperial European calendar, 20 March 1988. The employment of the new Iranian historiography needed, and in these calendar pages received, a sustained temporal progression of time with regular Islamic tempo. Unless time was so thoroughly Islamicized, the new historical narrative could not have easily followed.

1 Paul Ricoeur, Time and Narrative. 3 Volumes. (Chicago, 1983), esp. Vol. I, Pt. 1. 2 Ibid. Vol. I: 3.

what needs

to be done:

something on propaganda

Sixteen

IT IS OUR DUTY TO WORK TOWARD THE ESTABLISHMENT OF AN ISLAMIC GOVERNMENT. THE FIRST ACTIVITY WE MUST UNDERTAKE IN THIS RESPECT IS THE PROPAGATION OF OUR CAUSE; THAT IS HOW WE MUST BEGIN. IT HAS ALWAYS BEEN THAT WAY, ALL OVER THE WORLD: A GROUP OF PEOPLE CAME TOGETHER, DELIBERATED, MADE DECISIONS, AND THEN BEGAN TO PROPAGATE THEIR AIMS. GRADUALLY THE NUMBER OF LIKE-MINDED PEOPLE WOULD INCREASE, UNTIL FINALLY THEY BECAME POWERFUL ENOUGH TO INFLUENCE A GREAT STATE OR EVEN TO CONFRONT AND OVERTHROW IT... SUCH MOVEMENTS BEGAN WITH NO TROOPS OR ARMED POWER AT THEIR DISPOSAL; THEY ALWAYS HAD TO RESORT TO PROPAGATING THE AIMS OF THEIR MOVEMENT FIRST. THE THIEVERY AND TYRANNY PRACTICED BY THE REGIME WOULD BE CONDEMNED AND THE PEOPLE AWAKENED AND MADE TO UNDER-STAND THAT THE THIEVERY INFLICTED ON THEM WAS WRONG. GRADUALLY THE SCOPE OF THIS ACTIVITY WOULD BE EXPANDED UNTIL IT CAME TO EMBRACE ALL GROUPS OF SOCIETY, AND THE PEOPLE, AWAKENED AND ACTIVE, WOULD ATTAIN THEIR GOAL. YOU HAVE NEITHER A COUNTRY NOR AN ARMY NOW, BUT PROPA-GATING ACTIVITY IS POSSIBLE FOR YOU, BECAUSE THE ENEMY HAS BEEN UNABLE TO DEPRIVE YOU OF ALL THE REQUISITE MEANS.[1]

Upon his return from exile to Iran in February 1979, and at the graveyard of revolutionary martyrs, Ayatollah Khomeini felt compelled to address the question of radio and television: "We are not opposed to radio. We are opposed to prostitution. We are not opposed to television. We are opposed to that which is at the service of foreigners, used to keep our youth backward, wasting our human resources."[2] More than a month later, in Qom, he made it absolutely clear that radio and television "ought to educate all the nation." He was fully aware of the range of public audience that radio and television reached. "People understand things with their ears and their eyes. Both the illiterate and the literate individuals can thus understand. And this is quite crucial." Khomeini insisted that, as the monarchical regime used radio and television to promote its evil ends, so too must the Islamic Republic "for its Islamic responsibilities." Radio and television, he thought, constituted "a public university." They had to be de-"Westoxicated." "It is the responsibility of radio and television to treat people as teachers do students." They had to "feed people nutritiously." Radio, television, and cinema all had a common pedagogic purpose, leading people to a "pure" society.[3] In this chapter, our purpose is to consider some of these observations and see how Khomeini sought to "Islamicize" Iranian radio and television and thus have

them used effectively for revolutionary and propaganda purposes.

"Instruments of propaganda," Khomeini declared in April 1979, "ought to rectify themselves so that, God forbid, they would not go against the wishes of the people." These instruments ought to be at the disposal of the public good, as defined by its religious leadership. "Printed material, cinema, television, radio, journals, all these are to serve the country. They ought to be in service (of the Islamic Revolution)."[4] He was fully aware of the power of public media: "Radio and television can rectify a nation and they can (equally) lead it to corruption." He repeatedly reminded the employees of radio and television that theirs was "the most sensitive organ in this country." The range of publicity available to radio and television was virtually limitless. "Radio and television exist in all the villages of our country, and in the smallest villages of other countries too." There were limitations to the traditional modes of propaganda that Khomeini recognized very well: "Save for radio, a religious orator cannot reach beyond the four walls that surround him." He was equally aware of the necessity of reaching a wider audience beyond the immediacies of the Islamic Republic: "If you broadcast in foreign languages, talk about the problems of Iran." The negative propaganda of foreigners ought to be countered with the positive propaganda of the Islamic Republic, telling the truth "as it is." To perform this task, instruments of propaganda had to cleanse and rectify themselves first: "Corruption of radio and television is the corruption of the society (at large), and should these organs be corrupted it would be the corruption of the society (at large, too)."[5]

Khomeini placed the significance of propaganda highest on his revolutionary agenda. He considered radio and television as even more important to the Islamic Republic than various ministries.[6] In his judgment, "the way people pay attention to radio and television they do not pay attention to any other organ."[7] "If radio and television are not Islamicized, it means that Iran is not Islamicized."[8] The function of these organs of propaganda was not merely to report the news "as it actually is" and Islamically: "Radio has to guide."[9] Addressing the executive director of Iranian Radio and Television in July 1983, Khomeini advised that "you ought to ensure that every single step that you take is for Islam, so that (in effect) you are performing an act of worship."[10] He went so far as to assert that "the sanctity of radio and television (voice and vision) ought to be preserved."[11] Consolidation of these instruments of propaganda for Islam was urgently needed because the enemy was in full charge of negative propaganda: "We ought to be careful. The propaganda of these enemies are more harmful to us than wars. We should not take these propaganda simplistically."[12] In arguing for

263

خجسته سالروز پیروزی انقلاب اسلامی
وپیروزی نور بر ظلمت مبارک باد.

16.1 This poster is based on a photograph capturing Ayatollah Khomeini's descent from the Air France plane which brought him back home after living 14 years in exile. In the background is the flag of the Islamic Republic, and the statement reads: "May the auspicious anniversary of the blossoming of the Islamic Revolution and the victory of light over darkness be blessed."

propaganda, he appealed to the highest authority: "Propagate for God, because propaganda is a very important thing."[13]

You know that if something is said and broadcast on radio and television what an impact it has all over the country, indeed wherever this voice reaches. Now you are fully aware that this organ is used throughout the country, in villages and cities, by children and adults. This is different from other kinds of news and media. You should not consider radio and television as similar to other forms of public communication. These have a particular feature in that children of 2, 3, or 4 years to old men look at it or listen to them and they have an effect on their spirit. Everyone is influenced (by radio and television). As you know, since the inception of radio and television in Iran, these organs have done the greatest damage to this nation's honor, making it dependent, as they have, on superpowers. During the reign of this boy (that is, the Shah), he misused these organs more than his father in propagating corruption... God forbid, had he continued to reign for a few more years, we should have kissed Iran goodbye. Even one word which is said on these organs, even one sentence, and it can create havoc in the bazaar... these organs ought to be under the control of knowledgeable people, those who are deeply aware of the problems. Anything that is being broadcast has to be under their supervision. They have to see every word and sentence and ascertain its accuracy... These are the kinds of organs that can perform the greatest of all services, or else commit the highest treasons. Of all the organs of propaganda, radio and television are most important. If they are reformed, the whole country can be reformed, and if, God forbid, they are corrupted, it can lead a country to corruption. These are more important than schools. They are a nationwide public school... Even one sentence can create such problems that you cannot rectify it in a year.[14]

Khomeini's revolutionary messages were propagated through a range of diverse and yet complementary mechanisms. As he concluded his scholastic learning in the 1920s and 1930s and began his teaching career in Qom, his courses in Shiʿi jurisprudence, philosophy, and mysticism attracted many students. Although in these scholastic courses there are established curricula to be followed, the clique of students around Khomeini increasingly assumed a militant posture in accordance with his revolutionary disposition. As his *Velayat-e Faqih* indicates, there are pertinent topics in traditional Shiʿi jurisprudence to occasion radical political commentaries and thus create an ideologically significant level of discourse in the context of juridical learning. Whether it is in the collection of his legal edicts, *Tawzih al-Masaʿil*, or in polemical tracts written against secularism, or in patently political treatises like *Velayat-e Faqih*, or even in mystical reflections like *Jihad-e Akbar*, Khomeini always seized upon every opportunity to air his political opposition to the *status quo*. Thus, whether in the form of lectures to his immediate students or in the body of his published books and treatises, he took full advantage of his position of authority to speak for Islam.

Immediately surrounding Khomeini were a group of devoted students and followers. Some prominent members of this group, like Murteza Motahhari and Hussein Ali Montazeri, became leading figures of the Islamic Revolution. Many other students became the immediate disciples of Khomeini both in Qom and in Najaf. When in 1964 Khomeini was forced to flee Iran he left behind a group of dedicated student followers who kept a vigilant eye on events for him. He kept in close contact with these students and through them propagated his active political and ideological agenda. Beginning in 1965 he formed a new body of student followers in Najaf, and also formed a larger group of students who propagated his ideas in Europe and the United States. These were members of various Muslim student associations who had become increasingly attracted to his ideas. When in 1971 some of Khomeini's Iranian students were deported from Iraq they went back to Iran and presumably joined the group of active propagators of his revolutionary message. Thus, whether in the immediate or more distanced sense of the term, student followers of Khomeini were among the prominent agencies of propaganda that circulated widely his revolutionary ideas.

One of the most effective modes of propaganda available to Khomeini was his public sermons, of which perhaps the most famous were those he delivered in 1963, during his first bid for power. After the commencement of his period of exile in Iraq, the possibility of reaching a much wider audience was opened up through his systematic correspondence. He was always in relentless contact with his closest allies, especially with the Muslim student associations in Europe and the United States. But perhaps the most effective mode of propaganda, which Khomeini utilized to its fullest extent, was the publication of religious edicts and declarations. As a highest-ranking cleric, an *ayatollah*, Khomeini was in a position to be asked his "legal opinion" (*fatwa'*) and to issue a binding political statement. He extended this model to issue declarations on unsolicited occasions.

As the revolutionary momentum grew stronger, and as the international community became ever more aware of Khomeini's leadership, the attention of the news media gave him a unique opportunity to air his discontent with the *status quo*. An avalanche of interviews with the leading news organizations of the world — American, European, Australian, Japanese, etc. — became unprecedented occasions for propagating revolutionary sentiments. Central to Khomeini's reawakening of the Islamic consciousness was a compelling seriousness, a refusal to allow frivolity, a stark identification of the previous regime with corrupting laxities: "There is no joking in Islam, no licentiousness. Everything about it is serious."[15] The content of Iranian television had to be totally Islamicized to reflect this seriousness. Anything which was anti-Islamic was to be avoided and discarded by Islamic television, the most effective way of reaching Iranians and convincing them of their serious responsibilities as Muslims. Speaking as the authoritative voice of Islam, Khomeini occasionally conceded that

Iranian television had succeeded to a large extent in becoming "Islamic," "but still not as good as Islam wants." Iranian radio and television were to "satiate" the eyes and ears of Iranians with "good virtues and the necessary issues of the Islamic Republic."[16] To achieve such grave and serious objectives, Iranian radio and television had to be "purified"[17] from all anti-revolutionary elements. Even those who had apparently rediscovered their Islamicity were not to be totally trusted and accepted.

"Purity" became a central concern of Khomeini's in Iranian audiovisual propaganda. Muslim activists were to be on the alert to detect the slightest "impurity" and root it out. The kind of radio and television which for decades has been at the service of the "satanic regime" could not be expected to be "purified" immediately. Occasionally Khomeini showed a tolerant and conciliatory attitude towards these "corrupt" elements from the ancien régime: "If people of evil intent were in these organizations, admonish them, and if admonition were not effective then purify (that is, dismiss) them." Those who were to be immediately "purified" included "the leftists." They were to be substituted by "responsible, Islamic youths." The technical expertise of those who were being dismissed was of no concern: "The damage of an evil expert is more than the damage of an evil non-expert."[18]

16.2 Children were the principal targets of Islamic propaganda.

The views of Khomeini on propaganda in radio and television were so central to the Islamic Republic that they were codified explicitly in the Constitution of the Islamic Republic. "In the mass media (radio and television), the 175th Article of the Constitution of the Islamic Republic stipulates, "the freedom of publicity and propaganda is guaranteed, based on Islamic principles." The article proceeds to establish that "these media will be managed under the collective supervision of the three branches of the judiciary (the Supreme Juridical Commission), legislative, and executive, the specifics of which will be established by law."[19]

In July 1982 the Parliament of the Islamic Republic ratified a general "Guideline to Govern the Policies of the Iranian National Radio and Television." Legalized in this Guideline were the principal doctrines of Khomeini on how the mass media were to be effectively used for propagating the revolutionary purposes of the Islamic Republic. The Guideline (Khatt-e Mashy) consists of nine sections (fasl), the first of which establishes the general principles governing the policies of the National Radio and Television. According to this Guideline, "Islam" is to govern all the programs of the National Radio and Television, and there should be nothing in it that is "against Islamic principles." "The revolutionary spirit is to reign supreme upon every social institution." "Independence, freedom, and the Islamic Republic" are the three main tenets of this revolutionary spirit. Central to the objectives of the National Radio and Television is giving widespread expression to the ideas of the jurist/leader, that is Ayatollah Khomeini, and his constitutional successors. These organs of mass communication must prepare the groundwork for the ideological objectives of the Islamic Republic which is summarized in the slogan of "Neither East, nor West." Like "a public university, the combined coverage of radio and television ought to propagate the ideological, political, social, cultural, economic, and military" objectives of the revolutionary regime. In all these efforts, "human dignity" is to be protected, "according to Islamic principles." There are three kinds of majority in Iran which ought to be represented and addressed most emphatically: the ideological majority, that is the Muslims; the economic majority, that is the poor people; and the majority in terms of age, that is children and young adults. Islamic radio and television should unite Iranians from all walks of life in their most common denominator, that is their belief in Islam. The authorities in charge of radio and television should be in constant communication with their audience so that they can best express their concerns and ideals. In the Tenth Article of this First Section, there is a clear indication of how alert the authorities of the Islamic Republic are in effectively reaching out to mobilize people's deepest religious convictions. "In order to penetrate and influence (nufuz) the thought and sentiments of the society," reads the article, "the (Radio and Television) organization is obligated to do whatever is possible to present its message through the use of indirect expression, and in attractive and artistic forms, compatible with the dispositions and proclivities (ahwal wa Ruhiyyat) of the different groups of people." It is within this context that the Guideline proceeds to suggest that radio and television ought to advance people's creative imagination, their sense of hope and confidence. It also stipulates that the spirit of "sacrifice and perseverance" should be strengthened in people. Expansion of radio and television coverage should be programmed in accordance with "cultural, political, and geographical" priorities. The Fourteenth Article establishes that radio and television should do the necessary ground-work for "accelerating" the implementation of the programs of the three branches of the government.[20]

In the Second Section of the Guideline, certain rules and regulations are established to govern the broadcasting of news and other informative items. In this section, there is a concerted effort to block any possibility of counter-propaganda targeted against the legitimacy and/or institutional foundations of the Islamic Republic. Publication of anything which has "propaganda purposes for misguided and anti-revolutionary groups" is forbidden. More generally, anything which "causes injury to religious sentiments, national unity, or causes disturbance in society" cannot be broadcast. The Third Section deals with ideological issues. Islamic radio and television must "elevate the level of people's Islamic awareness." More specifically, "the propagation and dissemination of the genuine Islamic culture" is the responsibility of radio and television. The "genuine Islam" must be propagated not just nationally but internationally. Islamic philosophy, mysticism, and law must be compared against a critical evaluation of "similar schools of thought in the world." "Non-Islamic and misguided" ideas must be debated publicly on radio and television, and their incoherence demonstrated to the public.[21]

The Fourth Section addresses all the principal "cultural programs." "Islamic value systems" must be substituted for the value systems of "East and West." This should lead to a realization of "the Islamic self-consciousness." Conditions must thus be prepared so that noble human virtues are attained. "Trivial art" ought to be substituted by "committed and revolutionary art," which answers man's quintessential needs. Priority should also be given to sports that, in addition to promoting a healthy body, are beneficial to military and defensive objectives. But such sports as are contrary to "Islamic principles" are to be avoided. The younger generation should also be warned against harmful and dangerous addictions.[22] Social issues are the subject of the Fifth Section. The people are central to the continuity of the Revolution. Their active political participation must be encouraged. Religious minorities are to be accepted and dealt with in a brotherly fashion. "The superior status of women from the Islamic perspective" is to be explained, and "false values" about family relations replaced by "ethical virtues."[23] The sacrifices of the early and later revolutionary martyrs of Islam must also be glorified.

In the Sixth Section of the Guideline, the ideologues of the Islamic Republic sought to extend and institutionalize Khomeini's political ideas into the chief governing organs of the regime.

Intellectual and ethical foundations for the implementation of the Constitution of the Islamic Republic must be cultivated. All illegal acts must be discouraged. The arrogant superpowers must be identified in contradistinction to the oppressed people, and that through the "presentation of the ideological, political perspective." Emphasis must be put on "the Islamic identity of the Revolution," its anti-imperialist character, and "the endeavors of the enemy to alter this identity." Comparative assessments of the Islamic Revolution in relation to other revolutions ought to be made available to the people, and political debates among "legal parties" encouraged in order to "clarify the genuine political perspectives of Islam."[24]

Article Fifty-six in the sixth section of the Guideline is devoted to the responsibility of the Islamic radio and television for "foreign propaganda." The identity and the political and social foundations of the hostile world-mongers and superpowers must be presented to the people. Less hostile, more hypocritical, governments are to be won over through a policy of "warning and alerting mixed with attraction." The indifferent governments ought to be informed and turned into allies. Friendly governments, "which are mostly popular," must be encouraged into more active co-operation. The propaganda policy towards other Islamic governments should be directed towards the establishment and consolidation of a united Islamic front. Liberation movements, especially if they are Islamic, should be protected and encouraged. The people of different countries ought to be distinguished from their respective governments and subjected to a specific course of propaganda. Islam must be introduced to them "as the only genuinely revolutionary and liberating ideology." This will pave the way for "exporting the Islamic Revolution to (other) Muslim (countries) and people of the world."[25] All these activities must be performed under the general framework of the foreign policies of the Islamic Republic.

The Seventh Section specifies the policies that should be followed in the economic domain. The groundwork must be done in order to eliminate all aspects of economic injustice "according to the economic policies of the Islamic Republic of Iran." The people should be discouraged from luxurious indulgence in too much consumption. They must be encouraged to save and to live a modest life. Agricultural and industrial production should be encouraged so that the country achieves self-sufficiency. Specific attention must be paid to "the professional training of workers and farmers because they are the cornerstone of production in the country." Section Eight addresses the mission of the Islamic propaganda machine in reducing the bureaucracy. "A simple and consolidated bureaucracy" must be created which is compatible with the course of the Islamic Revolution of Iran."[26] A healthy relationship must be encouraged between the government bureaucracy and the people it is meant to serve.

The Ninth and final Section of the Guideline specifies the responsibilities of the Islamic radio and television in military matters. These organs are to help in the military training of the general population and the creation of "the twenty million (strong) army."[27] The ideological training of the military personnel is to be specifically addressed. The different divisions and forces within the Islamic army are to be encouraged to be unified and coordinated. And thus the major principles of Khomeini's revolutionary ideas on the necessity of propaganda became institutionalized in the very organs of the Islamic Republic of Iran.

1 KHOMEINI, ISLAM AND REVOLUTION: WRITINGS AND DECLARATIONS, TRANS. AND ANNOTATED BY HAMID ALGAR (LONDON, 1985), P. 126. 2 ANON. (ED.), SEDA VA SIMA DAR KALAM-E IMAM KHOMEINI (TEHRAN, 1363/1984), P. 21. 3 IBID., PP. 21-2. 4 IBID., P. 23. 5 IBID., PP. 25-6. 6 IBID., P. 27. 7 IBID., P. 29. 8 IBID., P. 30. 9 IBID., P. 32. 10 IBID., P. 40. 11 IBID., P. 41. 12 IBID., P. 45. 13 IBID., P. 43. 14 IBID., PP. 36-9. 15 IBID., P. 67. 16 IBID., P. 68. 17 IBID., P. 73. 18 IBID., PP. 73-4. 19 IBID., P. 223. 20 IBID., PP. 225-7. 21 IBID., P. 228. 22 IBID., PP. 229-30. 23 IBID., P. 231. 24 IBID., P. 232. 25 IBID., PP. 232-4. 26 IBID., P. 234. 27 IBID., P. 235.

the Kingdom of Christ to flourish more perfectly [than it does] lest we fall asleep, to which we are too much inclined. If the Church were at peace and the Gospel received without contradiction, and if there were no kings or princes who were not opposed to it, we would promptly become accustomed to our ease and Jesus Christ would reign as a consequence of our belief and not by his power. God therefore wishes that the Kingdom of Jesus Christ should be placed in the midst of his enemies in order that we might be kept on a short rein. *John Calvin*

the war

Part Three:

IN ISLAM, THERE ARE TWO KINDS OF WAR:

one is called jihad, which is the conquering of [other] countries, with specific conditions stipulated for it, and the other is war for the independence of the country and expulsion of foreigners. Jihad, which is the acquisition of [other] countries and the conquest of [other] lands, is contingent upon the formation of the Islamic government in the presence, or following the command, of the Imam. Should this be the case, Islam has made it incumbent upon all men who have reached puberty and are not invalid or incompetent or foreign slaves to be ready to conquer [other] countries and disseminate Islamic law throughout the world that the islamic conquest of [other] countries is very different from the conquests of lands by worldly conquerors. They want to conquer the world for their own personal gains. Islam wants to conquer the world for the benefit of the people of the world themselves. When they conquer the world, they disseminate justice and reasonable, God-given rules. They want and conquer the world for their utterly base material life. Islam wants to conquer the world for the spiritual life and the preparation of the people of the world for the most glorious and blissful life in the other world.

AYATOLLAH   KHOMEINI

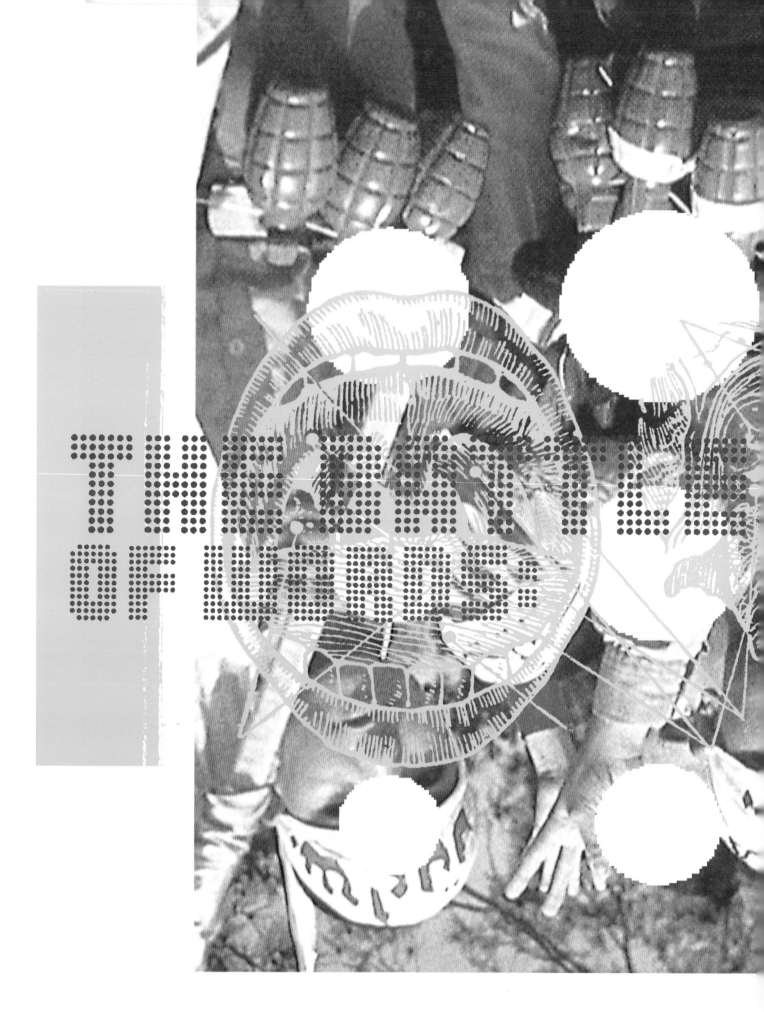

Seventeen

khomeini on
WAR ✛ SACRIFICE

FIRST OF ALL I OUGHT TO THANK THE GENTLEMEN CLERICS AND THE GENTLEMEN ORATORS WHO HAVE COME FROM TEHRAN AND, AS I AM TOLD, FROM QOM. IT IS AN HONOR TO SEE THEM. WE WISH THEM SUCCESS IN SERVING ISLAM AND THE MUSLIMS. THERE ARE MANY THINGS TO BE SAID, BUT I SHALL JUST MENTION ONE THING ABOUT THE GENTLEMEN CLERICS AND ORATORS... THE DEPTH OF THIS TASK WHICH IS LAID UPON YOU, AND THE DEPTH OF MOURNING SESSIONS [FOR THE SHIᶜI MARTYRS] HAVE NOT BEEN ADEQUATELY RECOGNIZED. INDEED SOME PEOPLE MAY NOT HAVE UNDERSTOOD ANYTHING [ABOUT THE IMPORTANCE OF THESE OCCASIONS OF MOURNING FOR THE SHIᶜI MARTYRS].[1]

17.1 Re-awakening Shiᶜi militant memory.

In his meeting with a group of Shiᶜi clerics, public prayer leaders, and orators in late June 1982, some two years into the Iraq–Iran war, Khomeini thought it appropriate to map out the extent to which they could help him reawaken the Shiᶜi collective sensibilities best suited to revolutionary and war purposes. He reminded his clerical audience that the annual and cyclical acts of collective commiseration for the historical atrocities committed against the Shiᶜi Saints and Infallibles had effects and functions far beyond what was immediately noticeable. "Gradually, the political dimension of this matter is becoming evident, and, God willing, it will become even more apparent."[2] The political uses to which these collective acts of remembrance, reminiscences about the actual and fantastic events in Shiᶜi sacred history, could be put thus became paramount in the revolutionary consciousness that Khomeini sought to create and sustain for immediate war purposes. In this chapter we shall review some of the salient features of Khomeini's position on resuscitating the Shiᶜi sentiments necessary for generating a self-sacrificial consciousness.

As Khomeini understood, and instructed his audience, the historical significance of these annual gatherings of commiseration were meant to give political and doctrinal cohesion and solidity to the Shiᶜi communities. That these communal gatherings were the focal point of the sacred memory had also functioned as a proper form of political organization against all kinds of adversities. "When I was captured in Qom for the first time, and taken into custody," Khomeini remembered, "some of these [secret] agents (who had come to capture me) told me in the way that, as they were coming to arrest me, they were afraid of these tents that were in Qom (where the poor people lived). They were afraid that should these people find out, they would not have been able to fulfill their mission." He continued: "those people are non-entities. The great superpowers are afraid of these tents."[3] The appeal to "the downtrodden," "the tent-dweller," was the most effective edge of Khomeini's rhetoric, which thrived on reactivating a sacred memory and then putting it at the service of what needed to be done. Central to that memory was a cyclical calendar of remembrance that never let go of a repoliticized imagination.

Of utmost importance in that calendar, in Khomeini's estimation, were the three months of Muharram, Safar, and Ramadan, particularly the central days of Tasuᶜa and ᶜAshura in the first month. During these months religious sensitivities are at their highest. No deliberate organization is necessary to gather people from all walks of life in villages and towns around a focal point of passionate remembrance of the Shiᶜi martyrology. There is an effective political organization behind these cyclical gatherings for apparently religious purposes. When Shiᶜi Imams had been specific in their instructions to have people commiserating with them in public places, Khomeini interpreted, it was not because they were in need of such acts of collective piety. Quite the contrary. It was the Shiʿites themselves who benefited greatly from these gatherings, were reminded of their common sacred heritage, and were encouraged to mobilize their power to oppose their enemies.

Khomeini lashed out against the "Westoxicated" intellectuals who denigrated such religious gatherings and commiserations. He equally criticized his fellow-clerics who had not taken full advantage of the political ramifications of these events. The religious implications of the events were self-evident for Khomeini: "Important," however, "is the political dimension." He went so far as to assert that the political dimension of these events was the original intent of the Shiʿi Imams: "Our Imams designed it that way from the very inception of Islam." This would bring Muslims "under one flag" and "under one idea." The June 1963 uprising, Khomeini assured his audience, would not have been possible without the

political effects of these pious recollections of things as they happened to the Shiʿi Imams. It was precisely these circumstances which trained young men and women who were willing and eager to sacrifice their lives for the sake of Islam. It was the political effect of such collective participations in the memory of the martyred Shiʿi Imams that created mothers who offered their young children for sacrifice without the slightest reservation.[4]

If the true significance of such commiserations were observed and understood, Iranian Muslims would not be known as "the people of misery," but as "the people of epic." If all the secular intellectuals, and all the "Westoxicated," and all the superpowers were to unite, they would not be able to create the June 1963 uprising. Only Shiʿism, only the collective belief in the sacredness of the Islamic cause, could bring Muslims together in their common revolutionary purpose. If the secular intellectuals were to understand the social and political dimensions of these gatherings, they would organize their own sessions of public crying and commiseration. The Shiʿi clerics ought to make it abundantly clear to the people that had it not been for the enduring effect of such commiserations, Iranians would not have had a revolution. Iranians were robbed of their human dignity. What gave them back their collective dignity was the Islamic Revolution which they carried out precisely in the utilization of the political implication of the Shiʿi sacred memory.

On the surface, these commiserations might appear useless and denigrating. But "we are a nation who destroyed a 2,500-year-old power precisely with these commiserations."[5] What the Shiʿi saints and martyrs had left for them, Khomeini told a group of Muslim soldiers and militia in March 1982, was a model of revolutionary behavior for all ages and generations to emulate.[6] "The household" of the Prophet — that is Muhammad himself, Fatemeh his daughter, Ali his son-in-law, and Hasan and Hussein his grandsons — were graced with divine blessings to provide the world with an unending source of inspiration for heroic and revolutionary behavior. Khomeini's followers ought to learn from these exemplary models not to be anxious about their meager resources, and to fight against their enemies no matter how powerful. The reason Iranian soldiers and militia were victorious in their battle against Iraq, despite the fact that Egypt and Jordan were helping the enemy, was precisely this indubitable moral conviction in the righteousness of their cause, inspired by the revolutionary model of the Shiʿi martyrs. The righteousness of Khomeini's cause, in war against Saddam Hussein for example, did not derive from any particular exigency of the situation itself. That righteousness was rooted in a history long

17.2 Idealizing the Muslim revolutionary.

before the Iraq–Iran war. The righteousness of the Iranian cause against the Baʿathist Iraqis was rooted in the righteousness of Imam Hussein's cause against the Umayyad caliph:

If today all those who have power, and all those who simply talk gibberish, write, deliver speeches, or conspire against you and against the Islamic Republic, they would not be able to conceal the truth. You are right! Just as Imam [Hussein], the Prince of the Martyrs, was right. He put up a fight with a very small number [of supporters]. Although he was martyred, and his children were martyred, he still kept Islam alive, and he made a mockery of Yazid and of the Banu Umayyads. You too are the Shiʿites [that is, followers] of His Same Excellency. You too, in such battles as those of Abadan… [etc.], did something miraculous.[7]

In the full grip of his own passionate rhetoric, Khomeini sometimes gave an even higher significance to his own time than to the time of the Prophet Muhammad or that of Ali. He generally praised the youth and repeatedly said how happy and proud he was to be living in a time when the young generation was so heroic and self-sacrificing. But at one point, speaking to a group of religious authorities from northern Iran in March 1982, he went so far as to say: "Today, the volunteers willingly anticipate martyrdom in the battle fronts [with Iraq]. Even during the time of the Prophet (God's blessings and benedictions be upon Him) and Amir al-Muʿminin [Ali] (God's peace be upon him), such was not the case."[8]

Abulfazl Ali

17.3 Championing a righteous cause.

Khomeini used the authority of the Qur'an and other canonical sources to remind his audience that even the military instructions of the Prophet and Ali were not always carried out precisely. Concomitant with the reawakening of the sacred memory, Khomeini considered his own time a unique and unprecedented moment in Islamic history. "The true Islamic government" had never been fully realized, he contended, "or it existed only in early Islamic history for a short time, and then no more."[9] Contemporary Iranian society had no historical antecedent of which the counter-revolutionaries could be aware and thus they could not conspire against it. There was a Divinity, Khomeini was convinced, that shaped Iran's revolutionary ends. The counter-revolutionaries "cannot open their eyes and see that in every corner of Iran some extraordinary things are taking place which could not have taken place with the ordinary hand of man." The instruments of battle at the disposal of the (revolutionary) Muslim Iranians, totally oblivious to the counter-revolutionaries, were "faith, monotheism, Islam, and the Qur'an." An excellent example of how God intervened on behalf of Iranians in history, Khomeini observed, was the failure of the American rescue mission to free the hostages: "They came to Tabas, and thought they could land their forces and on the pretext of taking away the hostages conquer Iran. Well, God, Exalted and Supreme that He is, sent the sand and the storms and defeated them."[10]

Khomeini claimed an exclusive interpretative power for himself in understanding Iran, Islam, and their history. All the counter-revolutionaries, from the opposition groups inside Iran to the superpowers (at the time there was still a Soviet Union) to Saddam Hussein, shared an ignorance of Islamic history in general and of Iranian society in particular. It was in its close approximation to the Shiʿi ideals that Iranian society was best understood. More than anything else, Khomeini accused his counter-revolutionary adversaries of ignorance, of not knowing Iranian society, of failing to understand the close affinity of Iranians to their Shiʿi ideals, aspirations, and expectations. Propaganda, Khomeini believed, was instrumental in this close approximation of the Iranian reality to its Shiʿi ideals. He advised the minister of Islamic guidance that propaganda was much more effective than arms in a mobilization of revolutionary sentiments. "Every subject-matter," he instructed him, "has to be constructed anew, and then preserved until it is perpetuated." This program called for a total reconstruction of the Iranian Islamic consciousness so that Iranians would know not only that they were not inferior but that they were actually superior to non-Muslims. This, in Khomeini's view unprecedented, Islamic awakening which he helped to consolidate and identify was a sign of divine approval and of the nearing of the Twelfth Imam's reappearance. No other explanation could account for this sudden, historically unprecedented rejuvenation of Islamic consciousness.[11]

How did he reconstruct this consciousness and put it to political use? Let us read him a little more closely:

275

17.4 Re-sanctifying the modernity of Muslim militancy.

Amir Ali Javadian

17.5 Children mobilized for war.

One after the other, I have received the pride-inspiring news from the battle fronts against the satanic forces. The pen is incapable of expressing my feelings. I congratulate the Islamic armed forces and ask God to grant them final victory. God's gracious greetings be upon you, the dear ones who have made us proud, for the great victory that with the help of God's angels and the assistance of His Most Exalted Sacred Presence you have brought for Islam and for our dear homeland Iran, the country of the Most Exalted Indication of God [the Twelfth Imam], may all our souls be sacrificed for Him! The ever-expanding munificence of God Almighty be upon those fathers and mothers who in their pure bosoms raised you, the brave ones in the battlegrounds and the warriors against the carnal soul in illuminated nights! Congratulations to you all, the brave youth, for seeking God's contentment! Victorious are you all upon the highest spiritual and physical, concealed and manifest, fortifications! God's gracious blessings be [also] upon His Indication [the Twelfth Imam], may all our souls be sacrificed for Him, for such precious soldiers and warriors in the path of God who saved the honor of Islam, honored the people of Iran, and made the fighters of God's Way proud! The great people of Iran and the offspring of Islam are proud of you courageous warriors. Solicitations be upon you who made your nation sit upon the wings of angels and distinguished it among all the nations of the world! Solicitations be upon the nation for such courageous youths, and upon you for such a thankful nation that raised up prayers and jubilation for your victory. From afar, I kiss the hand of you fighters, shielded as it is by the hand of God, and I take pride in this obedient kiss. [see Fig. 18.9] You have performed your duty to our dear Islam and to our noble homeland. You have cut off the greedy hand of the superpowers and their mercenaries from your country. You have courageously rebelled in the path of the nobility and honor of Islam. "O how I wish I were with you, and I would have been graced with a great blessing!" Benedictions be upon the noble generals and

warriors, and upon all those who fight for the glory of the country and of Islam! And cursed and hated be the hypocrites and those gone astray, those who wanted to put an ammunition depot of such warriors on fire! And God's anger and woe be upon those godless ones who by helping the cursed Saddam wanted to rescue him! Boundless gratitude be to God for your success in inflicting an ignoble defeat [upon the enemy], and for having the armies of the infidels dishonored in the presence of God Almighty, hated by the Muslim nations! I ask God Almighty for the final victory of you dear ones, and for the defeat of those who oppose truth. Benedictions be upon you, and God's munificence be upon the martyrs of God's way and upon those who sacrificed themselves in the battle fronts of truth against falsehood! And peace be upon the most righteous obedients of God! Ruhallah al-Musavi al-Khomeini.[12]

As Khomeini reawakened the sacred memory of his followers, thus exciting and mobilizing their religious fervor, ready and ripe for revolutionary uses, a crucial issue raised was the problem of hundreds of thousands of young men and women who were killed either in the course of the Revolution or in the battle fronts of the Iraq–Iran war. Khomeini could not ignore these massive casualties, Iranian women and men in their prime sacrificing their lives at his mere command. He felt obliged to address this issue. In addressing it, Khomeini's conviction of the necessity of sacrifice and martyrdom in the course of a revolution became apparent. The two central notes of "sacrifice" and "martyrdom," furthermore, linked the concrete and difficult realities of a revolutionary turmoil to that higher spirit of sacred imagination in the context of which he could account for all the human misery he had, in effect, expected his followers to suffer.

"The essence of revolution is self-sacrifice." Khomeini's dictum went deep into the most sacrosanct corners of the Iranian Shiʿi consciousness. "Constitutional to a revolution," he decreed, "is martyrdom and the readiness for martyrdom." The distinction between "martyrdom" and "readiness for martyrdom" was quintessential. Being martyred could be accidental, a possible consequence in one's pursuit of political ambitions. But "readiness for martyrdom" was an essential psychological compulsion, fortified by religious conviction, to engage in revolutionary acts of self-sacrifice. Khomeini fully recognized the political necessity of this readiness and rhetorically linked it to the most compelling forces of the Shiʿi sacred sensibility. The men of imagination from which Khomeini borrowed readily created a sustained atmosphere of shared conviction in which the revolutionary sage and his devoted followers could remap the world. "To be sacrificed and to give sacrifice in the way of the Revolution and its success," he said, with an eye on both the young and their parents, "is inevitable, especially [in] a revolution which is for God and His religion, for the sake of the downtrodden, and for the cutting off of the designs of world-mongers and tyrants." All the politically mandated objectives — representing the downtrodden, opposing world-mongers and tyrants, etc. — were linked, without the slightest hesitation, to the more metaphysically determined convictions of fighting for God, His religion, etc. "In every communal gathering...." Khomeini decreed, "we are expecting sacrifice to help God, and we expect martyrdom." In this "expectation" (intezar in Persian), there was almost an element of demand, as if there would be a great sense of loss and disappointment should martyrdom not occur. Thus, as Khomeini understood and propagated the concepts of sacrifice and martyrdom, they were not the unfortunate, regrettable, preferably avoidable consequence of a revolutionary movement. They were, as he said, the constitutional and necessary forces that in effect created the revolutionary momentum. Without them there would not be a revolution. They had to occur. Thus conceived, there was of course a need to hang them on metaphysical concepts for them to remain valid and significant. But their actual occurrence was not even to be left to chance. The occasion had to be created. "Sacrifice for a great revolution," Khomeini thought, "is the sign of a victory, a getting closer to the objective."[13] To drive the point home, he appealed to the archetypal figure of all martyrdom in Shi{c}ism, Imam Hussein:

It is said of the Prince of World Martyrs that the more his noble companions were killed and the closer he got to the high noon of {c}Ashura, the more his most gracious complexion became excited, his happiness intensified. With every martyr he offered, he got one step closer to victory. The aim is [one's] conviction, to struggle for it, and revolutionary victory, not life, and in this world not all the despicable distractions of it.[14]

This is how Khomeini saw Hussein. And in the mirror of that vision he saw himself.

In Khomeini's remapping of the Shi{c}i sacred memory there was a necessary contraction of time and space whereby the events and sentiments of the hagiographical sources were approximated to current events and vice versa. For example, he compared and thus transhistorically exchanged those who died for Imam Hussein with those who fought for the Islamic Revolution he led. When Islam was in danger 1,400 years ago, Shi{c}i Imams like Hussein came to its rescue. Now it was the turn of contemporary descendants of the same Imams, that is the Sayyid, to do similarly. This comparison and contraction sanctifies the present and gives a sense of purpose to the past. The result is the transfusion of two concurrent streams of consciousness — sacred and profane, real and imaginary, present and past — that culminates in the mobilized sentiments charged for immediate revolutionary purposes.

The boundaries of this remapped Shi{c}i martyrological consciousness are not and should not be limited to Iran. Khomeini had wider claims on the world community. In June 1982 he received a group representing "The Liberating Movements of the World." To them he delivered a speech outlining an argument for the unification of all Muslim countries against their non-Muslim enemies, particularly Israel. First he launched a bitter attack against what he considered to be deeply rotten states of the Middle East, who had become "deaf, dumb, and blind" to the mounting difficulties and miseries of the Muslims. He was particularly aggravated by the lack of response to the Israeli invasion of Lebanon.

17.6 Giving symbolic momentum to Khomeini's revolutionary vision, murals encouraged the military march towards Karbala.

17.7 The young Iranian soldier with his commanding images of militant piety. This poster is based on a photo by Kazem Akhavan [see Fig. 18.3]

He held the United States chiefly responsible for this attack. He denounced the Camp David accord, condemned King Fahd, mourned the loss of Muslim lives in Lebanon and Iran, accused the leaders of Islamic countries of "deaf, dumb, and blind" complacency, and sympathized with Muslim people who suffered in their own countries.[15] Unless Muslim people were awakened to their responsibilities, learned from the exemplary conduct of Iranians, and earned their rights, the misery would continue. Khomeini's frustrated anger against the leaders of Islamic countries who sat idly by while Muslims were being killed, maimed, robbed, and altogether humiliated was expressed with vengeful fury: **To whom shall we turn with such miseries except to the presence of God Almighty? To whom shall we complain about these governments except the presence of God Almighty? How can we express our grievance from those who proclaim holy war against Iran, which is standing upright and wants to oppose all [super] powers and wants to see Islam mobilized in the world, and yet remain silent about Israel which is fighting against Islam and clearly says, "From Nile to Euphrates is mine," and which considers the two sacred precincts to belong to it? Where can we take these pains? To whom shall we express these miseries? To whom shall we grieve of this deadening silence, this silence that condones the criminals, this silence that encourages the tyrants. Whom shall we ask to grace us with favor and break this silence? Are you few in numbers? Do you not own such great wealth? Do you not know the value of your oil? Are you small in territory? Do you not control places of great strategic significance? All the necessary facilities exist. But one thing is lacking. And that is faith. There is no faith.[16]**

Then the exemplary model, the reawakened Shiʿi lead, is offered: "The Iranian nation had nothing but had faith. Faith made it victorious over all powers. The leaders of all [other] Muslim countries have everything but they do not have faith. That which made our country, our nation, victorious was faith in God, and love of martyrdom, love of martyrdom in opposing unbelief, opposing hypocrisy, safeguarding Islam, safeguarding the Qur'an."[17]

Khomeini then proceeded to give his foreign guests a mission: to go back to their country and take "the Iranian message" with them. Other nations ought to do for themselves what Iran had done for herself. They should not wait for their leaders, who were all lackeys of the United States. "They are buying camels for their zoos, while Iran is so afflicted."[18] Khomeini was very angry that one of the local sultans in the Persian Gulf area, Qabus of Oman, had apparently purchased some camels for his zoo. "To whom shall we turn with this grievance? They buy fourteen camels from abroad for the zoo of such and such sultan in the region. They want to transport them there by aeroplane. These people are stealing everything we have, and then they buy camels! I do not know when these ears will be opened. Will they be opened by [Gabriel's] trumpet? When will these eyes be opened, and when will these tongues be speaking? "Summun bukmun ʿumyun fahum la yaʿqalun." Everything has to do with la yaʿqalun. "Summun bukmun ʿumyun" comes after "la yaʿqalun."[19]

To bring its Shiʿi message to the world, Iran was willing and able to do what was necessary, Khomeini declared. Iran was ready to go through Iraq and fight Israel.

The funny thing is [Khomeini said to his foreign revolutionary guests] that our government suggests [to the Iraqis], "Let us go and fight your enemy … because we have lost hope in you [doing that]…" And then they say, "You have to forgive all we have done so that we will let you in [to go through Iraq to fight Israel]…" Is this not a calamity which has afflicted Islam, that a sacrificing [Iranian] multitude wants to go and fight with the enemy of the Arabs, with the enemy of Islam, enemy of the Two Sacred Precincts, enemy of the whole region (because they themselves are sitting idly by and are indifferent, or even in agreement with them), [and then] they go and fight for them? It is just like a person who is drowning in the sea and somebody goes to rescue him and he says, "What will you give me so I will let you resent me?…" This is one of those strange things that history will remember, that in order to save the Arabs, because Israel is particularly hostile to Arabs, to save the Two Sacred Precincts, to save the Islamic countries, which are all threatened by Israel, and to fight against this rotten cancer, Iran wanted to march on and [then Arab] countries asked for bribery from it. These are things that will remain in history, marks of ignobility that shall always remain on the forehead of these people.[20]

The call for open revolt is clearly sent, through these emissaries, to all oppressed people of the region, of the world.

Until such time as Islamic countries and Muslim peoples follow that model which was implemented in Iran, until they pour into the streets and demand that their governments confront Israel, never believe for a moment that the deaf and the blind will ever come to their senses. Nations ought to use and demand that the armies of their region, and the governments of their regions,

come to the help of Palestinians and Syrians who have been victimized, to help to get rid of this cancerous tumor. If they [that is, the people] too remain spectators to see what happens, if they too are indifferent, and have the excuse that the governments ought to do this, if that is the case, they too do not have a proper answer to give in God's presence.[21]

Following the example of Iran was not just a matter of historical necessity for other Muslims. It was a matter of religious and moral obligation:

Iran is the exemplary model for all [other] countries. God Almighty might very well set Iran as an exemplary model [against which to judge] all those who have condoned tyranny, succumbed to tyrants, and have not revolted. If they believe in God and in the Day of Judgment, they have to have an answer ready for God Gracious and Exalted that He is. In that day, America and Israel cannot do anything for you. And if they do not believe in such ideas, they have to have an answer ready for the victimized peoples of the world, an answer for the future generations who, God forbid, will be trapped because of things that they [their present ancestors] are doing; they want to have an answer ready. If they take religious values for nothing, then they should consider their own military interests. Just for a short period of government, they should not accept ignominy under the boots of Israel. Muslims ought to rise. They ought to rebel. God Almighty has said… Do not say that you are alone. We have to rise individually, and we have to rise collectively. We have to rise all together. We are all bound by duty to revolt for God, to revolt for the protection of Islamic countries, against these two cancerous tumors, one the corrupt Baʿath Party of Iraq and the other Israel, both of which stem from America… There is no excuse that we do not have any weapon. The weapon that you have the world does not have, and that is the weapon of oil. The world needs your weapon. It is the life-vein of the world. This is the weapon that God Almighty has put at your disposal. Use it for God, Almighty and Majestic that He is… I hope that these governments will give as much importance to Islam as they to do their zoos… I hope that God Almighty will support the Muslims of the world and deliver them from the tyranny of the superpowers. And peace be upon you, and God's grace and bounty.[22]

1 KHOMEINI, SAHIFAH-YE NUR (TEHRAN, 1361/1982), VOL. 16: 207. 2 IBID. 3 IBID., P. 208. 4 IBID., P. 209. 5 IBID., P. 210. 6 IBID., P. 67. 7 IBID., P. 68. 8 IBID., P. 71. 9 IBID., P. 74. 10 IBID., P. 75. 11 IBID., P. 87. 12 IBID., PP. 96-7. 13 IBID., P. 219. 14 IBID. 15 IBID., PP. 197-8. 16 IBID., P. 198. 17 IBID. 18 IBID. 19 IBID., P. 199. 20 IBID., PP. 199-200. 21 IBID., P. 200. 22 IBID., P. 201

on the
path of war

WAR-FRONT BILLBOARDS

Eighteen

Our university is in the trenches; the entrance exam, the hejrat [holy journey]; the lessons, the jihad [holy war]; and the diploma, the shahadat [martyrdom].

BILLBOARDS WITH THIS SLOGAN LITTERED THE FRONT LINES DURING THE IRAQ-IRAN WAR. IN NO OTHER WAR IN HISTORY HAS THE ART OF PERSUASION BEEN EMPLOYED TO THE DEGREE USED BY THE IRANIANS IN THEIR EIGHT-YEAR-LONG WAR AGAINST IRAQ. IN HIS *IRANIAN MILITARY IN REVOLUTION AND WAR*, SEPEHR ZABIH OBSERVES: "IN THE COURSE OF THE FIRST TWO YEARS OF THE ISLAMIC REGIME, A MASSIVE INDOCTRINATION OF THE ARMED FORCES WAS BEGUN, AND AS A PART OF THE PROCESS, NEARLY EVERY UNIT OF THE ARMED FORCES WAS PLACED UNDER THE COMMAND OF A REGULAR OFFICER AND A CLERIC LEADER.

Mahmoud Badrfar

282

18.1 Sign on the battlefront: "Smile Brother Smile"

In addition, the Office of Propaganda and Indoctrination was organized at every level of the armed forces."[1] Of all the devices used to persuade the population to sacrifice their lives for Islam, signs and billboards must be given particular attention. These billboards, small and large, carried slogans and graphic images and were erected in unprecedented numbers and fashion throughout the front lines and across the battlefields, along supply routes and in the rear. They were produced by artists from a variety of groups, such as the propaganda units of the armed forces, Revolutionary Guards, and Volunteers; the cultural units of the Martyrs Foundation; and the propaganda units of the Jihad for Construction. Thanks to the publication of these war-front slogans by the Art Department of the Islamic Propagation Organization in the form of a book entitled Tabloneveshteha, the breadth and depth of this propaganda are now documented. The visual aspect of the war-front slogans is documented in Profiles of the Revolutionary Art: The First Collection: War-Stricken Area.[2] In this chapter we shall examine some of the central features of these slogans.

Muhammad Reza Rafii Rad

In the two volumes of *Tabloneveshteha* there are 773 slogans, battle-cries, invocations, catch-phrases, buzz-words, and vilifications of the enemy. They are alphabetically arranged in two volumes. The first volume has the English title, *The Front's Culture: Placards*. The English title of the second volume is *The Battlefront's Cultural Lexicon: Signboard Inscriptions*. In addition to billboards, the inscriptions and graphic images documented in these publications appear on the headbands, helmets, and battledress of the combatants. They are also painted on the sides of trucks, tanks, armored personnel-carriers, and bunkers. This is clear evidence that visual propaganda, omnipresent in the Iranian urban environment, was equally ubiquitous in the war theatre. According to Sayyid Mahdi Fahimi, the editor of both volumes:

The billboards could serve as a memorial to the culture of the front. They were found in those places where the hearts of our heroes were beating—in the mountains, on the plains, in the deserts, in the riverbeds and ditches, in the date-palm groves, in the stony wastelands, in the ravines and mountain passes, along roads, and in the trenches... These signboards and billboards sometimes planted a smile on the lips of the Muslim fighters, sometimes they lifted the burden of exhaustion from the shoulders of the Iranian combatants, and sometimes they made the stars the guests of the firmament of their hearts.[3]

The billboards exposed the soldiers to psychological warfare, directed not by the enemy but by the Iranian leadership. They were written and arranged in such a way as to express many popular and personal feelings: "The fighting boys lived for many years and died having the billboards in front of and beside them. No doubt the graphic and written expressions and sentiments on the billboards made lasting impressions on the tablets of the hearts and pages of the minds of these Basijis [Volunteers]."[4] The slogans and graphic images were reproduced many times, sometimes by the thousands, and studded the front lines as much as the burned-out tanks, abandoned military vehicles, and bomb craters.

The strategic circumstances of the war must also be considered. The long desolate miles of fortifications along the Iran–Iraq front line were, for the most part, static. The adversaries were dug in, facing each other, for many years. Had it been a blitzkrieg type of war, there would have been no time to erect these billboards at the front. The testimony of Iranian soldiers about them is quite telling. A Mr Rahimi states: "We were moving to the front line in trucks. My spirits were low until I saw a billboard saying 'You are going to Karbala. I am also coming and together we shall pray there.' This put me in high spirits. Other billboards, inscribed with the names of Imams, especially those with the pictures of our leaders and the Imam [Khomeini] were very effective in strengthening our morale."[5]

Kazem Akhavan

18.3

Seifullah Samadian

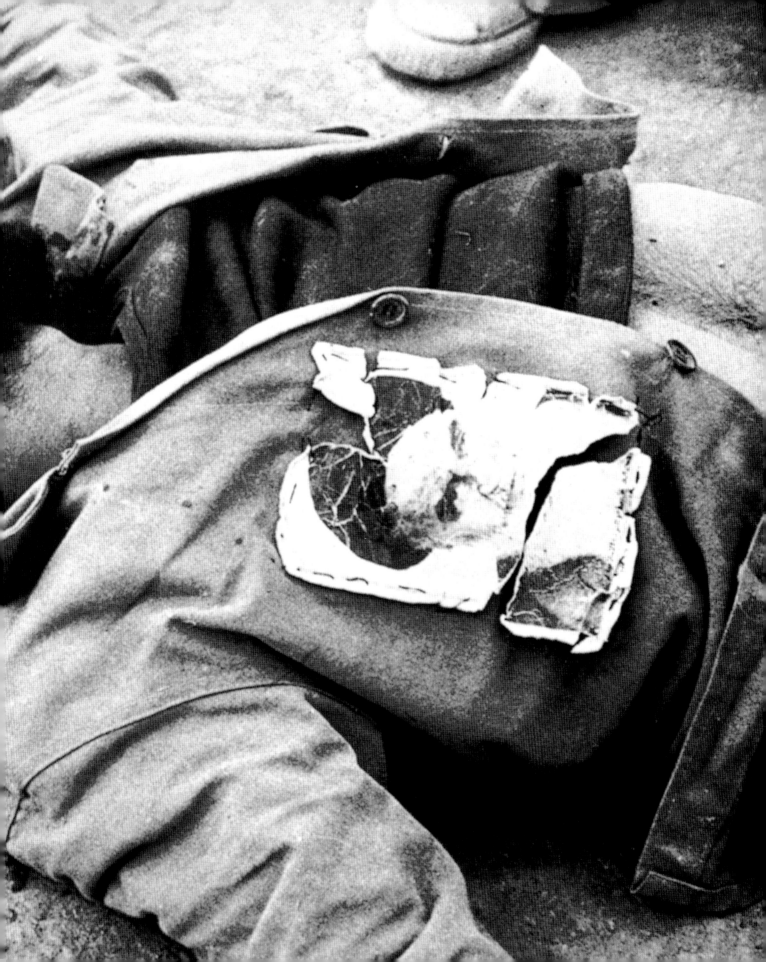

Another man, Murteza Rezai, says:

We were at Seh Rah-e Husseiniyeh. It was very hot. The officer in charge of propaganda ordered his men to erect a huge billboard at the positioning intersection. In order to complete the assignment we went to find a big board. Soon, however, we realized that a board as large as the officer had asked for did not exist. So we resolved to fashion one ourselves. At the front, thank God, there are enough wooden boards scattered around. We used the big wooden casings of Katusha rockets. We opened up four casings, each one three meters in length, and built a big board. Then we smoothed the surface and painted a picture and wrote a slogan: "The fragrance of God's paradise is the fragrance of Hussein." After the hardship of making this billboard was over, we erected it on the spot. It was so colossal that as soon as it was up the enemy planes flew in to attack it. They returned to attack it on several occasions. Since the enemy was against our propaganda, they were very persistent in attacking this billboard. Our men started to complain that they were going to be killed on account of the billboard. Finally we moved it to another spot and they continued to attack it there. This event will stay in my memory for ever.[6]

Another, anonymous, soldier is quoted:

In the action for the liberation of the strategic town of Faw along the banks of the river Behmanshir, we prepared several billboards featuring pictures of the Imam [Khomeini] and proclamations of the leaders and went to set them up along the route of military activity. We had just finished erecting two boards when enemy aircraft flew in and started a bombardment. A rocket hit the ground only 200 meters away from us. We thought that our fate was to become martyrs in setting up the billboards. That day we set up all the billboards that were assigned to be erected as far away as Khosrow Abad. The next day, as we went to continue with our work, there were no traces of the boards we had erected the day before. The enemy considered them to be military targets for their rockets and shells. Only the twisted metal rods which had formerly supported the billboards, now full of holes, remained as a testimony to our work. We laughed at the enemy for this.[7]

Yet another nameless soldier gives this account:

During the action code-named "Khaybar," we went to erect billboards along the "Khaybar Bridge," which played an important role in the success in reaching a particular island. Shortly after we started setting up the boards, the Iraqis began shelling the bridge. Every minute the shells were falling around us. The shells were exploding everywhere. We were unable to retreat. One enemy shell landed in the midst of some men who were pinned down. In the flash of the explosion, a slogan on a metal board caught my eye: "Praise be to God for the continuous good health of the Imam." This slogan was a very dear and famous one at the front. This event made a deep impression on me as I reflected on the fact that some 100 men in the clutches of death under enemy fire had forgotten

18.5 The road to Jerusalem passes through Karbala. In the arch of the Karbalah mausoleum is seen the mosque of the Dome of the Rock.

themselves as they invoked God's intercession for their Imam's good health.[8]

Devotional statements praising Ayatollah Khomeini and his leadership also appeared in great numbers, often accompanied by his picture. They too were on huge billboards as well as on headbands, helmets, battledress, and even rifle bats. The most common were *Allahu Akbar Khomeini Rahbar* (God is Greatest, Khomeini is the leader) and *Allahu Vahed Khomeini Qaed* (God is one, Khomeini is the leader). These short rhyming couplets were very popular, as Khomeini's leadership was connected with God's unity and greatness, showing God's will and His blessing on the cause. These very slogans made their first appearances in the form of graffiti during the first days of the Revolution. Another slogan which was very popular during the initial stages of the Revolution and then transferred to the front was *Ma hameh sarbaz-e toyim Khomeini, gush beh farman-e toyim Khomeini* (We are all your soldiers, Khomeini. We are awaiting your commands, Khomeini). The first line of this slogan also appears on 5,000 and 10,000 rial banknotes issued by the Islamic Republic of Iran. *Labbaik ya Khomeini* (Here am I waiting your commands, O Khomeini) was a declaration of

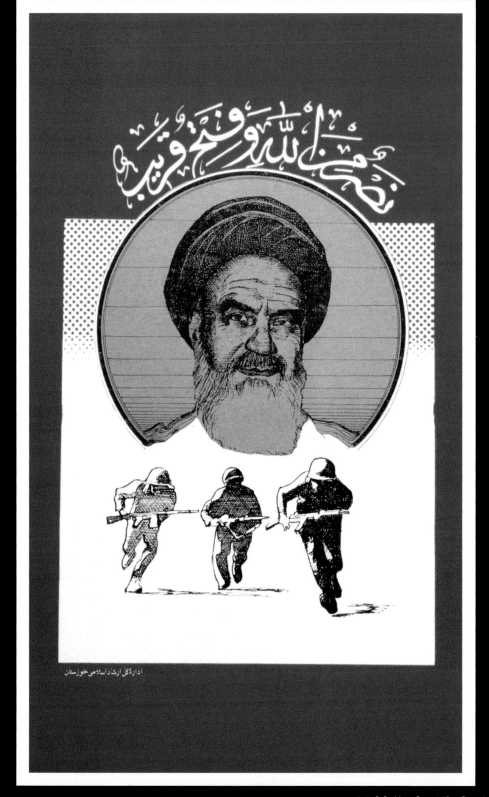

18.6 A letter from the front: "My dear ones, I congratulate
you on the third anniversary of the springtime of freedom.
Don't worry about me. I will never break the firm covenant
which I have made with God since we are men of war and

السلام عليك يا اباعبدالله

18.7 "Salutation to thee O Hussein." A profession of faith is on the red flag.

servitude and was very often found inscribed on the personal effects of the Iranian combatants. This invocation is derived from a recitation called *talbiya* which the pilgrims approaching Mecca continually recite: "*Labbaik allahuma labbayk*—Here I am, O my God, here I am! Praise and blessing belong to Thee and power." Total devotion to Ayatollah Khomeini is also declared in the following slogan: *Ya Khomeini rahseparim ta shahadat* (O Khomeini, we are proceeding even until martyrdom). A romantic notion is to be found in the following slogan: *Bi eshq-e Khomeini jehan cheh arzeshi darad* (Without Khomeini's love, what value has this world?). According to Fahimi: "Imam Khomeini's (may he rest in peace) utterances and guidelines were so numerous on the billboards, and so much attention was paid to them, that even when they were not connected with his name, they stood out from the others."[9]

The main thrust of the slogans employed in the theatre of war was to motivate the Iranian combatants to fight the "irreligious" enemy who had imposed this war on them. In these slogans the Iranian soldiers were described as heroes engaged in the sacred defense of Islam, that is, of the truth. Dying for these principles was described as being sweeter than anything else in this world. Postcards from soldiers at the front to their families were written for them beforehand and printed by the Office of Islamic Guidance. This is an example of a postcard prepared in the province of Khuzistan, preceded by an epigraph in both Arabic and Persian: **"The heart finds its repose in the remembrance of God." My dear ones,**

I congratulate you on the third anniversary of the Springtime of Freedom. Don't worry about me. I will never break the firm covenant which I have made with God, since we are men of war; and since Truth is victorious, we, too, are victorious.

There is space left for only a signature and the address. On the reverse side of the postcard is a picture of men running forwards with their rifles. At the top and dominating the picture is the head of Ayatollah Khomeini. [Fig. 18.6]

The war could only be compared to the battle of Karbala, fought by the Imam Hussein in 680 CE. In the foreword to the second volume of the *Tabloneveshteha*, Fahimi alludes to the fact that the origin of the front culture of the "Imposed War" is to be found in the story of Imam Hussein. The centuries-old tradition of identification with Hussein and his suffering and death was the primary motivation used in the war-front slogans. The billboards with graphic images of the battle at Karbala, Hussein's tomb, and the accompanying slogans served as reminders of the Karbala tragedy. This was an important tool for the clerics, who played a role in the Iranian armed forces similar to that of political officers in the Soviet and Nazi armed forces. They created a special chemistry of readiness, even of desire, for martyrdom. The headbands of Iranian combatants were, for the most part, inscribed with short invocations such as "O Hussein!" or "O Hussein, the Oppressed!" Sometimes the headbands were covered with badges that identified the individual soldier with the events of Hussein's martyrdom such as "The Karbala Soldier," "The Karbala Traveller," "The Karbala Lover," "Frenzied with Love for Karbala," "The ʿAshura Epic-maker," "The Karbala Pilgrim," "May I Sacrifice Myself for You, O Hussein."[10] Sometimes these epithets were written in Arabic. One could argue that the headbands played an even greater role than the slogan-covered displays, because the bearers had to live up to the content of the phrases written across their foreheads. Other slogans reflected similar sentiments:

O God! O God!	*"Fear" does not exist!*
Keep Khomeini Alive	*Iran is opposing Infidelity*
Until the Mahdi's Revolution!	*As tall as eternity!*
Karbala!	*Islam is Victorious!*
We are Coming!	*With full force*
In the Path of Karbala	*We shall liberate Iraq!*
We must cross the River of	*We are Going to Qods*
Blood!	*[Jerusalem]*
God is Greatest!	*Through Karbala!*
Khomeini is the leader	*Martyrs are Candles*
In the Lexicon of Martyrdom	*Of the Muslim Community!*

In a letter (dated late in August 1985) published on the dust-jacket of the first collected volume of war-related murals, Ali Akbar Hashemi Rafsanjani, then Speaker of the House (now President of the Islamic Republic), summarized the essential points of the propaganda art directed at the massive participation of Iranians in the war against Iraq. What this art reflected, he pointed out, was the very objectives of the Revolution which had preceded the war. That Revolution had initiated the legitimate government of Islam, he believed.[11] "Independence, freedom, social justice, holy war against universal blasphemy, expansion of the Islamic ethics and culture, defence of the downtrodden, the struggle against the foreign domination, the domination of the superpowers and the colonialists" were among the chief objectives of the Islamic Revolution, and they were amply represented in the revolutionary art.

Rafsanjani believed that the same art had served well the mobilization efforts in the Iraq–Iran war and demonstrated its true nature. The purpose of this war was "to defend the Revolution, Islam, and the country, to open the road towards Quds [Jerusalem], conquer Karbala, liberate the Iraqi Muslims, eradicate the barrier [in the path of] Islam and the Islamic Revolution, to punish the aggressor who has sold out [to foreigners], to teach a lesson to other lesser evils, so that they would never think of repeating the crimes of the Iraqi Baʿathists and their cowardly supporters." The same revolutionary art united all the diverse groups, classes, and organizations that had joined to defend their Revolution, faith, and country. This art reflected, Rafsanjani believed, the true nature of the Islamic Revolution, and the war that ensued. It encouraged a spirit of wishing to be a martyr, to follow the commands of Khomeini closely, to trust the religious leadership, to defend the weak, to hate the powerful, to sympathize with the Muslim world, to despise the counter-revolutionaries, to have hope, to expect the appearance of the Twelfth (Hidden) Imam, to wish for martyrdom, to love the homeland, to pray, to exercise, to study, to love, to write, to be content.[12]

Five years into the Iraq-Iran war, the Artistic and Cultural Bureau of the Office of Propaganda of Qom Seminary published a collection of war-related murals in which the compilers, Hasan Mahmoudi and Ibrahim Suleymani, gave an overview of the revolutionary art which had now assumed a new twist and responsibility. In an introduction to this collection of war murals, the compilers provided something of a guideline for all revolutionary artists interested in murals. What is remarkable about this introduction is that its authors give detailed ideological and technical instructions as to how revolutionary murals are to be painted. "Among our reasons in publishing this collection is to introduce the artists of every town to the artistic objects of other towns and thus to encourage and praise them for their work."[13] The authors proceed to give a detailed account of the varieties

18.8

18.9 Khomeini's messages on billboard. The text reads: "From afar, I kiss the hand of
you fighters, shielded as it is by the Hand of God, and I take pride in this obedient kiss."

of murals that have appeared in war zones—Kurdistan, Bakhtaran, and Khuzistan:

These pictures which appear in the roadways leading towards the war-fronts, or in the streets of war-afflicted cities, or on the walls of military camps, have had an extremely effective

role in the war. They create an amazing zest and delight in the hearts of the warriors. What these pictures speak of are the truthful words of the Islamic front. They are the mirror of their holy war, of the objective of this war, encouraging and enticing the warriors, as well as identifying the enemy and his fallacious reasoning.[14]

The introduction contains instructions as to what themes are to be portrayed: "holy war, the purpose of the holy mobilization for the war," or one of the specific themes that identifies and characterizes the Revolution, such as "the struggle of the Islamic Revolution against the colonialism of the East and West." Under all circumstances, the effectiveness of the revolutionary mural must be kept clearly in mind. Vague, indirect, and superfluous paintings should be avoided at all costs. "What is significant is to consider what a passer-by can take away in his memory and mind."[15] The artist must study religious texts as seriously as he examines the techniques of other artists. Murals with a theme or a scene are preferable to portraits with no specific message. Revolutionary posters should not be merely copied. Every artist must let go of his unique imagination, and create something unique. The location of the murals must be selected carefully so that passers-by can clearly see the complete picture. But the ultimate objective should be brevity of message, deliberate and emphatic brush-strokes, clear-cut shapes, and brilliant colors. Every mural should be framed by solid colors, selected from one of the dominant colors of the picture. The compilers proceed to give specific instructions about the texture of the wall and the materials that should be used to give the mural a more enduring quality. They conclude by promising that very soon they will publish a book on the techniques of wall-painting and distribute it among revolutionary artists throughout the country.[16]

1 Sepehr Zabih, The Iranian Military in Revolution and War (London and New York, 1988), p. 17. **2** Hasan Mahmoudi and Ibrahim Suleymani (eds.), Jelvehha-i az Honar-e Enqelab (Qom, [1985]). **3** Sayyid Mahdi Fahimi, Farhang-e Jebhe: Tablonev-eshteha (Tehran, 1369/1990), vol 1: 7. **4** Ibid. **5** Ibid., p. 66. **6** Ibid. **7** Ibid., p. 65. **8** Ibid., p. 64. **9** Ibid., p. 17. **10** Compare these to the slogans found on the helmets of American soldiers in Vietnam: "Born to Kill," "Born to Lose," "War is Hell," etc. **11** Mahmoudi and Suleymani (eds.), Jelvehha-i az Honar-e Enqelab, dust-jacket. **12** Ibid. **13** Ibid., introduction. **14** Ibid. **15** Ibid. **16** Visual coverage of the war against Iraq is best documented in the five volumes of The Imposed War, published by the War Information Headquarters, Supreme Defense Council of the Islamic Republic of Iran. The first volume was published in February 1983, the fifth in September 1987. Another important photographic album of the war is Talashi dar Tasvir (Tehran, 1362).

291

islam
ON THE MOVE:

Nineteen

EXPORTING THE Islamic revolution

UPON THE SUCCESSFUL ESTABLISHMENT OF THE ISLAMIC REPUBLIC IN IRAN, THE IDEOLOGUES OF THE REVOLUTION WERE ADAMANT IN EXPORTING IT BEYOND THE BOUNDARIES OF THE COUNTRY. ISLAM, THESE DEVOTED IDEOLOGUES THOUGHT, IS A UNIVERSAL TRUTH, AND ALL THE PEOPLE OF THE WORLD MUST SHARE IN ITS FRUITS. KHOMEINI HIMSELF ON A NUMBER OF OCCASIONS EMPHA-SIZED THE IMPORTANCE OF EXPORTING THE IDEOLOGY OF THE ISLAMIC REVO-LUTION. "ALL PEOPLE SHOULD PREPARE THEMSELVES TO STRENGTHEN, GOD WILLING, ISLAM IN THIS COUNTRY," HE COMMANDED ONCE, "AND GOD WILLING, IT WILL BE EXPORTED FROM THIS COUNTRY TO OTHER COUNTRIES, AS IT HAS ALREADY BEEN EXPORTED. DO NOT THINK [FOR A MOMENT] THAT IT HAS

In Memory of Martyrs Kh. Istambuli
17 June 1982

19.1 Egypt: Stamp comme-morating the "martyrdom" of Khalid Istanbuli, the man who assassinated President Anwar Sadat.

NOT BEEN EXPORTED. IT HAS BEEN EXPORTED. RIGHT NOW, THERE ARE MANY COUNTRIES WHOSE PEOPLE HAVE BEEN AWAKENED AND ALERTED."[1] "WE MUST BE ADAMANT," HE INSISTED, "TO EXPORT OUR REVOLUTION TO THE WORLD. WE MUST ABANDON THE THOUGHT THAT WE DO NOT EXPORT OUR REVOLUTION"; "TAKE AND IMPLEMENT ISLAM ALL OVER THE WORLD, TO EVERY COUNTRY. RAISE THE FLAG OF ISLAM [EVERYWHERE]"; "WE ASK FOR NOTHING BUT FOR THE IMPLEMENTATION OF THE ISLAMIC RULES THROUGHOUT THE WORLD."[2]

After Khomeini, the ideologues of the Islamic Revolution articulated the specific ideological foundation of propaganda that would promote the cause of the Islamic Revolution throughout the world. Tracing the roots of "propaganda" (*tabligh*) in the Qur'an and other canonical sources, one particular ideologue was emphatic about the universal nature of the Islamic Revolution and the necessity of exporting it throughout the world. There is a great discrepancy, Muslim ideologues believe, between the propaganda generated in the world superpowers and that produced by weaker countries. The United States of America spends millions of dollars every year, they insist, propagating its ideals and interests throughout the world. "The Voice of America has altogether 822 hours of programs every week, [broadcast] in thirty-eight languages." In "unholy" regimes, such as that of the United States, "the only purpose of propaganda is to influence public opinion so that the minds and thoughts of the masses are distorted from their divine nature. The objective is to attain their goal, which is to make people stupid, colonize them, keep them in a weak state, and then plunder and rob them." Contrary to such "unholy" objectives, "in Islam, the principal goal and objective of propaganda is to move people towards God, expand Islamic values, that is to say, to make

known the exalted and liberating values of Islam, cleanse men's spirits of the dust of the propaganda of the East and of the West, and to save them from the rotten depth of corruption and darkness."[3] To achieve this end, the Islamic Republic included in its national budget a specific clause to support radical Islamic movements in Lebanon.[4] According to Article 154 of the Constitution of the Islamic Republic, Iran will support "the righteous struggle of the weak against the powerful everywhere in the world."[5]

When the Soviet Union was still around, Muslim ideologues believe that the world superpowers disagreed on just about everything except the elimination of "Islamic fundamentalism," a term they literally translate from English without the slightest critical assessment. All the powerful propaganda against Islam will, in their view, amount to nothing. With help from the Divine Will, Islam will prove victorious. These ideologues believe that there is a coalition of superpowers that exists to prevent the rise and expansion of Islam. The academic study of "Islam" and "Iran" by so-called "scholars" and "Iranists," they hold, is to promote a more accurate understanding of the Islamic Revolution in Iran, in order to be able to curtail its growth and expansion. The United States' fear of the consequences of the Islamic Revolution reached a point

19.2 Afghanistan: Mocking the Soviet occupation of Afghanistan.

19.3 The Middle East: Promising to liberate Jerusalem.

where "Reagan commissioned Harvard University to organize an international conference and invite statesmen, Islamic scholars, and Iranists to discuss this issue: how is it possible to prevent the expansion of the wave of Islamic revolution?"[6]

The operative force behind all these movements, according to the collective belief of these ideologues, is something called "The Universal Order of Tyranny" (*nezam-e estakbar-e jahani*), which entails specific reference to the United States but with occasional inclusion of the (then) Soviet Union, Europe, and Israel. This order, they believe, has hidden and obvious hands everywhere. It detects liberating movements and destroys them. Right now, they assure their audience, the Universal Order of Tyranny is frightened by the success of the Islamic Revolution in Iran and seeking ways of curtailing and eliminating it.

The Islamic Revolution must be propagated patiently. "Marx and Engels published the principles of their ideas in 1848 in the form of a manifesto. If we look at issues superficially, we have to conclude that since these ideas did not create any particular movement in Europe in the course of the next ten or twenty years, they were defeated, whereas in 1917 the principles of Marxism were utilized by Lenin in Russia and led to the establishment of the Soviet government."[7] Muslim ideologues must learn from the Marxist example, and "given the freedom of expression... which is relatively present in the modern world... [we] ought to take advantage of this situation in order to propagate divine values and concepts."[8] Sometimes there is official resistance to the propagation of the revolutionary Islam, but "it has been observed that when a line of thought cannot directly challenge the dominant ideology, then it uses other different methods, such as art, in order to express its ideas and points of view, disguising them in the official and legal form and thus gradually presenting and making them available. Now this [form of] art may be poetry, painting, cinema, caricature, etc. As an example, we may note how Shiʿism has historically used such arts in order to preserve ʿAshura and the culture of resistance."[9]

297

19.4 The World: The promises of a universal Islamic Revolution.

1 FOR THIS AND OTHER SIMILAR PASSAGES, SEE JAVAD MANSURI, JANG-E FARHANGI ʿALAYH-E ENQELAB-E ISLAMI (MASHHAD, 1369/1990), PP. 8-10. **2** IBID., P. 10. **3** IBID., P. 22. **4** IBID., P. 24. **5** QUOTED IBID. **6** IBID., P. 28. **7** IBID., PP. 42-3. **8** IBID., P. 43. **9** IBID., P. 44

Certainly God does not make known his will to us in order that knowledge of it should perish with us, but that we might be witness to posterity, and that posterity should pass on what was received from our hands, so to speak, into the hands of their descendants. Therefore, it is incumbent on fathers zealously to communicate to their own children what they have learned from God. In this way the truth of God must be propagated among us, so that no one may savour it privately but that each may edify others according to his own calling and mode of faith.

John Calvin

Part Four:

conclusion

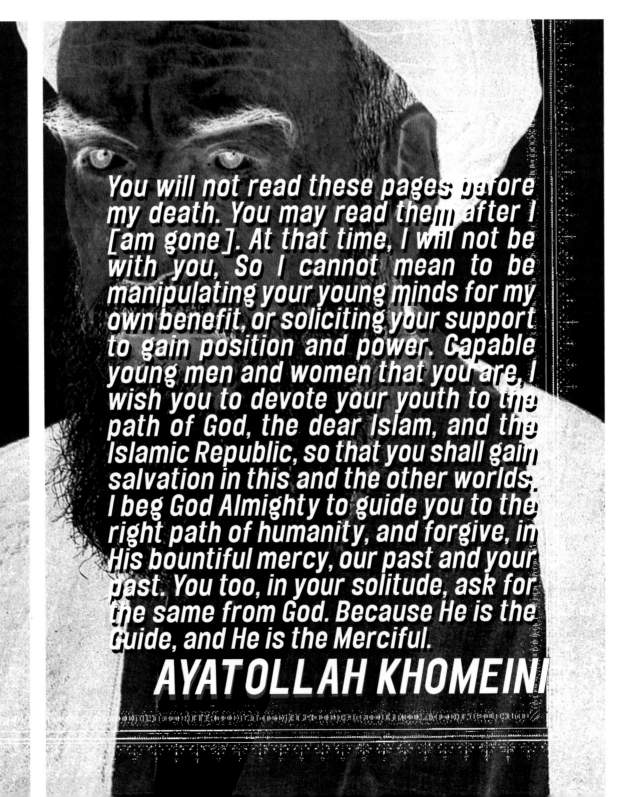

Brothers!

You will not read these pages before my death. You may read them after I [am gone]. At that time, I will not be with you, So I cannot mean to be manipulating your young minds for my own benefit, or soliciting your support to gain position and power. Capable young men and women that you are, I wish you to devote your youth to the path of God, the dear Islam, and the Islamic Republic, so that you shall gain salvation in this and the other worlds. I beg God Almighty to guide you to the right path of humanity, and forgive, in His bountiful mercy, our past and your past. You too, in your solitude, ask for the same from God. Because He is the Guide, and He is the Merciful.

AYATOLLAH KHOMEINI

Twenty

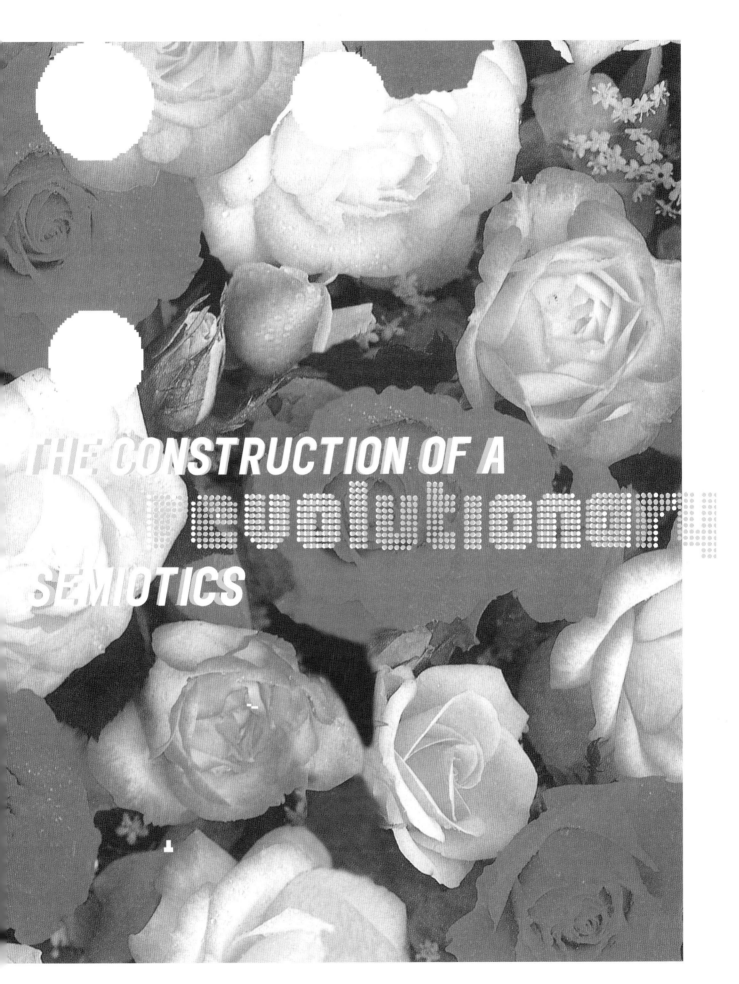

THE CONSTRUCTION OF A

revolutionary

SEMIOTICS

EVERY REVOLUTIONARY INSTANCE IS A MOMENTOUS OCCASION FOR A RECONSTITUTION OF SYMBOLIC ATTENDANCE UPON A POLITICAL CULTURE'S UNIVERSE OF IMAGINATION. EVERY SYMBOLIC ORCHESTRATION OF SIGNS AND THEIR SIGNIFICATIONS IS GEARED TOWARDS A(N) (UN)CONTROLLED PRODUCTION OF MEANING. UNDER REVOLUTIONARY CIRCUMSTANCES, THE COLLECTIVE REBELLIOUS SPIRIT REACHES OUT FOR A PARTICULAR REMOBILIZATION OF ALL THE SYMBOLICS OF THE HIGHEST FOR THE PRODUCTION OF A MAXIMUM LEVEL OF MOBILIZING MEANING. ANY SYSTEMATIZATION OF THAT SYMBOLIC PRODUCTION OF MEANING WILL HAVE TO ACCOUNT FOR THOSE MOMENTOUS HISTORICAL OCCASIONS WHEN THE SIGNIFIERS AND THEIR SIGNIFIEDS NEGOTIATE A NEW RELATIONSHIP, UNDER THE SUPREME AUSPICES OF A (RE-)EMERGING POLITICAL SEMIOTICS. IT IS ALWAYS AGAINST THE MEANINGFUL PARAMETERS OF A SIGNIFICANT AND TRUSTWORTHY CONTEXT, COLLECTIVELY ACCREDITED WITH AHISTORICAL AUTHORITY, THAT ITEMS OF SIGNIFICATION ASSUME THEIR MEANING AND LEGITIMACY. SEMIOTICALLY, REVOLUTIONS ARE MASSIVE OCCASIONS FOR RENEGOTIATING THIS ITEM—CONTEXT DIALECTICS.

As all signs are things that stand for something else, there is always the necessary human intermediary through whose cognitive faculties this act of signification takes place. Revolutions are collective acts of interference whereby the dialectics of the signs —the human cognitive faculties—and the signifieds are reconstituted. Whatever the medium of expansion—a word, a sound, an image, etc.—the revolutionary renegotiation of symbolics demands, and historically occasions, a reunderstanding of things past for things to come. The "logic" of correlation between the signifier and the signified escapes all reasons and rationalities. The color red may represent leftist (communist) radicalism, or Shi'i martyrdom, or bloodthirsty despotism, or provocative eroticism, or any number of other possible constructions of meanings, passions, sentiments, totally dependent on a received or concocted universe of signification. Such conclusions might be iconic, indexical, natural, or cultural, as C. S. Peirce observed. But all such occasions are subject to renegotiation when the political culture reinvents its dominant semiotics.

There is a range of interpretations available to the text of the signifiers Umberto Eco once identified as *opera aperta*. Eco's *Against Interpretation* is an attempt to measure the limits of that openness. There are inherent limitations that a political culture, however enduring or volatile, invests in the open-endedness of its possible orchestrations of symbolics. Even under revolutionary circumstances, there is a relentless mechanism of control that does not completely let go of its interpretive constituency, all the while that the process of renegotiation for new correlative arrangements between the signifiers and the signified is under way.

Long processes of reinvestments of meaning are needed before the inherently incomplete signifiers enter successfully their moment of signification. Generations from Al-e Ahmad to Khomeini will have to reconstruct Islam successfully before the Islamic Revolution of 1978-9 can count on any measurable mobilization of fresh and agitated sentiments. Every construction of truth behind the signifiers is the end-product, an *ex post facto* deliberation, of a succession of dialectics that through a culturally sanctioned process of interpretation links the constellation of symbolics to their symbolized. As signs invite interpretations, the interpretants seek their self-legitimacy by reading them. The result is a dual process of self-legitimation whereby the signifiers and the signifieds establish the boundaries of a semiotic culture. As the nuclear representations of a collective organization of meaning, "social signs" are the most reliable indices of a culture— whether at its stable moments of self-assurance, or at its volatile occasions of rebellious (un)certainty. Through any individual or collective constellation of these representational symbolics, as successfully demonstrated by Clifford Geertz in cultural anthropology, we gain the most reliable access to the dominant "culture" of a given society. Semiotic expressions find their legitimate meaning by virtue of the tribute they pay to their cultural point of origin. Called *paradigm* (Kuhn), or *episteme* (Foucault), or any other name, they contribute to the construction of a context within and against which all meaning and significance is made possible.

Nowhere is the extended function of the semiotic culture more noticeable than in the revolutionary rejuvenation of old myths into new, and ever more powerful, ones. Every process of remythologization of a (political) culture involves the deepest, as well as the most immediate, patterns of its symbolic significations.

20.1 During the war with Iraq, the martyrs' fountains were the regular features of Iranian towns. The red-dyed water in the fountain symbolised the blood of the martyrs. This photograph represents such a fountain in the center of the city of Meshhad. In the background is visible a photographic portrait gallery of the local martyrs.

Michael Coyne

Kazem Akhavan

20.2 A grief stricken mother at the tomb of her young martyred son at the Beheshtabad cemetry in Ahvez.

There is no political revolution without a necessary ideological reconfiguration of a semiotic culture most immediately underlying that revolution. Revolutions are the political antennae of successful registrations of mobilizing significations. Unless revolutionary messages are first coded by their ideological signifiers and then decoded by their immediate, and politically significant, constituency, there will simply not be any revolution. As Erving Goffman demonstrated, it is through an operative functioning of the "frame" of symbolic receptivity that that decoding is made collectively, as it is collectively made, possible. What Goffman calls "frame," and in another language H.-G. Gadamer calls "fore-projections," establishes the *a priori* principles under the authority of which all possibilities of understanding are (implicitly or explicitly) anticipated.

Social persons ordinarily live and create operative meanings within the cognitive and signifying principles of any number of legitimate (received) framings. Revolutionary circumstances create their own framing fore-projections. There is a meta-biological significance to drinking a glass of water in a Shiʿi Muharram procession that has scarcely anything to do with quenching one's thirst. Often glasses of water are drunk without reference to the biological fact of thirst or the lack of it. In the Muharram procession, drinking a glass of water is a symbolic reidentification with the martyrs of Karbala some hundreds of years ago. The same Shiʿi person a few hours or days earlier or later has a perfectly mundane

biological relationship to that same glass of water. Contextual framing of the signifiers are constitutional to all political cultures and their social functions.

Framing and fore-projections are regenerative. Particularly under revolutionary circumstances, every framing of particular signifiers leads to more powerful, even uncontrollable, conditionings of collective behavior. The controllability of such interpretative unfoldings of meaning and significance is always subject to the hermeneutic elasticity of a given political culture. The cultural participant can continue to interpret and believe and act accordingly only to the degree that such abiding interpretations are plausible and (historically) relevant.

Collectively constructed framings, or historically received fore-projections, are at once emancipatory and debilitating. As they release the possibility of any number of understandings, they preclude, simultaneously, any number of other (mis)understandings. Cultural members cannot think the unthinkable thought. There is an uncontrollable act of selectivity in framing the constituent forces of an interpretative choice. This selectivity has to do with the active and passive forces of tolerance that any collectivity can endure. No human collectivity can tolerate the conscious recognition of all its simultaneously historical memories.

Revolutionary ideologies are the architects of the new semiotic enterprise within the framework of which all knowledge and sensation, all understanding and signification, are made possible. They bring together a mystifying combination of previous facts and future fantasies, of previous myths and future anxieties. Such is the stuff from which framings of the present facticities are made. Every structural rearrangement of the semiotic culture unfolds the hitherto unanticipated potentialities of a given symbolic narrative. As a symbolic narrative, Shiᶜism has given historical rise to any number of cognitive (doctrinal, juridical, theological, philosophical, gnostic, literary) patterns of signification. "The Islamic Ideology" is the most recent, and the most historically relevant, cognitive pattern of signification to come out of Shiᶜism in its modernity.

In any act of semiosis, for example from Shiᶜi theology to "the Islamic Ideology," all the historically relevant combinations of signifiers, the signifieds, and their intermediary patterns of cognitive signification are simultaneously changed. Any act of revolutionary hermeneutics fundamentally alters the terms and the spirit of all its father-figures, mother-models, ancestral legitimacies. This act of collective metamorphosis, a relentless unfolding of what Goffman considered serial meanings and sequential framings, puts the audience in direct contact with the deepest and most culturally consequential of symbolics. The culturally and situationally specific dialectic that takes shape and finds momentum in a shared space between the ideological symbolizers and their mobilized audience takes advantage of every concrete event (for example, a confrontation with the army, a concession by the government) in order to verify its historical relevance and legitimacy.

305

Such a constant and relentless conception of communal interaction, particularly activated under a transformative situation, fundamentally alters our understanding of the revolutionary process. What enters a revolutionary moment is not a set package of historically validated conceptions of order, fidelity, justice, leadership, etc. Quite the contrary, from the scattered remembrances of past and present loyalties gather particular elements of a revolutionary interaction that dictates its own future as it unfolds and expands. It is in a third space, between the leaders' ideals and the crowds' conceptions, that the dialectics of communal consensus takes shape. It is precisely this volatile, transfigurative, and rearguable nature of cultural symbolics that makes them conducive to ideological refabrication for the highest possible degree of revolutionary mobilization.

Cultural symbolics—the color red, Qur'anic calligraphy, the shape of a circle—are historically received conceptions of anxiety-controlling activities. Against the infinite possibility of any number of other shapes, colors, and verses, these terms of collective certainty sustain and cover reality so that life can proceed with some illusion of order and trust. But, left to their archaic staleness, they will grow to their exotic irrelevance. What resuscitates them into contemporary relevance is the air and blood of material historicity, aspects of some daily anxiety, some collective despair, that needs expression. Individuals enter these symbolics, as they in

turn animate individuals, with diverse and expansive conceptions, expectations, aspirations, and anxieties. The collective festival has a logic, and insanity, of its own.

There is, of course, no exaggerating the precise mode and degree of participation in communal gatherings where cultural symbolics are used. There is always a considerable margin of discrepancy among the different participants' conception of what exactly is happening in a symbolically significant communal gathering. Meaning and signification are always created collectively. But what exactly is the meaning of a communal gathering and all its diverse symbolic references? Who exactly is in charge of regenerating old symbolics with new significations? And how are the reconstructed symbolics thus resignified, received, registered, and decoded? Take a Friday prayer and its sermon: is this a religious event with a political overtone, or is it a political meeting with a religious undertone? The communal context goes far enough to establish the bare skeleton of the decoding fore-projections. But much discrepancy still remains to allow for the private concerns of the individual participants to collide or conform with their public conceptions.

From Goffman we have learned the significance of fronts, poses, voices, and guises through which conceptions are made and perceptions are projected. Revolutions are made or broken through gestures and voices, eye contact, and pictures. A symphony of colors and shapes, of voices and guises, of signs and symbols, of sentiments and memories, precedes, accompanies, and succeeds a revolution. All the material conditions of the world cannot move a people unless a mobilizing dialectic engages their deepest aspirations and anxieties to the most enduring symbolics of their communal remembrances they call their culture.

305

The semiotics of every revolution is the most public term of its collective self-perception. A revolution sees itself in the mirror of the images it creates. A revolution is the images it creates. Revolutionary images are not spontaneous. They are premeditated in the deepest and most enduring layers of a people's collective imagination. The revolutionary semiotics teaches its mobilized participants what to believe by telling them, in sign language, what signifies what. Red signifies blood, noble blood, that is. It is good, so teaches the revolutionary semiotics, to shed one's blood for the revolutionary cause. The heavens will turn dark in mourning once the revolutionary man sacrifices his red blood. The posters will celebrate, the people will sing in praise, the heavens will open wide, the birds will fly and soar — all black and white and in abundance for the glory of the noble red. The revolutionary semiotics gives the revolution its name, calls it by its attributes, locates it in its history, defines it for its participants—waves high its primary and most irreducible colors.

Signs cannot mean unless they are culturally and socially located. Culture provides the more enduring weights of a collective symbolic. Society is the more historically nuanced and responsive context of all acts of semiotic signification. People may forget what the color red meant 200 years ago. But with a vague and unrelenting memory, a carefully constructed, historically cornered, reference can go very far in all the necessary nuances of a cultural *farbenlehre*. Fabrication of signified and implied meaning in a semiotic act borrows heavily from the cultural context of its creation, yet it is most immediately linked to historical realities that animate and mobilize its targeted audience. The linkage between the signifier and the signified, always culturally controlled, can, and does, receive periodic resuscitation through revolutionary reidentification with its collectively imagined origin.

Truth and falsehood, fact and fantasy, right and wrong, all dichotomous bipolarities of power and morality yield to the commanding act of signification. The same fabrication of symbolics that is designed to propagate the "true" Islam are remanipulated to designate "the reactionary mullahs." Ideological signification is central to all denotative and connotative forces of cultural symbolics. Any reconfiguration of colors and shapes, memories and melodies, signs and symbols, rhythms and meters, can claim a measure of belief and obedience in a reactivated collective consciousness. The ideological bent of all acts of signification begin to gain their momentous power from the properly manufactured framing they receive from their individual or collective constructions. "Truth" or "lie" is irrelevant. What matters is the power of convincing that links the signifier, the sign, and the signified together, and with them locks the targeted audience into the grip of the manipulator of the whole act of signification. The codifier, particularly under mobilizing revolutionary circumstances, leaves no, or minimum, room for mis- (that is, unwanted) interpretation. The target should need no rekeying for the necessary instant interpretative (re)action. In the semiotic reading of "truth," we have not so much the "representation" of reality as the "construction" of it. There is no "reality" other than the one thus constructed to be represented. The representation of reality is the reality. There lies the quintessential truth about the power of visual mobilization that reaches for faculties and sentiments of conviction much deeper than a mere act of propaganda. No propaganda is successful as propaganda. It is as "truth" that acts of propaganda find their power and disguise.

The primary function of the iconic (re)construction of reality under revolutionary circumstances is to ward off all alternative claims on the revolution and secure a monopoly of interpretation (and thus appropriation) by it. Through the revolutionary rhetoric of semiotic (re)codification, attributes are given to the movement with such matter-of-fact certainty as if given and unquestionable. That this is an "Islamic Revolution," that Khomeini is its leader, that Iranians are participating in it as Muslims, are all preparatory frameworks to ascertain the equally natural appellation of "the Islamic Republic" as the ideal form to be derived from these circumstances. That this is an "Islamic" revolution, and not "Iranian," that Khomeini (a cleric) is its leader, and not any number of other secular candidates, that the future regime should be called

the "Islamic" Republic, as opposed to any number of other kinds of republics (or monarchies?) are attributions of ideological preference that shape and overshadow the event for the precise liking of the Muslim ideologues. That an Iranian may not necessarily feel "Muslim" on one fine revolutionary day, that a republic of a more secular certainty might be wished for, and that the universal authority of a Shiʿi cleric might very well be questioned, are all in the range of possibilities that the Islamicity of the Revolution consciously recognizes as rivalrous and ideologically denies as illegitimate.

But even in this dominant theme of Islamicity and Muslimhood, there is no "original" pattern to return to. There is an historically (re)created, ideologically forceful, and politically convenient conception of "Islam" and "Muslim" that the new codifiers/officers of the faith persistently propagate. From explicit denotations to implicit denotations, the ideological leitmotif of a semiotic act is that quintessential organization of prejudices that the initial codifier of a poster or a stamp deliberately seeks and yet conceals in a veneer of matter-of-factness which presents the purpose of the statement not as an argument or suggestion or "propaganda," but as a simple, even understated, truth. It is in this concocted, perfectly artificial, way that the recipients of a pregnant text are provided with suggestive avenues leading to one (re)definition of their mythological origin or another. An iconic representation of Ali, with a huge beard, handsome face, kind and compassionate eyes, sitting on his knees and holding his sword (Dhu al-faqar) in his hand and on his lap, with the underlying subtitle of "There is no young man like Ali and there is no sword like Dhu al-faqar," becomes a compelling mobile shrine in the face of which myths of Shiʿi virtues are reawakened.

The theatricality of a revolutionary movement acts out publicly the collectively inculcated virtues of a community. This collectivity does not just make a revolution; it is, in its essence and attributes, made by it. When "the Muslim people of Iran" pour into the streets of their capital and welcome their great revolutionary leader, coming home from his exile in the suburbs of a "Western capital," the whole history of "the Islamic Revolution" is thus officially appropriated and narrated. The participating actors in this massive, and quite serious, theater become what they are collectively held to be. There is no escaping this ideological construction of identity. Upon the moment of its political success, "the Islamic Revolution" Islamicizes everything about the event. The event is either "the Islamic Revolution" or nothing, no revolution, a mere disturbance perhaps. The colossal staging of revolutionary virtues makes its participants in the collective image of their relevance and significance for the "good" of the cause. Upon the theatricality of a revolution there is an almost voluntary suspension of belief, a gradual dissolution of private realities into the vast and expanding domain of collective acts. As the revolutionary observers become the participants, just about that magical moment when the streets of public protest and action become the rooms of the most intimate practices of conviction and piety, the mass staging of a real passion play leaves no room for any audience. Everyone is on stage, acting out what they think others think they are. Upon this massive stage, the colossal (re)politicization of fantasy, there is an innocence, as there is no conscious, or necessarily self-conscious, fabrication of a lie. There is a genuine conviction on the part of every revolutionary artist, at least in the moment of the creative imagination, that a martyr flies to heaven, a white pigeon of infallible piety. Without that conviction, without that deep and enduring engraving of the momentary act into (what always appears to be a) permanent character, no revolutionary theater can claim real blood, spilled over the stage of its historical production.

The Iranian Revolution of 1978-9 reveals, in the most spectacular way, the deepest, most energetic, volcanic forces of the Islamic culture of Iran. Never does a nation so completely and thoroughly reveal its innermost anxieties as in a revolution. Prosperity and affluence, opulence and placid social conformity, conceal under the most charming civilities forces and ferocities that most fundamentally animate a culture. A revolution, to the contrary, is the opening up of the deepest and hardest wounds of a people's historical endurance. A revolution also reveals how utterly arbitrary the collective construction of reality, of truth, of trust, of significance, is. The semiotic manipulation of shapes and colors, of memories and fantasies, is at the heart of (the revolutionary) man's conception of his being self-consciously in the world. The historical borderlines between truth and falsehood, reality and fantasy, begin to lose their received authority the moment the brutal artificiality of conviction makes itself apparent.

In the village of Aiello, Calabria, deep in the southernmost Mezzogiorno of Italy, the local branch of the Communist Party changes its old name and logo, splashes a green tree under the hemispheric red of a crescent "Partito Democratico della Sinistra." The former proud title of the Communist Party of Italy is reduced, abbreviated, miniatured into a circle, and delegated nostalgically to the lower center of the huge banner. The red, green, and white of the Italian flag communicates and underlines all this metamorphic opera. In the provincial capital of Ahvaz in southern Iran, in a neighborhood near the old part of the city (Ahvaz-e qadim), two local thugs who had spent all their youth intimidating their neighbors, go to their roof, mount a flag of the Islamic Republic on their door and hang a sign that reads "In the Name of God Most Sublime." That is in black. Under it in red: "The Local Branch of the Islamic Republic Party." The rhetorical orchestration of symbolics to convince and mobilize is at the heart of not just revolutionary moments but any other radical need to believe in a comforting framing of reality.

20.3 Chewing-gum wrapper spells out: "Salutations to the warriors of Islam, Death to America!"